THE ENGLISH
Cottage Garden

THE ENGLISH
Cottage Garden

ANDREW SANKEY

THE CROWOOD PRESS

First published in 2021 by
The Crowood Press Ltd
Ramsbury, Marlborough
Wiltshire SN8 2HR

enquiries@crowood.com
www.crowood.com

British Library Cataloguing-in-Publication Data
A catalogue record for this book is available from the British Library.

ISBN 978 1 78500 949 5

Cover design: Kelly-Anne Levey

Graphic design and typeset by Peggy & Co. Design
Printed and bound in India by Parksons Gaphics

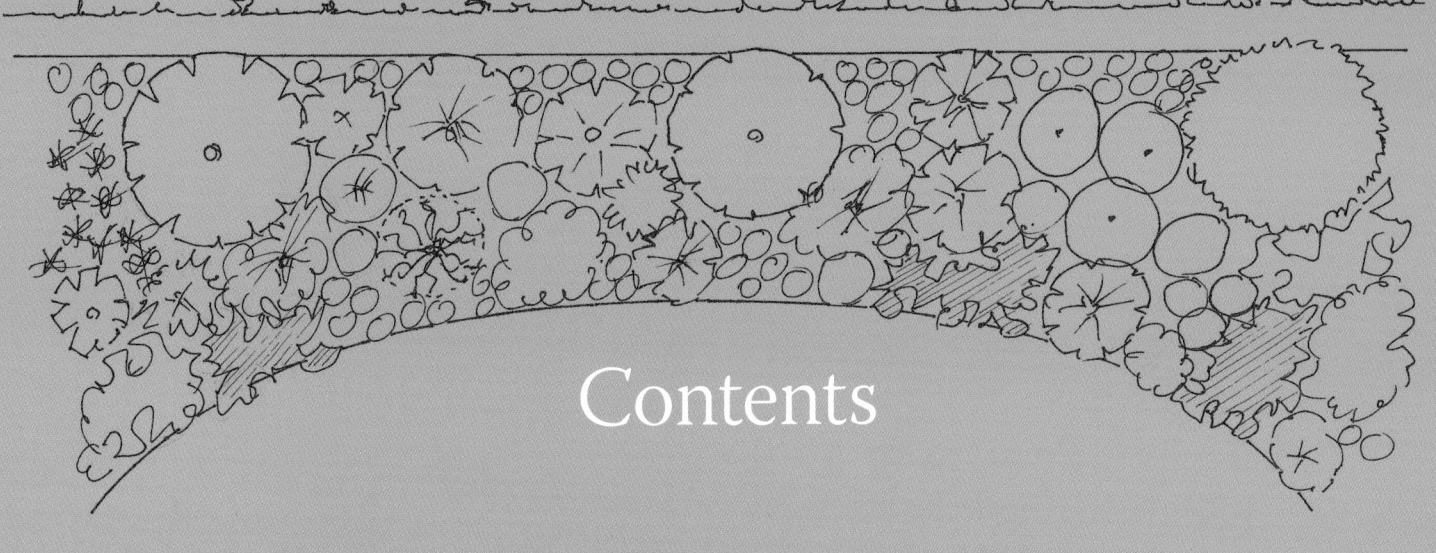

Contents

Preface

My first introduction to the style of the English cottage garden came when I was given a copy of Margery Fish's book, *We Made a Garden*. Having been enthralled with the book, I then travelled down to Somerset to see her wonderful cottage garden at East Lambrook Manor. Shortly after this, Geoff Hamilton started to construct his cottage gardens for the BBC *Gardeners' World* programmes and it soon became apparent that this was the style of gardening I myself wished to adopt.

Not long after this I moved to Lincolnshire and started my own garden design/landscaping business, and I soon realized it was difficult to obtain the more unusual plants required for a number of my garden designs, in particular plants for dry shade positions. This encouraged me to look for a larger garden with the potential to run a small specialist nursery. This resulted in purchasing a Grade II listed cottage (built in 1852) with a good-sized old cottage garden. Although the original garden (like many in Lincolnshire) had once been an extremely long strip stretching back to the village

pond, the plot that came with the cottage was much reduced. Nevertheless, at almost half an acre it was more than enough for me to manage. Luckily the garden was pretty much a blank canvas, having a couple of large old fruit trees, a vegetable patch, various outbuildings and a chicken hut; and this afforded me the opportunity to make something special of the garden.

It was here that my love for cottage gardens blossomed. Over-time I re-designed the garden, I created different rooms/areas, spring and summer borders, and began experimenting with colour schemes and companion planting. I joined the Cottage Garden Society and then helped form the Lincolnshire branch, eventually becoming chairman. Within a few years I opened the garden under the National Gardens Scheme; I then started writing articles and lecturing on different aspects of the cottage garden.

This book is the culmination of my years working on my own cottage gardens, designing and creating cottage gardens for clients, experimenting with companion planting and lecturing widely on the subject. I very much hope you enjoy it.

A very small back garden in Cambridge planted up in a cottage garden style

Introduction

The cottage garden is a unique style of gardening that has developed in England since the medieval period and now reflects the very essence and charm of our English villages. The much-romanticized cottage garden with its glorious drifts of traditional flowers, roses, gnarled old fruit trees and neatly clipped front hedges is the image that immediately springs to mind. However, if we set aside this idealistic Victorian image for a moment and focus on the older cottager's garden, we discover a garden plot used primarily to grow vegetables and medicinal herbs with a few chickens and pigs. The layout of these simple productive gardens was determined by its location (region), its soil, the availability to acquire new plant introductions, but more than anything else, the individual owner's desire to create a garden that not only provided for all the needs of his family, but had attractive flowers to mark the passing of the year and to yield intoxicating scents to lift the spirits.

In these modern times we have no necessity to grow food to live on, to keep valuable animals, to grow herbs for medicinal use or to plant large fruit trees for a late season crop. With these original elements not required you might wonder why the cottage garden has remained highly fashionable, and more importantly, still hugely relevant. The answer is that many of the other original features that contributed to the character of the old cottage gardens are still immensely suitable and easily transferable to the modern garden. Cottage gardens were generally small plots with cottagers having little time to garden (normally only after a long day's work) and little or no money to spend on them. This resulted in a garden where the flowers needed to be tough and able to thrive without much attention; where there was no wasted space and plants were pushed in together and allowed to self-seed (creating a typical profusion of cottage flowers); and where every garden was individualistic, due to each cottager having to work with plants that suited their particular site and soil.

A modern gardener inherits many of these same problems – a small sized garden, a limited budget to spend and little time to devote to the garden due to the pressure of work. The cottage garden style is therefore a wonderful solution to the modern way of life and the ever-decreasing size of gardens. The timeless appeal of the cottage garden and its old-fashioned flowers that are tough, floriferous and often highly scented, match the criteria for a flexible, easy maintenance and year-round interest garden. This style of garden can be adapted by the individual owner to suit his/her own requirements; whether that be a keen gardener wanting a garden full of plants, an inexperienced gardener simply requiring a pleasant oasis to sit and relax in after work, or someone more interested in cooking requiring a garden with a few vegetables, herbs and flowers in pots.

The instantly recognizable cottage garden style can happily be designed to create that essential 'chaotic mix' of flowers in any shape or size of garden. A cottage garden doesn't necessarily require a beautiful thatched cottage, as this style of garden can easily be adapted for long back gardens of terraced houses, larger lawned gardens of country properties or even the tiny gardens of newly built modern town houses.

The aim of this book is to provide both inspiration and a comprehensive source for garden design ideas and solutions, techniques, features, planting schemes, and in particular, plant combinations that can be used to create the modern *cottage garden style*. Although the introductory chapter deals with the history of the cottage garden, the main focus of the book is on creating a cottage-style garden – which traditional features are suitable, how to attain a cottagey feel to the planting, how companion planting works, how to create colour-schemed borders and which plants should be used to suit different garden situations.

The subject matter within this book – which includes garden design ideas, examples of planting schemes and ideas on how to improve an existing garden – although centred upon cottage-style gardens, is also relevant to all other gardens. With this in mind, the book will be of interest not just to cottage gardeners, but to any amateur or professional gardener wishing to extend their knowledge of gardening techniques and plants, and students studying general gardening or garden design courses. I therefore feel sure that this book will be a useful addition to the library of all enthusiastic gardeners.

Chapter 1

The History of the Cottage Garden

The 'cottage garden' is quintessentially English. It immediately brings to mind a quaint thatched cottage with a beautifully scented rose rambling over its door, a neatly clipped hedge with a picket gate and paths with scented flowers spilling over in sweet disorder.

However, the highly romantic style of today's cottage garden with its borders of traditional flowers intermingled with trees, shrubs, and newer varieties of plants, which are now usually planted in beds around lawns, is a relatively modern form of the cottage garden. This is in complete contrast to the enclosed medieval yard, where beds of vegetables and herbs were simply grown to ensure the poor peasant-cottager could survive on a basic diet of bread, pottage and ale.

Cottage gardens in the past were never consciously designed but evolved over the centuries to fulfil the needs of the poorer classes (labourers, cottagers and village craftsmen) who generally lived a 'hand-to-mouth' existence. With little or no wealth to speak of, they took advantage of the native flora, new vegetable introductions and the discarded flowers from the lord of the manor or farm owner for whom they worked.

A beautiful thatched cottage with a garden planted in the traditional cottage style, with roses climbing up the cottage walls and a profusion of flowers spilling over the border under the windows.

THE MEDIEVAL GARTH

Unfortunately, only the important fashionable gardens of the royal and wealthy were ever considered worthy of recording, making it more difficult to trace the early development of the cottage garden. Written evidence about what they grew and how they grew it is scarce. We do, however, know something about the monastery gardens in Europe and can safely assume techniques and flowers filtered down to the peasant-cottagers who worked the land. We can be certain that these early gardens had limited varieties of vegetables and herbs which would have been common throughout Britain. A poor cottager had little need of decorative flowers which weren't considered essential, although I'm sure a few native plants would have been welcome.

The Domesday Book (1086) tells us there were vast numbers of garths in England. The word 'garth' is an early term for a plot or garden, and they would have varied greatly in size, some being tiny and some of possibly a few acres. The garth was always enclosed: either with a dead hedge, wattle hurdles, a paling fence (vertical posts driven into the ground) or a 'thorn' hedge.

Within this enclosure were raised beds for vegetables and herbs. A separate area would have been fenced off for the pig(s) to prevent the animals from eating the precious roots. In the early medieval period, the word 'vegetable' wasn't used – it comes from the French *vegetablis* meaning to grow and entered the English language sometime in the fourteenth century. Vegetables were called root herbs, worts, leaf beet, or simply referred to by their names – onions, garlic, leek, beets. All these would have been

The medieval hovel and Saxon garth.

Reconstruction of a thirteenth-century flint cottage with wattle enclosure for basic vegetables and herbs, at the Weald and Downland Museum.

grown in raised beds approximately 1m (3ft) in width being edged with wooden planks or a low wattle fence. This method was probably passed on by the monks, as it was a vital part of the ordered layout within the monastery vegetable and physic gardens. It allowed the free-draining beds to be worked on from either side without compacting the soil.

The small cottages of either wattle and daub or stone, had an earthen floor and thatched roof (no chimney). It was a basic shelter supporting a large family, and during the winter months sheltering the precious animals as well. The village craftsmen and small farmers had similar but larger buildings on a greater area of land and possibly a barn to accommodate the animals. However, everyone gardened and grew the same vegetables and herbs and in general lived on a diet of cabbages, onions, kale and roots (turnips and skirret).

Apart from the vegetables, cottagers had a pig(s), chickens and a few essential herbs they considered worthwhile, which they grew in the garden or up against the cottage. These herbs had three uses: culinary, medicinal and strewing. The strong-tasting herbs were always used for the pot or to flavour ale. Healing herbs were gathered from hedgerows, meadows and woods, but it would have made sense to have the most frequently used medicinal herbs close at hand in the garden, and we know that the monastery and castle gardens had raised beds filled with certain physic herbs. The strewing of herbs mixed with rushes upon the floor was commonplace and helped repel vermin to some extent.

William Langland's *Vision of Piers Plowman*, in 1394, states that the 'croft' (possibly half an acre behind the cottage) provided a harvest of 'peas, beans, leeks, parsley, shallots, chilboles [some sort of small onion], chervil and cherries half-red'. Geoffrey Chaucer, throughout his *Canterbury Tales*, makes mention of 'beds of wortes' (root vegetables) and medicinal herbs in the yard.

The *Feate of Gardening*, a poem from the late Medieval period by Master Jon Gardener, is unique in that it is the first practical guide to gardening. There has been much speculation as to who Gardener actually was, but more important is the information in his work, as he mentions over 100 plants grown in gardens during the period. There is guidance on sowing and setting of worts, seeds and vines; on grafting apple and pear trees; and on when to harvest. I shall not go through the full list of trees, herbs and flowers in the poem, but would like to mention some of the flowers in the section beginning 'Of other herbs I shall tell'. This includes rue, sage, thyme, hyssop, borage, mint, savory, yarrow, comfrey, valerian, honeysuckle, lavender, cowslip, strawberries, daffodil, primrose, foxglove, hollyhock and peony. It illustrates the use in gardens of both native and newly introduced plants in this period.

A large swathe of native foxgloves in English woodland.

Long beds of herbs the Tudors would have grown for culinary, medicinal and strewing purpose in the Tudor Walled Garden at Cressing Temple Barns.

If we summarize the medieval plot, we can confidently say it contained basic vegetables, some essential herbs, possibly a few native wildflowers, a few animals (pigs and chickens) and a compost heap. There are no fruit trees just yet (as fruit would simply have been gathered from the wild in season) and no flowers purely for decoration, although wild plants may well have self-seeded around the garden. In this period, *all* plants had to be of use.

THE TUDOR AND ELIZABETHAN GARDEN

With the end of the Wars of the Roses and as relative peace returned in Tudor England, gardens began to change. Henry VIII and his court embraced the new knot designs within gardens and welcomed new and interesting flowers and herbs. Vegetables began to be pushed out of the privy garden (private show garden) and instead flowers that were more decorative than useful took their place. Orchards full of new varieties of fruit trees (often purchased from France) became a gentleman's pride and joy.

However, it was with the long reign of Queen Elizabeth I (1558–1603) that peace and prosperity created a climate of stability that the country had never seen before, and gardening became a great pastime that all classes would benefit from. There was improvement in housing, farming and diet. Herbals, gardening and husbandry books were printed for the first time throughout this period and give us an insight into the advances made in both garden design and the wonderful plants introduced from Europe and the New World. During this golden period the cottage garden starts to take on the form that we recognize as the English cottage garden today.

The nosegay garden, full of flowers and herbs found in all gardens of the sixteenth century.

Thomas Tusser explains the essential work on a farm month by month and gives us a particularly good snapshot of the vegetables, herbs and flowers which he suggests should be grown by the Yeoman farmer's wife. *One Hundred Good Points of Husbandry*, although aimed at the relatively wealthy middle-class farmer, lists the flowers and herbs he believes are essential to any garden. These would eventually trickle down to the cottager/labourer throughout this period. Within his book are a number of different lists: seeds and herbs for the kitchen, herbs and roots for salads, strewing herbs and herbs for physic; but the most interesting is a list of herbs, branches and flowers for windows and pots – this particular list confirming the use of flowers for decorative purposes in addition to being useful plants.

The 1580 edition of Tusser's second book, *Five Hundred Pointes of Good Husbandrie*, includes: columbines, cowslips, cornflowers, daffodils, sweet briar rose, gilliflowers (red and white), carnations,

USE OF ELIZABETHAN HERBS

Herbalists, garden writers and poets extol the virtues of herbs for: medicine, cooking, strewing, celebrations, weddings, funerals, grave flowers, garlands, wreaths, nosegays, pest repellents, flavouring drinks, sweet waters, plague protection, lucky charms, cosmetics and love potions.

Strewing herbs were particularly important in the Elizabethan period and remained so until the mid-eighteenth century. A mixture of rushes and herbs were strewn on the floor to make it feel warmer, smell better and deter vermin, lice and fleas. Thomas Tusser, in his best-selling *One Hundred Good Points of Husbandry*, first published in 1557, had a section 'Strewing Herbes of all Sorts', which doesn't just include the usual herbs of rosemary, lavender, tansy and wormwood (*Artemisia*), but also includes flowers such as daisies, roses, violets, primroses and cowslips to add prettiness and scent. Queen Elizabeth I's favourite strewing herb was meadowsweet, and John Gerard extols this herb's virtues in his herbal of 1597, telling us:

> The leaves and flowers far excel all other strewing herbs, for to deck up the houses, to straw in chambers, halls, and banqueting houses in the Summer time; for the smell thereof makes the heart merry and delighteth the senses; neither doth it cause headaches as some other sweet smelling herbs do.

lavender of all sorts, larkspur, lilies, double marigolds, nigella, heartsease pansy, pinks of all sorts, rosemary, roses of all sorts, snapdragons, Sweet Williams, French marigolds, violets, rose campion, wallflowers, iris and even love-lies-bleeding. When Tusser states these flowers are suitable for windows and pots, I believe that the term 'windows' equates to 'for growing under the windows' – which of course would make sense as women generally planted the prettiest and most highly scented flowers under the windows for maximum enjoyment.

Tusser's list is a fairly comprehensive one but it has to be remembered that the Elizabethan farmer, particularly the English sheep farmer, may well have been as wealthy as most of the gentry due to the great demand for English wool. They might not have spent vast sums of money on the design of the garden, but they certainly wished for a well-stocked and well-organized garden. Of course, it needs to be remembered that the cottager's garden would have been a pale reflection of the one up at the big farm and would have had only a small number of the flowers listed. However, Tusser's list is backed up by other gardening writers, herbalists and poets (including Shakespeare). John Clare, known as the Northamptonshire Peasant Poet, mentions in his poem *The Cottager* (written in the early nineteenth century) that the cottager's meagre bookshelf still contained 'prime old Tusser'. This

THE SHEPHERD'S CALENDAR

> Bring hether the Pinke, and the Purple Cullambine,
> With Gellifloures
> Bring Coronation, and Sops-in-Wine,
> Worne of Paramoures;
> Strowe me the ground with Daffadowndillies,
> And Cowslips, and Kingcups and loved Lillies;
> The pretie Pawnce
> And the Cherisauce,
> Shall match the fayre flower Delice.

Edward Spenser (1579)

illustrates just how influential Tusser's book was to the cottager, even centuries later.

In his *Description of England* (1587), William Harrison tells us:

> If you look into our gardens annexed to our houses how wonderfully is their beauty increased, not only with flowers, but also with rare and medicinal herbs.

Another poet who describes the flowers commonly grown in an Elizabethan garden is Richard Barnfield, in his poem *The Affectionate Shepherd* (1594); although not all these wonderful flowers would have reached the cottage garden as this time, they would gradually filter down to become firm favourites in the next century. The part of the poem that describes the garden is as follows:

> Nay, more than this, I have a garden plot
> Wherein there wants nor herbs, nor roots, nor flowers;
> Flowers to smell, roots to eat, herbs for the pot,
> And dainty shelters when the welkin lowers:
> Sweet-smelling beds of lilies, and of roses,
> Which rosemary banks and lavender encloses.
> There grows the gillyflower, the mint, the daisy
> Both red and white, the blue-veined violet;
> The purple hyacinth, the spike to please thee,
> The scarlet dyed carnation bleeding yet;
> The sage, the savory, the sweet marjoram,
> Hyssop, thyme, and the eye-bright, good for blind and dumb.
> The pink, the primrose, cowslip and daffodil,
> The hare-bell blue, the crimson columbine,
> Sage, lettuce, parsley, and the milk-white lily,
> The rose and the speckled flower called sops-in-wine,
> Fine pretty king-cups, and yellow boots,
> That grows by rivers and by shallow brooks.

The dates given below equate to the plant being mentioned in a period herbal or gardening book.
If the date is 'circa' it means that the plant may well have arrived earlier.

Common name	Latin name	Country of origin	Date of introduction
African marigold	*Tagetes erecta*	Mexico (via N. Africa)	1535
Globe thistle	*Echinops sphaerocephalus*	Siberia	1542
Cotton lavender	*Santolina chamaecyparissus*	Spain	c.1548
Goat's rue	*Galega officinalis*	Middle East	1548
Winter aconite	*Eranthis hyemalis*	Southern Europe	1550–70
French lavender	*Lavandula stoechas*	Southern France	c.1550
Nasturtium	*Tropaeolum minus*	S. America (via Spain)	c.1560
Monkshood	*Aconitum napellus*	Central Europe	c.1560
Cupid's dart	*Catananche caerulea*	Mediterranean region	c.1560
Golden rain tree	*Laburnum anagyroides*	Southern Europe	c.1560
Virgin's bower	*Clematis viticella*	Southern Europe	c.1560
Yellow chamomile	*Anthemis tinctoria*	Mediterranean region	1561
Passion flower	*Passiflora incarnata*	S. America (via Spain)	c.1568
Globe thistle	*Echinops ritro*	Southern Europe	1570
French marigold	*Tagetes patula*	Mexico (via Spain)	1572
Larkspur	*Delphinium ajacis*	Europe	1573
Lemon balm	*Melissa officinalis*	Southern Europe	1573
Sweet William	*Dianthus barbatus*	Southern Europe	1573
Rock cranesbill	*Geranium macrorrhizum*	Balkans region	1575
Tulip	*Tulipa gesneriana*	Western Asia	1577
Candle larkspur	*Delphinium elatum*	Europe / Siberia	1578
Crown Imperial	*Fritillaria imperialis*	Turkey	1578
Yellow crocus	*Crocus flavus*	Europe	1579
Potato	*Solanum tuberosum*	Chile (Sir Francis Drake)	1586
Lilac	*Syringa vulgaris*	Balkans region	c.1590
Chimney bellflower	*Campanula pyramidalis*	Italy	c.1596
Sunflower	*Helianthus annuus*	S. America (via Spain)	1596
Busy Lizzie	*Impatiens balsamina*	India (via Silk Route)	1596
Yellow foxglove	*Digitalis grandiflora*	Turkey	1596
Hyacinth	*Hyacinthus*	Turkey / Middle East	1596
Auricula	*Primula auricula*	Europe	c.1597
Virgin's bower	*Clematis flammula*	Southern Europe	c.1597

Before the Elizabethan period orchards were only found in connection with monasteries, but they become important attachments to any garden of note during the sixteenth century. An orchard was often more than just a collection of fruit trees, often having drifts of wildflowers, bee skeps, and arbours in which to rest and shade oneself from the sun (as Shakespeare frequently tells us). Apple and pear trees became an integral part of the garden for the first time and possibly encouraged the cottager to copy the wealthy and include fruit trees in the larger gardens behind cottages.

New exotics from the Balkans/Turkey region and from South America became much sought after for display within gardens of wealthy courtiers. These incredible new flowers were highly expensive and only to be found in the best gardens at the end of the Elizabethan period, often planted in special raised beds or pots. The list of 'new' arrivals is impressive and includes the tulip, hyacinth, Crown Imperial, lilac, delphinium, sunflower, larkspur and catananche (Cupid's dart). These new arrivals when added to the commonly grown flowers and herbs from the medieval period form the basis of what we would refer to today as traditional cottage garden flowers.

There were of course some new vegetable arrivals. The potato, tomato and runner bean all arrived from South America via Spain. However, it would be centuries before any of these became generally grown in the cottage gardens.

THE SEVENTEENTH-CENTURY COTTAGE GARDEN

The design of the English garden followed the fashion in Europe, and in particular France, where formality was the key feature and topiary became ever more important. Yew and box were grown in their thousands to feed the demand for intricate designs laid out in symmetrical patterns called parterres. The vast formal designs that stretched over acres of levelled estate with wonderful water features and fountains couldn't be replicated in the smaller gardens of farmers or cottagers. However, a little topiary probably crept in, as can be seen from paintings of cottage gardens in the nineteenth century. The thorn or privet hedge surrounding the garden, or a yew tree placed up against the cottage wall could be clipped into an abstract form or perhaps peacocks either side of the cottage gate. A little topiary is still to be found in cottage gardens today but is more likely to be a train or cat in design.

Also, during the beginning of the seventeenth century the eight species of plants considered florists' flowers were being developed. It is believed that Huguenot weavers fleeing France brought with them the *Primula auricula* with its stunning markings and beautiful form. These plants needed care and attention but very little space, and being hardy, could easily be grown in pots by artisan cottage weavers and lace-makers in the north of England, who bred and showed their prize plants regularly. The weavers in Paisley developed particular varieties of pinks known as 'Paisley pinks' but many new varieties were being cultivated in the northern counties giving the cottage gardens many of its traditional flowers still to be found today. This art became known as 'floristry' and as well as the auricula and pinks, anemone, carnation, hyacinth, ranunculus, tulip and polyanthus were included. The first florists' societies were formed, and members met to display their flowers at 'florists' feasts' in the local pub.

Vegetables and soft fruit, too, began to be grown for show, and a particular favourite was the 'gooseberry'. This fruit

Crown Imperial.

Yellow foxglove.

Monkshood.

Cupid's dart.

was originally grown to make a 'green sauce' to go with the goose (to help cut through the fat). However, growing gooseberry bushes and showing the fruits became popular in the Midlands and North, where 'gooseberry clubs' sprang up. They too, met at the pub in late summer and competed for the biggest or weightiest fruit – something that still happens in a few places in the north of England today.

Sir Thomas Browne, a keen observer of life, moved to Norwich in 1637 and wrote a marginal note 'in the country a few miles from Norwich ... a handsome bower of honeysuckles over the door of a cottage of a right good man', next to one of his poems in praise of the simple healthy country life. We tend to think that cottage doors should be covered with English roses but actually it was more usual for a honeysuckle to climb over the doorway as the wonderful scent could waft into the cottage at night and also give protection to the cottage from evil and witches.

In 1677 the agriculturalist/horticulturalist John Worlidge wrote the book *Systema Horticulturae or The Art of Gardening* and said, 'scarce a cottage in most of the southern parts of England, but hath its proportionate garden, so great a delight do most men take in it.' Although this book is well and truly aimed at the wealthy end of the gardening scale and talks at length about design and features that should be incorporated in any good garden of the period – those being walks, arbours, fountains, grottoes, statues and other necessary ornaments, as well as the new 'exotic plants' required – there is a chapter devoted to 'Vulgar Flowers'. The introduction begins, 'There are many Flowers that either for scent or show are raised in the more ordinary Country Gardens', after which Worlidge goes on to list some of the vulgar (common) flowers grown. The list includes bellflowers, cranesbill, feverfew, toadflax, blew-bottles (cornflowers), nigella, candytuft, satten flower (honesty), scabious, foxgloves, gilliflowers, flower of the sun, rockets (hesperis or sweet rocket), double chamomile and common amaranthus (love-lies-bleeding). He also mentions pilewort or lesser celandine, which was more likely to have been grown for its use as a poultice. Scabious too, may well have been grown not just for its flowers but also its medicinal value to help with coughs.

By 1700, an average cottage garden might well be half-an-acre to an acre in size and enclosed within a quickthorn (hawthorn) hedge with native and self-seeded plants growing both beneath and over the top of the hedge. A reasonable variety of vegetables could be grown, herbs for culinary and medicinal uses and a few fruit trees. Some chickens, pigs and bees would be kept, and a climber would cover the cottage door. Finally, there would be a few beds of scented and decorative flowers under the cottage windows and possibly a pot or two of flowers that required special attention.

Sweet rocket.

Honesty seed-heads (satten flower).

Cornflowers.

Bellflowers.

Sunflower.

Feverfew.

THE EIGHTEENTH-CENTURY COTTAGE GARDEN AND THE ENCLOSURE ACTS

This century saw a rapid and complete change in garden design with a truly English idea: the 'natural' garden – better known as the English Landscape Movement. The formal gardens with their topiary, parterres, grand water features, terraces and flowers were swept away in favour of gardens that 'nature' would applaud: grass, trees and water (huge lakes), some with classical temples and grottoes depending on the designer. The immense new Palladian house was now to sit in a sea of green with a natural view in every direction as far as the eye could see. To achieve this illusion the 'common land' was taken from the villagers by way of the Enclosure Acts, and in some cases the whole village would be destroyed as it constituted a blot on the landscape! Nothing could stand in the way of the vast new parkland.

What of the cottage garden during this great upheaval? With the loss of common land, it was vital the cottage garden continued much as it had before by providing vegetables, fruit and herbs for the poor labourers and village craftsmen. However, they did gain from the 'big house', because where the old formal gardens were pulled apart and the plants discarded, the cottagers eagerly rescued these lovely flowers and ensured they proudly graced the cottage gardens instead. In this way many old varieties of flowers were saved and passed down from generation to generation being loved and admired in the cottager's plot.

An excellent insight into a cottage garden of this period comes from a pamphlet by Thomas Bernard in 1797 called *An Account of a Cottage and Garden near Tadcaster, with observations upon labourers having freehold cottages and gardens....* It is such a wonderful illustration of how a labourer and his wife coped and gardened that I have reproduced an extract of the account below:

Two miles from Tadcaster, on the left-hand side of the road to York, stands a beautiful little cottage, with a garden, that has long attracted the eye of the traveller. The slip of land is exactly a rood [¼ acre], inclosed by a quick hedge; and containing the cottage, fifteen apple trees, one green gage, and three winesour plum trees, two apricot trees, several gooseberry bushes, abundance of common vegetables, and three hives of bees; being all the apparent wealth of the possessor.

His name is Britton Abbot; his age sixty-seven; and his wife's nearly the same. At nine years old he had gone to work with a farmer; and being a steady careful lad, and a good labourer, particularly in what is called task work, he had managed so well, that before he was twenty-two years

A mid-eighteenth-century thatched cottage of mud and stud near Harrington Hall in the Lincolnshire Wolds.

of age, he had accumulated near £40. He then married, and took a little farm at £30 a year; but before the end of the second year he found it prudent, or rather necessary to quit it, having already exhausted, in his attempt to thrive upon it, almost all the little property that he had heaped together. He then fixed in a cottage at Poppleton; where, with, two acres of land, and his common right, he kept two cows. Here he had resided very comfortably, as a labourer, for nine years, and had six children living; and his wife preparing to lie in of a seventh, when an inclosure of Poppleton took place; and the arrangements made in consequence of it, obliged him to seek for a new habitation, and other means of subsistence for his family.

He applied to Squire Fairfax, and told him that, if he would let him have a little bit of ground by the road-side, 'he would shew him the fashions on it'. After enquiry into his character, he obtained of Mr Fairfax the ground he now occupies; and planted the garden, and the hedge round it, which is a single row, thirty-five years old, and without flaw or defect. Mr Fairfax was so much pleased with the progress of his work, and the extreme neatness of his place, that he told him he should be rent free.

Britton Abbot says he earns 12s and sometimes 15s and 18s a week, by hoeing turnips by the piece, setting quick, and other task work. He gets from his garden, annually, about forty bushels of potatoes, besides other vegetables, and his fruit is worth £3 to £4 a year. His wife occasionally goes out to work; she also spins at home. And takes care of his house and garden.

Two photographs showing a row of Chippenham Park Estate cottages. All cottages are well set back from the road and given the same frontage in which to grow fruit trees and vegetables.

The picturesque village of Milton Abbas today with the two rows of cottages hidden away in the valley so that they didn't destroy the view of the new landscape park. Each cottage had its own appointed garden front and back.

This account clearly illustrates a number of things – the devastating effects of enclosure on a village in England and the loss of common land; that a good thick hawthorn hedge was in general the hedge of choice to surround the cottage garden; that potatoes were now being grown as a crop in Yorkshire; that the garden had a small orchard of fruit trees, gooseberry bushes and beehives; and possibly most importantly of all, that it was the woman who tended the garden and herbs.

On those estates where the village was totally destroyed because it was sited too close to the house and therefore interfered with the new landscape, some considerate landlords took the decision to re-position the village out of sight, but, at the same time create a new architect-designed model village as a show piece. This gave the owner the opportunity to demolish what he considered the ramshackle, unsanitary, poorly constructed cottages and hovels and improve the lot of his workers and their health.

In his 1775 *Hints to Gentlemen of Landed Property*, Nathaniel Kent says:

The shattered hovels which half the poor of this kingdom are obliged to put up with are truly affecting to a heart fraught with humanity. Those who condescend to visit these miserable tenements, can testify that neither health nor decency can be preserved within them.

The Board of Agriculture (1790s) had similar worries and talked about reform of the poor labourers' housing stock, but although there was some concern, only a very few landlords would create a model village, and when they did so it was more for aesthetic reasons than worries about the plight of their labourers' living conditions. However, for the first time we have a designed cottage and garden which would try to combine 'utility and beauty'. All cottages would have the same area of garden enclosed by a neat hedge with a central path leading down to the door (all of which were painted the same colour). There might be a rustic structure or porch over the front door and to the side or back perhaps a wash house and pigsty. A large fruit tree might be planted in each garden and a brick privy down the end. The size and design of the garden varied according to how generous the landlord was but would have been large enough to grow a good quantity of vegetables, herbs, soft fruit bushes and flowers. This seemed like an improvement and although the cottages looked quaint from the outside, unfortunately they were often too small for the size of labourer's family and the gardens only just of an adequate size.

Possibly the first model village was built by Lord Orford at Chippenham Park, Cambridgeshire (1702–12) after he had obtained permission from the king to alter and enlarge his park. This required extending into the village, so a new village was designed by Adam Russell with gardens at the front.

Nuneham Courtenay, Oxfordshire, was created by Simon Harcourt, 1st Earl Harcourt in 1749. The name Nuneham means 'new village', with Courtenay coming from the thirteenth-century 'Curtenay' family that lived there. The 1st Earl demolished the old manor house, medieval church and unsightly clay cottages around the village green to create space for Nuneham House and its landscape park. The new semi-detached single-storey cottages were built out of sight of the hall and either side of the main Oxford road, each with its own garden.

Between 1773 and 1780 the village of Milton Abbas in Dorset was designed and constructed by the partnership of architect William Chambers and landscaper Lancelot Brown, after Lord Milton (Earl of Dorchester) decided that the beastly town of Middleton was going to interrupt his view of the new landscape. Instead, a lane consisting of thirty-six newly constructed thatched cob cottages, each housing two families, was tucked away in the wooded valley out of sight. Between each cottage was a horse chestnut tree creating a tree-lined avenue. Unfortunately, we know little about the gardens accompanying these cottages, but they surely had cottage gardens to provide for the families.

In the late 1830s a picturesque village was planned to accompany Harlaxton Manor in Lincolnshire, which was being built for the new owner Gregory Gregory. The gardens around each dwelling were reasonably large and all had a well. No two gardens were designed the same, but all were hedged, and it is thought planned and possibly planted by the estate's head gardener. Often a little topiary, prettily edged paths and a few fruit trees (still to be seen today) were added.

Many more model villages would be built in the nineteenth century for factory workers by employers concerned about the normally atrocious living conditions and, like all things, some were far better designed and had larger gardens than others. But new model villages were in general few and far between; most cottagers continued to live a very simple life in leaky, damp, extremely draughty and over-crowded dwellings with little warmth, no running water and holes in the thatch!

THE NINETEENTH-CENTURY COTTAGE GARDEN

The old proverb 'Poverty's no disgrace but 'tis a great inconvenience' sums up the beginning of this century when a number of factors would make things decidedly worse for the cottager. The Enclosure Acts were still gathering pace with seven million acres of land being enclosed by 4,000 Acts of Parliament between 1750 and 1870, thus wiping out virtually all the common land in and around rural villages and creating lasting hardship for the cottagers. In 1804 the Corn Laws were introduced, stopping the import of cheap grain so that British farmers could keep their prices high. This was good for farmers but devastating for poor labourers who struggled to buy bread. Food prices were higher but agricultural labourers' wages fell to the lowest level ever recorded. The 1840s became known as the 'Hungry Forties' as a series of poor harvests and potato failures exacerbated the situation and starvation became commonplace.

At this time the cottager relied entirely upon his garden to be self-sufficient in food to feed his large family, and at what seems a particularly difficult and desperate period for cottagers we still hear of well-tended and productive cottage gardens.

William Corbett, author of *Rural Rides* (1822), comments on what he sees:

> … in almost every part of England … the most interesting of all objects, that which is such an honour to England, and that which distinguishes it from all the rest of the world, namely, those neatly kept and productive little gardens round the labourer's houses…

With so many cottagers struggling to survive it seems ironic that this period, from the early to mid-nineteenth century, was also probably the heyday of the cottage garden. All the elements that were so essential to a traditional cottage garden were present:

- a good-sized hedged plot being both productive and pretty
- a mixture of vegetables, herbs and flowers
- colour and fragrance
- use of free or cheap materials throughout the garden
- something in flower in every season
- native plants and flowers loved by bees
- fruit trees – mainly apples and pears
- few shrubs (lilac possibly) and no lawn
- chickens and pigs commonly kept

It would be these flowery gardens that so delighted gardeners, writers and artists later in the century and had such a huge influence on Gertrude Jekyll and William Robinson, who enthusiastically proclaimed that the ideas gained from cottage gardens should be admired and utilized in the new garden designs that architects and gardeners were creating. It would therefore seem appropriate at this juncture to describe the two main distinct forms of cottage garden in England *c*.1830–60.

The cottage close to the lane

If the cottage was built extremely close to the lane (as many were in the Cotswolds) the small front strip of garden under the

This attractive cottage with a lovely display of typical flowers, would once have had a picket fence and gate at the front, and a substantial back garden for vegetables, herbs, fruit and animals.

cottage windows was considered the ideal position for the pretty mix of flowers. These tiny narrow areas were still often walled or hedged and had a picket gate leading to the front door. The little garden itself was crammed with flowers: tall hollyhocks, larkspur, scented mignonette, pinks, stocks, sweet rocket, marigolds, Sweet Williams, nigella, forget-me-nots, campanulas, columbines and Michaelmas daisies. The deep windowsills of the cottage could accommodate pots of polyanthus or auricula, and over the door would be a rose or honeysuckle.

Behind the cottage was the large area devoted to vegetables, herbs and large old fruit trees. Closest to the cottage would be an area for valuable herbs. Being near the cottage they were within easy reach for use in cooking and herbal teas. Flora Thompson's *Lark Rise to Candleford* illustrates this planting:

> As well as their flower garden, the women cultivated a herb corner, stocked with thyme and parsley and sage for cooking, rosemary to flavour the home-made lard, lavender to scent the best clothes, and peppermint, pennyroyal, horehound, camomile, tansy, balm and rue for physic. They made a good deal of camomile tea, which they drank freely to ward off colds, to soothe the nerves, and as a general tonic.

Also close to the cottage was the wash-house and probably a large bed of soapwort (*Saponaria officinalis*) – the plant used to clean clothes much the same as washing powders today. Outside the back of the cottage was the main vegetable area, which might have been one large area with vegetables grown in rows, or perhaps large beds with narrow paths running between them. Beyond

the vegetable plot was the less well-kept grassy area of a small orchard where large old fruit trees were grown. These would have been apple and pears mainly. The semi-shade created beneath the large spreading branches was ideal for native self-seeders like snowdrops, winter aconites and primroses in the early part of the year, which were quickly followed by bluebells, pulmonarias and foxgloves. Beehives were normally positioned near to the fruit trees for pollination and the chicken house was also generally kept in the orchard. Stacks of wood for the fire would be gathered into wigwams (so the outside kept the inside dry) and positioned close to the fruit trees. A little further on would be the pigsties, and then finally at the bottom of the garden, the outhouse. Here also might be the muck heap with all the vital pig muck added, which would be essential for replenishing the vegetable patch. In Lincolnshire, the last third of a long cottage garden was often a large 'bean patch' – being furthest away from the cottage as it required very little attention.

A cottage garden in Thimbleby, Lincolnshire

The cottages in the village of Thimbleby (one of which I visited in 2002 with the Lincolnshire Cottage Garden Society) were originally laid out in exactly the same way as described above. The village, mentioned in the *Domesday Book* of 1086, has one main street with thatched cottages sited virtually right on the road which runs down to the church at the far end. The narrow strips in front of each cottage are (even today) simply devoted to flowers, however, at the back of each cottage there was once a highly productive garden of approximately one acre.

The garden area nearest to the back of the cottage when we visited was devoted to vegetables in beds cut into the lawn in irregular blocks. Some old cottage flowers and shrubs rambled around both the cottage and the large vegetable patch, and beyond this there were three disused brick pigsties and some old-gnarled fruit trees. Further on still the garden became rather wild, as it had been let go somewhat, but was considered valuable for wildlife. Discussing the cottage garden with the owner, a lovely lady in her eighties, we discovered that she had never purchased a single plant from either a garden centre or nursery in her entire life. She explained that every plant in the garden had been given to her as either a cutting, seeds or a piece of root split off a friend's plant. It was delightful to hear that the old cottage method of exchanging cuttings and seeds was still alive in small rural communities, very much tying in with another of Flora Thompson's descriptions – 'As no money could be spared for seeds or plants, they had to depend upon roots and cuttings given by their neighbours.'

The thatched cottage is set right on the road and originally had a picket fence running along the front separating its narrow cottage garden from the lane.

The back garden is still the original size associated with the cottage in medieval times and was originally purely devoted to growing vegetables and fruit, and keeping pigs and chickens.

Trees, shrubs, raspberry canes, feverfew, a patch of potatoes and teasels can all be seen in the large back garden. A red shirt in the foreground acts as a bird scarer on the newly sown vegetable patch.

In true cottage garden fashion, everything in the back garden is mixed together – cottage shrubs, broad beans, teasels and buttercups.

A cottage garden in Hipsburn, Northumberland

It was pure chance that on a visit to Alnmouth I came across Ann Taylor's cottage garden in Hipsburn. This again is a cottage set close to the road but having a long productive back garden with cottage flowers near to the back door, a vegetable patch and a large area of grass beyond that. The grassed area at the end was originally part of the productive garden and probably had fruit trees and animals, but in more recent times had become part of a common area across the backs of all of the cottages. It was a delight to find a cottage garden laid out in such a manner.

Looking down the garden over the bright cottage flowers to the vegetable patch, and then beyond to the lawned area at the bottom.

The grass path leading down the garden from behind the greenhouse to the vegetable patch.

The cottage set back from the road

If the cottage was set back from the road then a very different layout became the norm. A central path would run from the picket gate down a straight line to the front door. Over the door was always a rustic porch or structure and climbing over this a rose or honeysuckle. On either side of the door and under the windows were flowery borders of highly scented and traditional cottage plants. Here the scent could waft into the cottage through the windows on hot summer's days and be appreciated inside. Or if the strips under the windows were too narrow, then an area of traditional flowers, herbs and self-seedlings were all crammed into a large patch.

To quote Flora Thompson again:

A cottage garden set back from the lane, c.1870.

Nearer the house was a portion given up entirely to flowers, not growing in beds or borders, but crammed together in an irregular square, where they bloomed in wild profusion. There were rose bushes there and lavender and rosemary and a bush apple-tree which bore the little red and yellow streaked apples in late summer, and Michaelmas daisies and red-hot pokers and old-fashioned pompom dahlias in autumn and peonies and pinks already budding.

ADAM BEDE

Adam Bede, written by George Eliot in 1859, describes a delightful large type of cottage garden:

> Adam walked by the rick-yard, at present empty of ricks, to the little wooden gate leading into the garden – once a well-tended kitchen garden of a manor-house; now, but for the handsome brick wall with stone coping that ran along one side of it, a true farmhouse garden, with hardy perennial flowers, unpruned fruit trees, and kitchen vegetables growing together in careless, half-neglected abundance. In that leafy flowery, bushy time, to look for any one in this garden was like playing 'hide-and-seek'. There were the tall hollyhocks beginning to flower, and dazzle the eye with their pink, white and yellow; there were the syringas and Guelders roses, all large and disorderly for want of trimming; there were leafy walls of scarlet beans and late peas; there was a row of bushy filberts in one direction and in another a huge apple-tree making a barren circle under its low-spreading boughs.

Whittaker's Cottage. This agricultural labourer's cottage at the Weald and Downland Museum in West Sussex was built in the mid-1860s and shows the small cottage garden of approximately 9m (30ft) wide mainly at the front of the cottage which is set back from the lane.

The central path would always be edged with plants to make a wonderful display running down towards the door. The plants chosen would differ according to the part of country where the cottager lived. It might be double daisies, marigolds, London Pride, cottage pinks, or, as my grandad had, garden auriculas.

Following the same line of the path would be rows of vegetables and potatoes, and behind these would be rows of raspberry canes and gooseberry bushes. A number of fruit trees would probably be placed around the outside edge of the garden near to the hedge and these would probably have climbers rambling up through them. A well, pigsty, chicken shed and muck heap would be placed wherever possible.

By 1870 England had moved from an agricultural nation to an industrial one. Victorian ingenuity and the growth of factories rapidly changed every part of society. There was new wealth being generated, a vast new middle class, a growing rail network and the accelerated expansion of towns and cities. With a sudden demand for land for workers' housing many towns expanded into the surrounding countryside and the villages started to be swallowed up. Hovel-like cottages were pulled down and the in-fill of large areas between cottages accelerated the loss of yet more common ground.

New farm machinery (threshing machines/ploughs) and an agricultural depression resulted in a great reduction in the need for manpower and many farm labourers became destitute. Thomas Hardy commented in a letter to Rider Haggard that village tradition was 'absolutely sinking, had nearly sunk, into eternal oblivion'. It is no surprise, then, that many labourers made the choice to

These gardens in Warwick are rare survivors of the allotment gardens of the Victorian period which provided tradesmen in the town (who lived above their shops) with both a productive plot and recreational area. These plots fall into the category of cottage gardens as they provided food, fruit, and herbs for the family but also an area that the family could enjoy on Sundays. The remaining sixteen historic plots give us an idea of how they looked, each having a summerhouse, lawn and flower beds, as well as the vegetable area. These allotment gardens were particularly popular in the Midlands where the town's craftsmen often lived in cramped and over-crowded conditions.

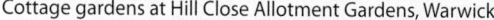
Cottage gardens at Hill Close Allotment Gardens, Warwick.

up-sticks and leave their homes and move to a town or city to work in the new factories where there was a chance of regular paid work. Anything seemed better than trying to survive on a pittance and a plot of land. Many cottage gardens were probably simply abandoned, although maybe a few favourite plants were taken. Relocated to long streets of new terraced housing with only a tiny back yard, many former cottagers wished to grow food to supplement their poor wages and luckily some progressive factory owners 'allotted' them some land for this purpose.

Allotments had first appeared in the late sixteenth century as common land was grabbed by the wealthy due to their need to create fields for their sheep (first enclosures) – English wool being superior to anything in Europe and therefore our greatest export. Commoners were then allotted land next to their tenanted cottage as part of their wages. This was still very much the case in the nineteenth century: as Flora Thompson in *Lark Rise to Candleford* mentions, the men of the village worked on either their gardens or allotments for an hour or two after their tea-supper. These allotment plots were divided into two, one half planted with potatoes and the other half wheat or barley – 'the garden being reserved for green vegetables, currant and gooseberry bushes, and a few old-fashioned flowers'. Allotments as we know them today took off at the beginning of the nineteenth century – the first Act of Parliament for land of 20 acres to be made available in parishes to help with the relief of poverty being passed in 1819. Later, in 1887, the Allotments and Cottage Garden Compensation for Crops Act was supposed to encourage local authorities to provide allotments if there was a demand. However, this Act wasn't strong enough and would require further Acts of Parliament through to 1950.

THE ROMANTIC COTTAGE GARDEN

From the 1880s onwards the cottage garden divides into two streams – the productive self-sufficient poor labourer's garden (being vegetables, herbs and animals), and the 'new' romantic, picturesque style of cottage garden of the middle class who wished for the idyllic country life. It is no surprise that a magazine called *Country Life* promoting this new healthy and romantic lifestyle was first published in 1897, and would showcase the talents of the young architect Edwin Lutyens and gardener Gertrude Jekyll, upon whom he called for the planting schemes. It is this 'new' second stream that forms the basis of the modern cottage garden today, and it was this period when a number of factors all came together to create the right conditions for a different form of the cottager's garden.

She would force nothing, graft nothing, nor set things in rows, she welcomed self-seeders, let each have its head, and was the enemy of very few weeds. Consequently our garden was a sprouting jungle and never an inch was wasted. Syringas shot up, laburnum hung down, while roses smothered the apple tree, red flowering currants spread entirely along one path; such a chaos of blossom as amazed the bees and bewildered the birds of the air. Potatoes and cabbages were planted at random among the foxgloves, pansies and pinks. Often some species would entirely capture the garden – forget-me-nots one year, hollyhocks the next, then a sheet of harvest poppies.

Laurie Lee also comments on the gradual loss of village life as the motor car became a common feature and the old village families started to disperse and move elsewhere to live and work. The erosion of village life is echoed by the loss of the productive cottage garden, as grocers, butchers and other trades become more prominent within the village.

But just when we find the traditional cottage garden disappearing, along comes the *Dig for Victory* garden during the Second World War. The government, needing everybody to pull together and produce much of their own food, advised that a garden or allotment of 10 rods (¼ acre) would be a sufficient area to grow five vegetables and keep some rabbits, chickens or perhaps a pig. In cities and towns across Britain back lawns were dug up, fruit trees planted, essential vegetables sown and some animals kept. This wartime garden with the lawn being transformed into a vegetable patch, yet at the same time the cheery decorative flowers being retained, basically created a cottage garden in an urban situation.

With rationing continuing after the war and a need for a vast amount of new housing stock due to the bombing, architects designed new housing estates and gave each semi-detached house a large garden. This enabled the owners to have both a lawned area for recreational use and a large area for vegetables, animals and compost bins. It gave post-war families the opportunity to be partly self-sufficient in the way that cottagers had once been and has resulted in many social houses having the luxury of such large gardens today.

THE MODERN COTTAGE GARDEN

The modern cottage garden is difficult to define, but it can be said with certainty that the greatest change is from a productive garden to one that is designed purely for pleasure. It is easy to see why – we no longer need to grow our own food to survive in today's society, although we may well grow vegetables for pleasure on our allotment or in the back garden. Keeping livestock in the garden has generally disappeared and those who do keep chickens only

Front garden of a cottage in Saltfleetby, Lincolnshire, planted in a modern cottage garden style.

A designed modern cottage garden with clipped box hedges making a formal feature path to contrast with the profusion of cottagey planting.

do so as a hobby or because they like the idea of fresh eggs and a few decorative hens scratching around. I have never found anyone keeping pigs in a modern cottage garden during my lifetime, yet even up to the Second World War the pig was a vital element of the cottage economy. The advancement in food production and importation since the 1950s has meant a major change in gardens throughout Britain. Supermarkets, butchers and corner shops sell all we need to eat without individuals having to grow it.

The rise of the motor car has also had a major effect, particularly upon front gardens. The design of the front portion of a cottage garden now has to accommodate at least one car (if not more). Room for a drive and perhaps a garage for this modern-day necessity has seen many of the old cottage gardens lose their traditional path from the gate to the front door, often being replaced simply by a large area of hard standing.

Something else that is extremely common in cottage gardens today that was rarely seen in the past is the lawn. Even the most ardent cottage gardeners today display their flowers in beds and borders around areas of lawn, and admittedly, I too had an area of lawn in my previous cottage garden. It must be remembered that the lawnmower wasn't invented by Edwin Budding until 1830 and those that had areas of grass before this time had to be wealthy enough to have them scythed regularly. But even if the cottager could afford a mower and the time to mow it, they still wouldn't have had a lawn, as it would have been a total waste of very valuable growing space.

Possibly the greatest difference today is that cottage gardens are *designed* to fulfil the owner's own desires and follow the latest gardening trends. What people require in a garden is often driven by gardening programmes, magazines, books, major flower shows, garden centres, garden visiting and what the neighbour has done. In the past the cottage garden changed very little over the years. Villages were generally self-contained communities with very limited outside influence. The garden was passed down from generation to generation with perhaps a few new plants added, as friends, family or neighbours exchanged seeds, cuttings or a

The turf maze forms a central feature in this Lincolnshire cottage garden.

piece off a good clump of a particular plant. Fashions in gardening change rapidly nowadays and we are bombarded with new plants with bigger heads, richer colours and longer flowering periods. It is no surprise then that the modern cottage garden covers a wider range of possibilities and many different ideas which to some extent depend on the style of house, size of the garden and the particular likes of the owner. Some try to be more traditional in their layout, with straight paths covered with overflowing cottagey-type flowers; others have wonderful garden structures, statues and summerhouses covered in climbers and designed to impress; some have an army of plastic gnomes; some have a formal knot garden brimming with herbs; some have a wildlife area with pond and native plants; some are plantsmen's gardens, full of unusual perennials and snowdrops; others have a large gravel garden with grasses and perennials. And *all* call themselves a cottage garden!

Two specific gardens helped revitalize the cottage garden style in the twentieth century: Vita Sackville-West's Sissinghurst and Margery Fish's garden of East Lambrook Manor. They are very different gardens, Sissinghurst being an extremely formal structure overlaid with a maximum of informality of cottage-style plantings and some colour-themed rooms, the 'white garden' becoming world famous and much emulated. East Lambrook Manor, on the other hand, is not as well-known and is more of an old-style cottage garden with meandering paths and many rescued old-fashioned cottage flowers crammed into every available inch.

So how do we find the modern cottage garden? A modern cottage garden 'style' can be achieved in a number of ways – which I aim to cover in the following chapters – but in essence, it is about trying to create that 'cottagey feeling' with the planting. It really doesn't matter if the house is old or new, the garden large or small, whether the garden has lawns or a large patio, or even whether traditional cottage flowers or their modern equivalents are used. In the end, it boils down to capturing those essential elements: a profusion of flowers jostling for space with each other; an exuberance of mixed planting spilling informally over paths, patios and lawns; and of course, roses over the door.

Chapter 2

Creating the 'Cottage Garden Style'

B y their very nature, cottage gardens should feel chaotic, disorderly and unplanned. However, to create what *you* particularly want within your own cottage garden, it is best to have some idea of what you wish to achieve – a plan that meets your requirements.

Should a cottage garden be designed? You might think not, as in the past it was often believed that a 'true' cottage garden was never designed, and that this is what set it apart from other gardens. But if you look more closely at the old cottage gardens, you'll discover that they did contain structure – their guide was common sense. First and foremost, the garden was enclosed. The hedge or paling fence enclosed and defined the garden, kept animals from getting in and devouring the valuable vegetables, and helped filter the wind. Essential well-trodden paths went where there was a need: front gate to front door; back door to wash-house, privy or pigs; and along under the washing line. Vegetables were planted in a specific area where the soil was sunny and suitable, and were sown in rows for ease of weeding and picking. Herbs were grown by the back door for convenience (culinary/medicinal), with the soapwort grown next to the wash-house for easy access. And flowers too, grown where their beauty and scent could be most appreciated and for ease of cutting. This 'need-based' layout is effectively a basic garden design.

STRUCTURE – KEY DESIGN ELEMENTS

The traditional layout of the cottage garden is not appropriate for today's society, as we don't require a large plot of vegetables, large fruit trees and pigs or chickens. The requirements of the modern cottage garden are very different: to create an oasis of flowers and scents, a recreational rather than productive space, an area for relaxation and entertainment, and to appreciate the natural beauty of the garden through the seasons. Whether you're creating a garden from scratch, simply wishing to re-think and improve upon an existing garden, or develop certain areas within the garden, some thought needs to go into the design.

An attractive timber-framed thatched cottage is *not* necessary to achieve a cottage garden style. The style can easily be adapted for any design of modern house or bungalow. And don't be tempted to think that you must have old-fashioned bits and pieces to give that 'old world' cottage garden feel. Modern materials will actually blend in better with a modern house and look just as pleasing once the planting has been introduced. The aim when creating a cottage garden is to make it look as if it 'just happened' naturally, although it's actually been designed thoughtfully.

Of course, the most important element in any cottage garden are the plants, but these should only be considered after the main framework of the garden has been worked out, and therefore planting schemes and choosing which cottage plants to use will be covered in the following two chapters.

Cottage border in the front garden of a modern house in Cambridge.

The first step in creating a cottage-style garden is to ask yourself what you want and then make a list. Typically, the elements might include lawn, sitting area, pergola, washing line, shed, arbour or compost bins.

Once you've decided what you require, you can begin by creating the garden framework – hedges, walls, lawns, paths and patio/sitting area. Getting the structure of the garden right is vastly important as it creates what is known as the 'bones' of the garden. A combination of good structure and clever planting will give you the correct cottagey feel. A good example of a strong structure overlaid with stunning planting is Vita Sackville-West's garden at Sissinghurst Castle in Kent. A visit to the garden would enable you to appreciate this and possibly give you some ideas.

ENCLOSING THE GARDEN

Hedges

The English cottage garden was always enclosed; and an enclosed garden is still required today, not so much to protect the vegetables as to give privacy. We all value our privacy and a place to relax. Some very lucky owners may have a walled garden which can be clothed with climbers and rambling roses to create a green haven. My own wish has been to have a walled garden, but I have never achieved this dream! Like me then, you will probably have no choice but to enclose your own garden with either a hedge or fence. Both have advantages and disadvantages. A hedge is a fairly inexpensive option, as you can buy young hedging plants and allow them to grow to the height required. Hedges are excellent for exposed sites, as they effectively filter the wind and prevent plants from being battered and bent over.

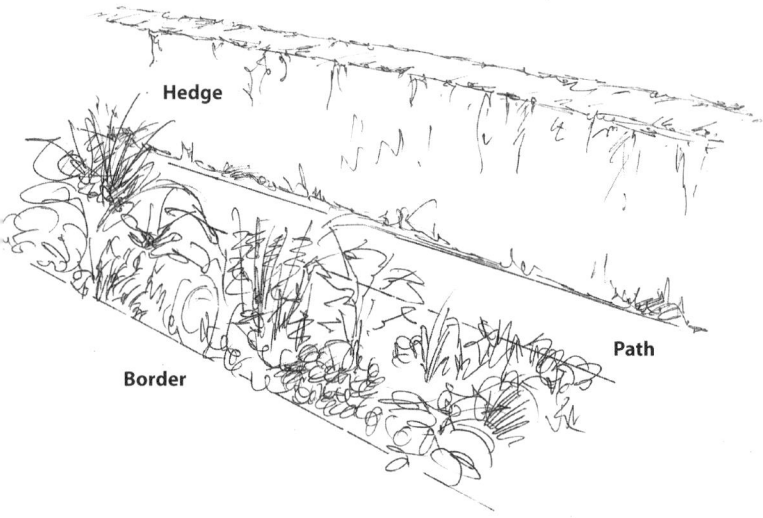

Hedge, path and border positioning.

A well-kept hedge is a traditional and attractive option around the perimeter of a garden; it can be shaped, is good for wildlife, and will provide a lovely backdrop for flower borders (particularly if a single-species hedge is used). The height of a hedge depends upon its position: a front hedge is often about waist height, whereas back garden hedges tend to be taller to give the necessary privacy. This is a very modern change from my parents' time, when their back hedges were deliberately kept short to allow the neighbours to talk over! What height should a hedge be? According to the law it should be no higher than 2m (6ft) to allow light into your neighbour's garden and back windows.

One of the disadvantages of a hedge is the regular cutting required, which obviously depends upon the variety chosen. The roots can also be problematic; they take up a great deal of water and nutrients from the surrounding soil, which vastly reduces the variety of plants you can grow beneath them.

If you opt to buy small hedging plants, you'll require a temporary wire fence or something similar until the hedge has filled out and attained some height. Another idea that should be considered is laying a path alongside a hedge. This does two important jobs: firstly, it gives easy access and a solid standing for step ladders (should you require them) from which the hedge-clipping can be tackled; secondly, it alleviates the scenario of problem roots. A path between a hedge and any flower border is a great solution that doesn't detract from the border itself, but also allows the border to be weeded and worked upon easily. In fact, when the border is in full flower, you wouldn't even notice the path behind it!

Chapter 6 (Green Structure) goes into detail on the various types of hedging and which types are suitable for various areas within the garden.

Fencing

Fencing seems to be a more obvious choice for the smaller modern cottage garden, as it takes up less space. It comes in many styles, is fairly easy to put up, and can be either preserved or painted. Fencing is as traditional as hedging, and the old wattle or woven fence has again become popular, although it is rather expensive. For really tiny front gardens, a picket fence is a great option, and comes in a variety of designs. This will set off the cottage-style planting beautifully, with flowers spilling under and poking through the 'pickets' (vertical boards). For the back garden, the ubiquitous 6-foot panel fence is the norm. Easily attainable from all DIY and garden centres, the panels come in a range of different variations, some stronger than others (price dependent), some vertical, some horizontal and some in a fancy weave. If you wish to make a short garden feel longer than it really is, then opt for the horizontal panels.

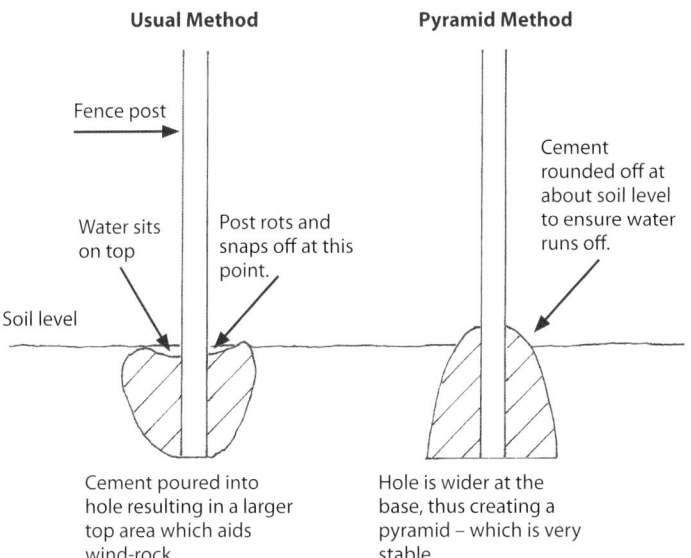

Usual Method

Fence post

Water sits on top

Post rots and snaps off at this point.

Soil level

Cement poured into hole resulting in a larger top area which aids wind-rock.

Pyramid Method

Cement rounded off at about soil level to ensure water runs off.

Hole is wider at the base, thus creating a pyramid – which is very stable.

How to cement the base of fence posts.

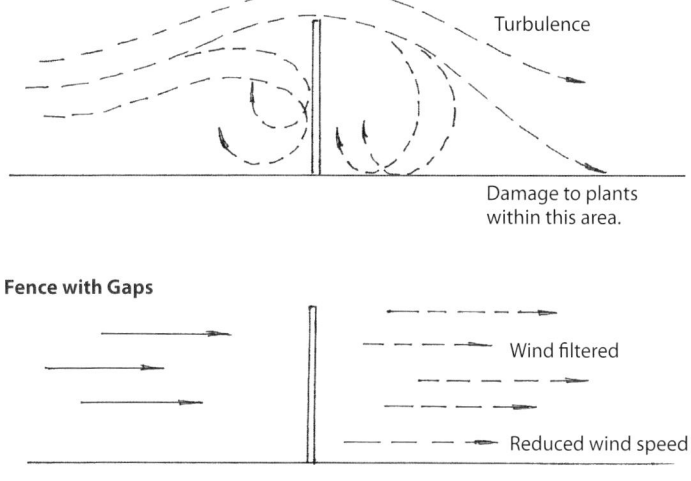

Solid Fence

Turbulence

Damage to plants within this area.

Fence with Gaps

Wind filtered

Reduced wind speed

The effects of wind upon different fences.

Picket fence with clematis, allium and lavender spilling through.

Cottage border with alliums, clematis, white camassia and hardy geraniums backed by a painted closeboard fence with trellis along the top.

If the panels are preserved and the posts are concreted in correctly, the fence should last many years. Whenever I put up fence posts I use the 'pyramid' method which ensures the post doesn't rot near the ground and snap off in high winds.

Painting the panels rather than preserving is another option – this is an individual preference. With such a vast range of outdoor paint colours it can be difficult to choose, but I would suggest either a blue/green or silver/grey colour as both complement flowers exceedingly well. This colour also helps give a general feeling of space in small gardens, whereas a dark-coloured paint or preserve tends to make the garden feel closed-in.

Another clever trick to give a feeling of space in back gardens is the use of trellis panels on the top of the fencing. You are essentially taking a 'borrowed view' from beyond the garden and bringing it into yours. The trellis panel along the top will give a view from beyond the garden, allow in more light, and create a structure for climbers planted at the base of the fence to climb through. Panels can either be purchased with integral trellis or you can buy trellis pieces to add to existing panels.

Fencing made up of either horizontal or vertical slats that allow the wind to filter through is a better solution than the typical closeboard or featheredge fencing that is commonly available. Solid panel fencing has the disadvantage of turbulence in strong winds that will batter the plants at the base of the fence, and actually decrease the life of the fence.

Treillage is a more elaborate form of trellising for supporting climbers. The French used large areas of wooden latticework (*treillage*) in the eighteenth century as architectural support for the display of climbing plants and as a background for shrubs

and hedges whilst they grew to the required height. Simple rustic forms of trellis work best for subdividing large cottage gardens or as rose supports along the back of a border.

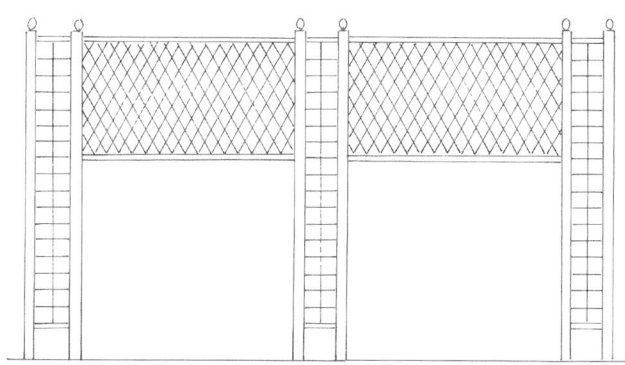

A treillage design for climbing roses.

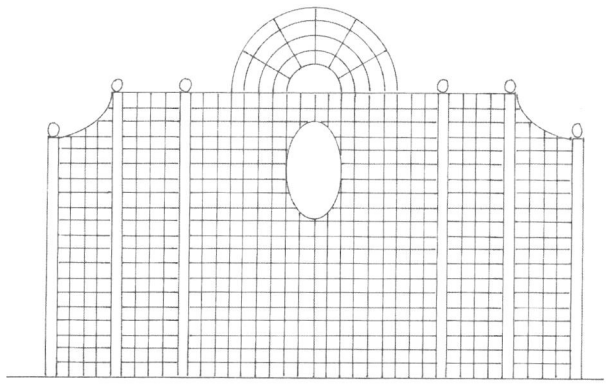

A more elaborate design for climbers, possibly for the end of a garden, which includes an oval window giving a 'borrowed' view.

Trellis panels are an alternative yet attractive solution for screening the garden boundary, but can also divide the garden into rooms or create secluded seating areas. Trellis ties in beautifully with the cottage garden style, filtering wind, allowing in light and acting as a wonderful backdrop for planting and climbers. The design of a seating area could include both solid fence panels and trellis panels – the solid panels around the actual seating to give maximum privacy, and the trellis panels attached slightly further along for planting opportunities. If all panels were painted the same colour it would tie everything together.

GARDEN COMPONENTS

Lawns

Large lawn surrounded with wide borders of cottagey planting.

Traditional cottage gardens never had lawns as the whole garden needed to be productive. Not until the invention of the lawnmower in 1830 did lawns start to become popular with the masses, and during the Victorian period, lawns with flower beds become an essential part of the garden. The lawn found its way into the new middle-class cottage-style gardens in the countryside, as illustrated in some of Helen Allingham's paintings, and in modern times has become a part of virtually every English garden. What can be better than a well-mown green English lawn? Creating the world's best lawns is something the British excel at; and in a garden

situation they are generally the largest element, creating a space that has many uses – sitting out, eating out, partying and playing games and letting the children play on. In a modern garden, the lawn also acts as a wonderful foil to set off the colourful borders of cottage flowers.

Decisions arise with the shape, size, situation and edging of any lawn. As a general rule of thumb, lawns tend to work best in larger gardens where there is more space. Families with children often try to buy houses with large gardens, to give themselves a sizeable lawn area. With large gardens there are two options: to keep the lawn as one sweeping mass, or to break the lawn up into areas to create a series of lawned rooms.

For the small town, city or seaside garden, it is worth asking yourself whether you really need a lawn. Here it is often better to completely dispense with the lawn and instead make the most of paths, cottage plantings and seating areas. In addition, without a lawn, there is no need for a bulky lawnmower and somewhere to store it!

If designing a garden to include lawn(s) it is worth bearing in mind that retaining the lawn as a 'whole' will cut down on the amount of time spent mowing and edging. Any lawn with island beds requires you to mow around and then edge each individual bed. This all takes time, whereas one large area is so much quicker and easier to mow up and down.

Grass gets very bare under trees and can prove problematic to mow with tree roots just below or on the surface. Tree roots spread outwards to at least twice the height of the tree, they take up a vast amount of water and prevent rain from penetrating the ground. It is best to design (or re-design) any garden so that the lawn skirts around under the tree and then source dry-shade-loving plants for the area under the spreading branches.

Examples of how gardens can be improved

The following two examples give some ideas on re-designing gardens to make life easier with regard to the lawn, whilst enhancing the overall design of the garden.

Example 1

The garden plan on the left shows the original garden with two large permanent fruit trees, A and B. They were planted as young trees in the original garden but as they've grown the lawn beneath has become bare. The owners then simply mowed around the base of the trees further out into the garden.

Three island beds have been cut out into the lawn at one time or another, making it more difficult to mow the lawn, and certainly more time consuming – one kidney-shaped bed, one teardrop bed and one circular island bed. Another obvious problem is the very narrow grass path that runs under the arch, which with constant foot traffic has turned into virtually bare soil, getting muddy in wet weather. This is a relatively high maintenance garden.

The garden plan on the right shows a re-design of the garden, retaining the two major trees, A and B. The lawn has been re-designed as one major area of grass that sweeps down the garden. The high-maintenance island beds have gone, and a summerhouse has been added at the bottom of the garden as somewhere to walk down the garden to and relax in. Tucked away in the right-hand corner, the summerhouse is a major feature that is only glimpsed from the patio outside the house. This is now a low-maintenance garden.

Example 1: Garden plan on left shows the original, high-maintenance design; garden plan on right shows the new, low-maintenance design.

Figure 1

Arch

Tree B

Tree A

Lawn

Patio

Figure 2

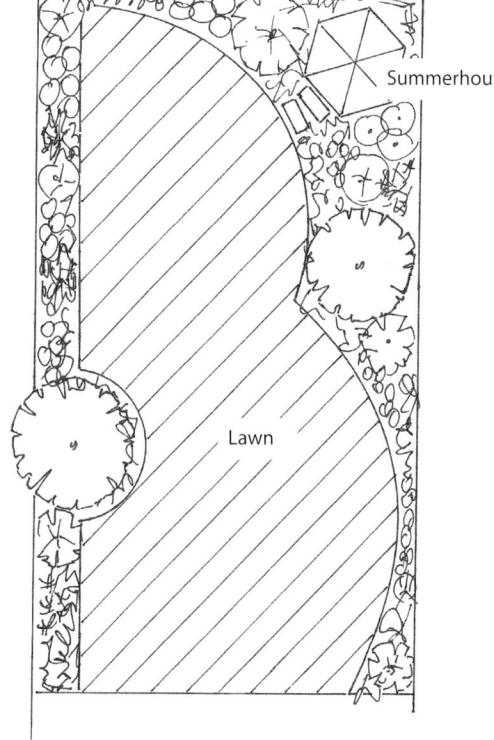

Summerhouse

Lawn

Figure 1

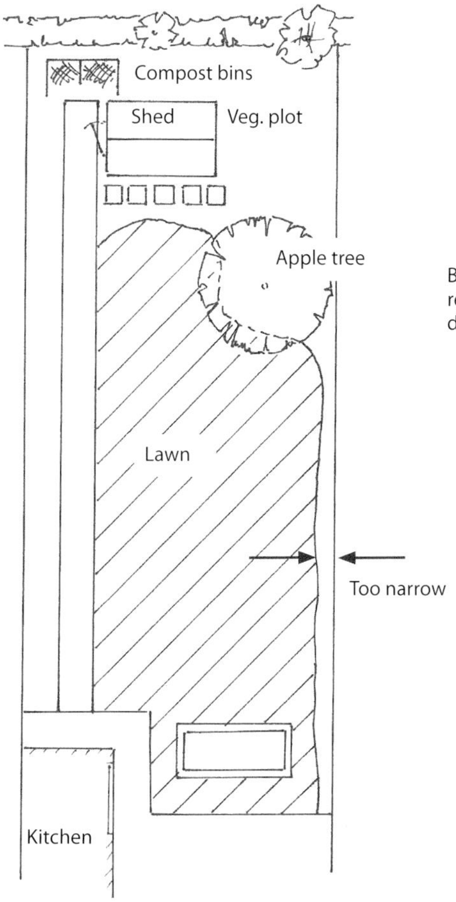

Compost bins

Shed   Veg. plot

Apple tree

Lawn

Too narrow

Kitchen

Figure 2

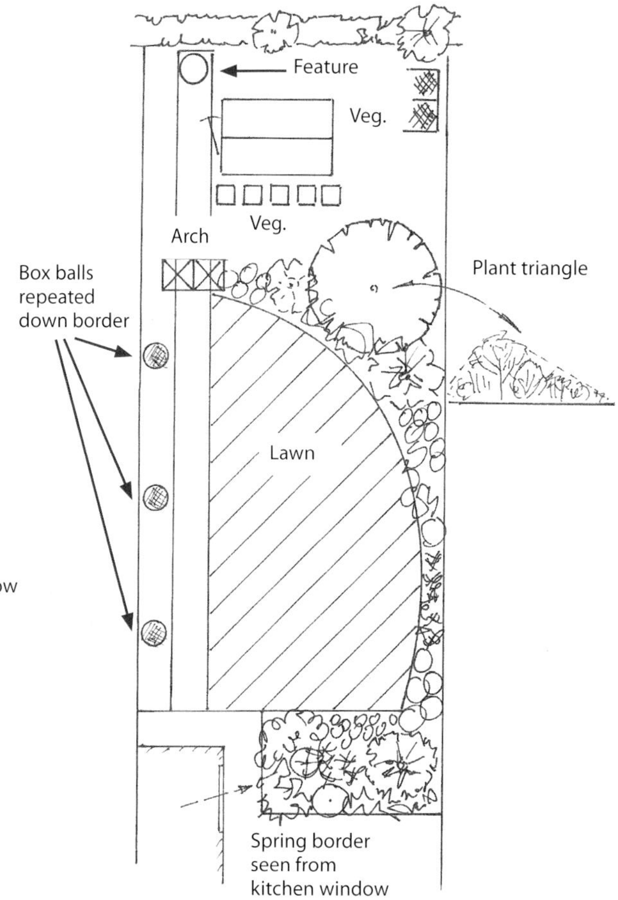

Feature

Veg.

Veg.

Arch

Box balls
repeated
down border

Plant triangle

Lawn

Spring border
seen from
kitchen window

Example 2: Garden plan on left
shows the original high-maintenance
design with no borders; garden
plan on right shows the new, low-
maintenance, more attractive design.

Example 2

The garden plan on the left shows the original garden which is behind a terraced house. It has a concrete path running the complete length of the garden to the compost bins, which sit in front of the mixed hedge. There is also a shed and a small vegetable patch at the bottom of the garden, and a large old apple tree close by. The lawn near the apple tree has been re-shaped over the years as plants have grown larger. The small concrete pond close to the house is difficult to mow around and doesn't hold water any longer. This is another high-maintenance garden with no good-sized borders.

The garden plan on the right shows a re-design of the garden with the lawn re-shaped for ease of mowing and to create a good-sized curved border using the old apple tree as the main feature. The main concrete path has been retained but the small concrete pond taken out and replaced by a spring flowering bed. The compost bins have been moved from the end of the path and placed closer to the vegetable patch, and are now out of view from the house. Instead, a decorative urn now acts as a vista-closer at the end of the path, being framed by the new arch with a climber. Clipped box balls have been repeated in the long border on the left-hand side to take the eye down the path. This is a more attractive, low-maintenance garden.

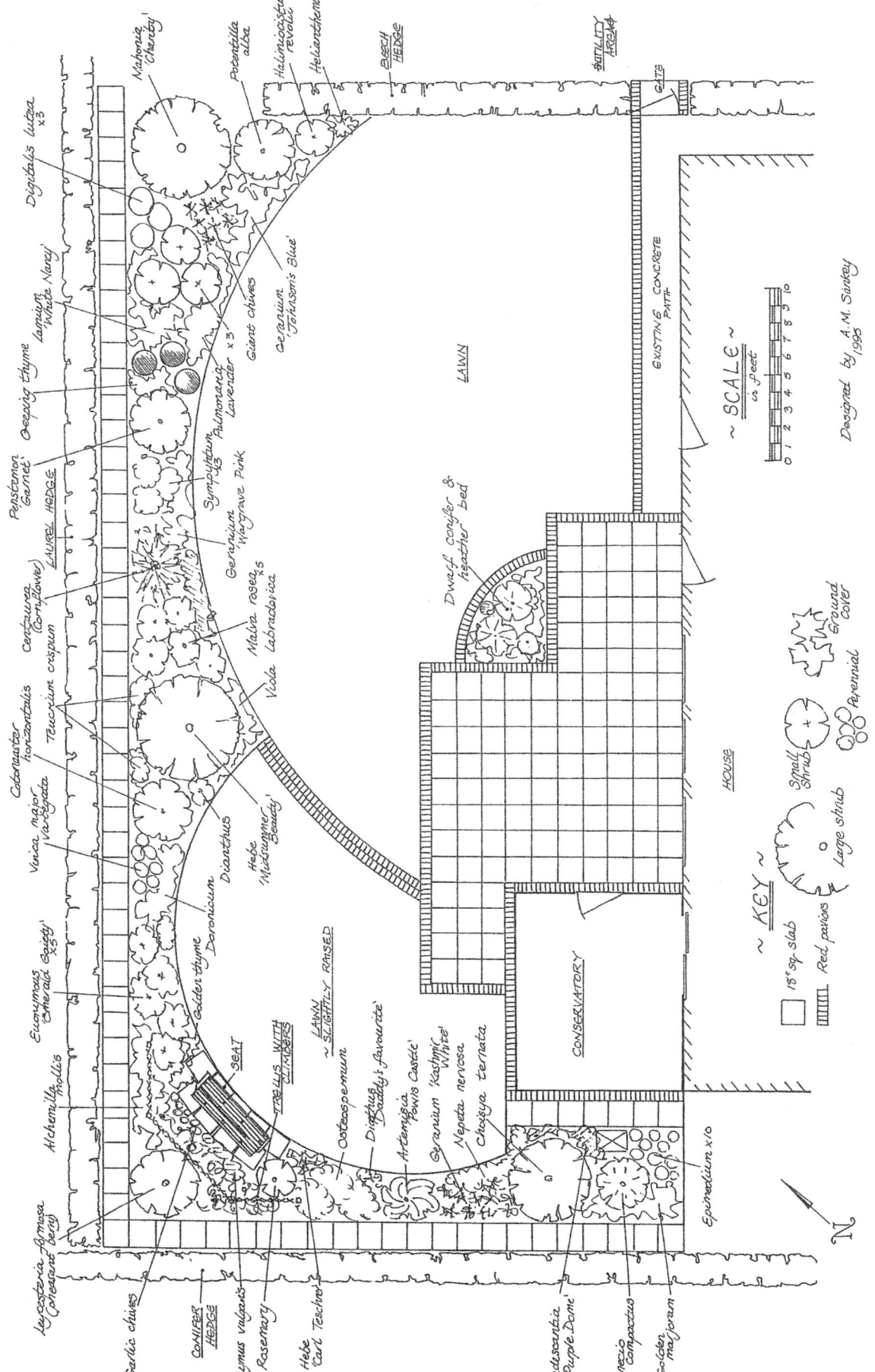

An example garden design plan of a large back garden with patio and lawn.

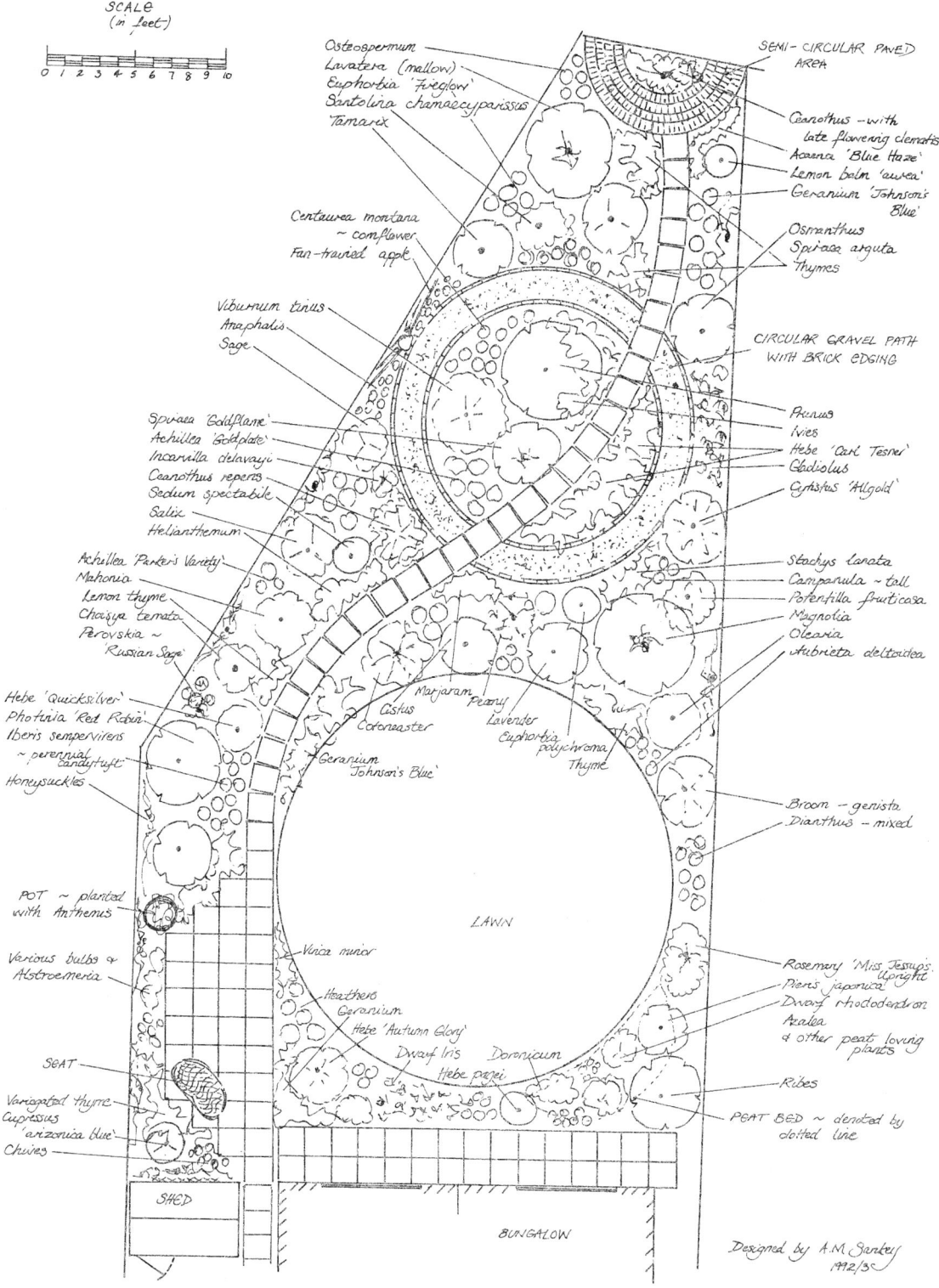

SCALE
(in feet)
0 1 2 3 4 5 6 7 8 9 10

Osteospermum
Lavatera (mallow)
Euphorbia 'Fireglow'
Santolina chamaecyparissus
Tamarix

SEMI-CIRCULAR PAVED AREA

Ceanothus – with late flowering clematis
Acaena 'Blue Haze'
Lemon balm 'aurea'
Geranium 'Johnson's Blue'

Osmanthus
Spiraea arguta
Thymes

Centaurea montana ~ cornflower
Fan-trained apple

CIRCULAR GRAVEL PATH WITH BRICK EDGING

Viburnum tinus
Anaphalis
Sage

Prunus
Ivies
Hebe 'Carl Tesner'
Gladiolus
Cytisus 'Allgold'

Spiraea 'Goldflame'
Achillea 'Goldplate'
Incarvillea delavayi
Ceanothus repens
Sedum spectabile
Salix
Helianthemum

Stachys lanata
Campanula ~ tall
Potentilla fruticosa
Magnolia
Olearia
Aubrieta deltoidea

Achillea 'Parker's Variety'
Mahonia
Lemon thyme
Choisya ternata
Perovskia ~ 'Russian Sage'

Marjoram
Cistus
Cotoneaster
Peony
Lavender
Euphorbia polychroma
Thyme

Hebe 'Quicksilver'
Photinia 'Red Robin'
Iberis sempervirens ~ perennial candytuft
Honeysuckles

Geranium 'Johnson's Blue'

Broom – genista
Dianthus – mixed

POT ~ planted with Anthemis

LAWN

Various bulbs & Alstroemeria

Vinca minor

Rosemary 'Miss Jessup's Upright'
Pieris japonica
Dwarf rhododendron
Azalea & other peat loving plants

Heathers
Geranium
Hebe 'Autumn Glory'
Dwarf Iris
Doronicum
Hebe pagei

SEAT

Variegated thyme
Cupressus 'arizonica blue'
Chives

Ribes

PEAT BED ~ denoted by dotted line

SHED

BUNGALOW

Designed by A.M. Sankey
1992/3

Plan for awkwardly shaped garden that narrows towards the bottom.

Circular lawns

For gardens that are long and thin, circles work best. A circular green lawn creates a feeling of space in small or narrow garden, as wherever you stand on the lawn you always have the diameter of the circle, and this appears to expand the area. For a long back garden, you might decide to subdivide the garden into rooms, and this can be achieved with a series of interlocking lawned circles.

Circles also work well for the awkwardly shaped garden shown in the diagram here, which narrows considerably towards the bottom. The circular lawn near the house creates an open room making the garden feel larger and creating a green canvas for a range of cottage flowers. A second circle repeats the design, tying the garden together, and creating a circular gravel path from which to view and work on the flower borders.

Paths

The old cottage paths always had purpose, taking the shortest route from one point to another. The front path from the gate on the lane to the door was always straight and dictated the layout of the front garden. This was generally edged with attractive flowers and had the rows of vegetables planted behind edging plants, following the line of the path. The major feature of any cottage path will be the exuberant flowers cascading over the edges to create that chaotic informality so typical to the style of the cottage garden. There is an opportunity to edge paths with scented plants or herbs, which when brushed against will release their gorgeous scent into the air. The Elizabethans often planted herbs along the edges of paths so that the ladies' flowing dresses would brush against the plants continually as they walked in the garden.

Like the old cottage gardens, ensure your main paths go where they are needed – from house to garage, back door to shed, to a seating area, to the compost bins and possibly the washing line. These paths should be attractive routes around your garden, perhaps running under a pergola or alongside the main lawn. However, be practical when laying down the main paths by making them twice the width you think it should be, as this allows for the profusion of cottage plants spilling over in the summer, yet still giving enough space to walk down. As a guide, make main paths 900mm (3ft) wide to accommodate the plantings along the edges. Major paths need to be wide enough for equipment such as lawnmowers and wheelbarrows.

See Chapter 7 (Traditional Features) for further information relating to paths, types of path and the choice of materials for paths.

A cobbled path weaving its way through the sumptuous cottage planting.

Good patches of cottage flowers spilling over the edge of the gravel path.

Steps

In gardens, different levels create interest, and in any garden with a slope, steps are an essential requirement. For cottage gardens you don't need anything too grand, but like paths, the hard landscaping required for steps opens up the opportunity to soften or informalize this feature. Gertrude Jekyll would always push frothy-type plants between the steps to soften the edges and create a cascading mass of pretty flowers. An excellent plant for this purpose, and a favourite of Jekyll, is the small white/pink-flowered daisy, *Erigeron*

karvinskianus. Not only does it provide that wonderful cottagey appeal, but it flowers from May right through to the first frosts, making it a most valuable addition to any garden.

Steps often act as a link between two areas of a garden, giving the user an awareness of something different to come. Steps are not just functional but are a feature in their own right. Arts and Crafts garden architects were so keen to have different levels within the garden to create interest, that they deliberately chose sloping sites so that terraces and steps could be included as features. If the site was flat, then a sunken garden was often included to ensure that

NARROW FRONT GARDEN OF A BUNGALOW IN LINCOLN

Requirements: A low-maintenance front garden with cottage-style planting.

The garden plan shows an interlocking circle design used for a narrow garden in front of a bungalow. The original north-facing narrow lawn with a long narrow border was totally dispensed with and a design which incorporates one main circular grass area introduced. The circles add a greater feeling of space and negate any hint of a long, narrow garden. The clipped box hedge circle adds evergreen formality, and the cottage-style planting adds interest, colour and scent throughout the whole year.

Cottage-style front garden of interlocking circles.

Brick edged circular lawn used to create width, tied in with the design of gravel circles which are informalized with the cottage planting.

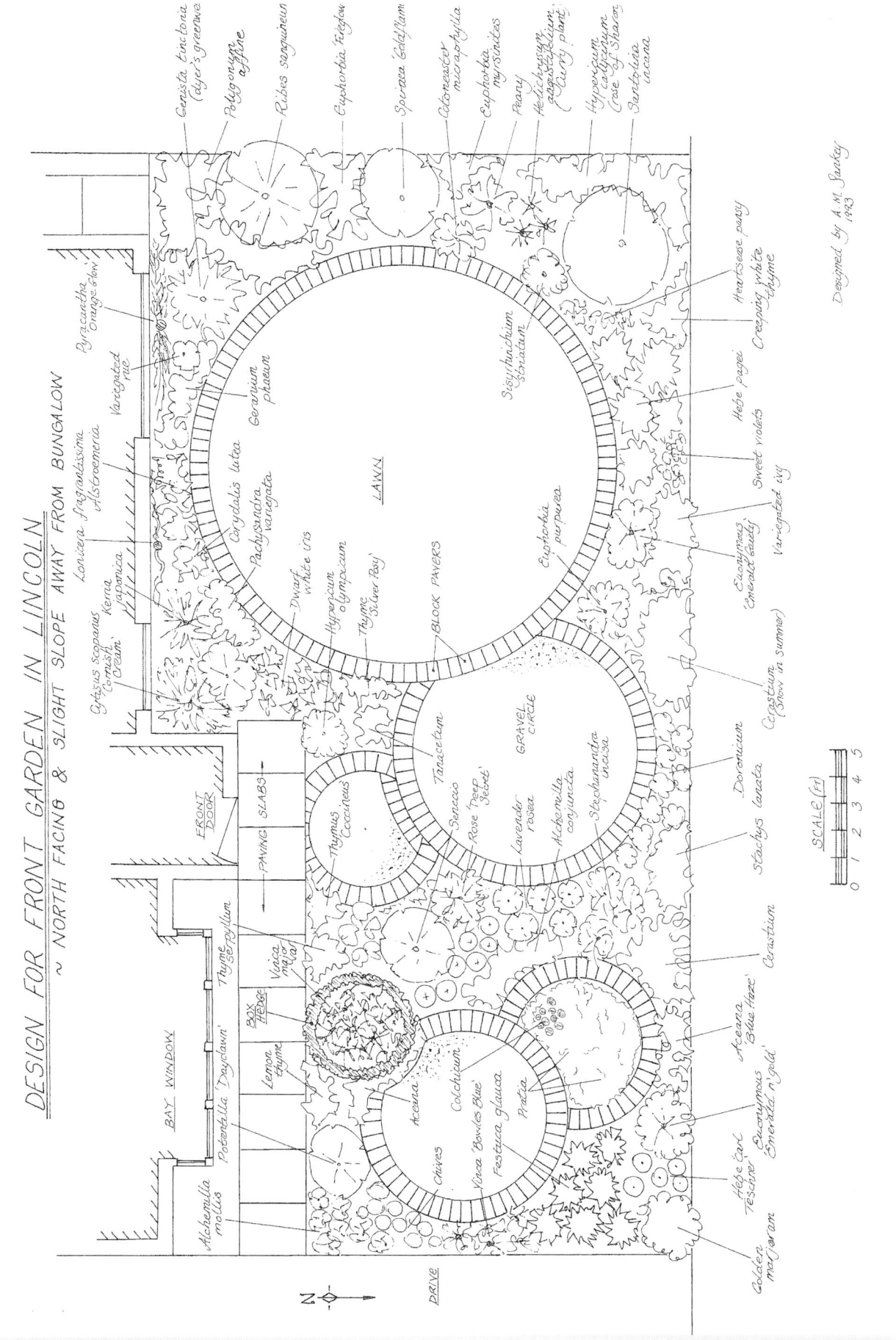

DESIGN FOR FRONT GARDEN IN LINCOLN

~ NORTH FACING & SLIGHT SLOPE AWAY FROM BUNGALOW

Designed by A.M. Sankey 1993

Genista tinctoria (dyer's greenwe)
Polygonum affine
Ribes sanguineum
Euphorbia Fireglow
Spiraea Goldflame
Cotoneaster microphylla
Euphorbia myrsinites
Peony
Helichrysum angustifolium (curry plant)
Hypericum calycinum (rose of Sharon)
Santolina incana

Pyracantha 'Orange Glow'
Variegated rue
Lonicera fragrantissima
Astroemeria
Kerria japonica
Cytisus scoparius 'Cornish Cream'
Pachysandra variegata
Corydalis lutea
Dwarf white iris
Hypericum olympicum
Thyme 'Silver Posy'
BLOCK PAVERS
Geranium phaeum
LAWN
Sisyrinchium striatum
Euphorbia purpurea

Heartsease pansy
Hebe pagei
Creeping white thyme
Sweet violets
Variegated ivy
Euonymus 'Emerald Gaiety'
Cerastium (snow in summer)

Thymus Coccineus
Senecio
Rose 'Deep Secret'
Lavender rosea
Alchemilla conjuncta
Stephanandra incisa
GRAVEL CIRCLE
Tanacetum
Doronicum
Stachys lanata
Cerastium

BAY WINDOW
Alchemilla mollis
Potentilla 'Daydawn'
Thyme serpyllum
Lemon thyme
BOX HEDGE
Vinca major
Acaena
Colchicum
Vinca 'Bowles Blue'
Festuca glauca
Prata
Chives
Golden marjoram
Hebe 'Carl Teschner'
Euonymus 'Emerald 'n'gold'
Acaena 'Blue Haze'

FRONT DOOR
PAVING SLABS
DRIVE

N

SCALE (ft)
0 1 2 3 4 5

Garden design for a narrow front garden, Lincolnshire.

Unpretentious steps
in this cottage garden
leading onto the lawn.

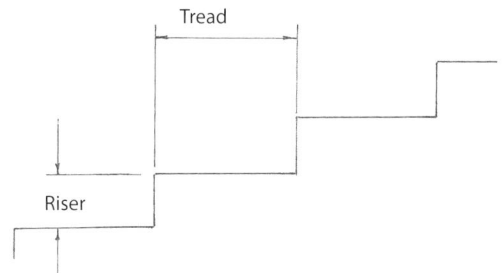

Plan and measure when creating steps.

interesting steps could be designed. Arts and Crafts gardens offer a great wealth of ideas for steps; many are not just straight but often designed as corner steps.

Ensure the width of any steps can accommodate two people side-by-side if they are to be a major central feature within the garden. Not only does width matter, but the height (or rise) and depth of each step as well. Do not have steps too high or too shallow, as it causes problems ascending and descending the garden. The steps should allow a person to move up and down easily without hesitation or having to actually concentrate on their feet. Looking down constantly to see where you are putting your feet results in little or no appreciation of any flowers spilling over the steps or flower borders on either side. For this reason, you'll

find garden steps are generally shallower than indoor stairs. If the garden is particularly steep, a handrail might be worth thinking about – if not for you, then for any visitors to the garden. Obviously, steps are dependent upon the height that needs ascending. The height needs to be measured and then you can start to work out how many steps will be required. According to building regulations the riser (the height of a step) should be 150–170mm, and the tread (the flat part for the foot) a minimum of 300mm, but ideally 450mm. Ensure you keep steps of a uniform height.

For an easier route, ideal for both wheelbarrows and wheelchairs, opt for a sloping path that zigzags its way to the top. This will require the zigzag path to have retaining walls to hold back the soil as you ascend. Old railway sleepers are often used for this purpose; however, you can also buy concrete blocks that key into each other and therefore don't require cementing. Make sure the path is wide enough, especially on the bends.

A variety of materials can be used for steps – concrete slabs, bricks or stone. For a softer look, use brick or timber risers for each step and then pea gravel, broken slate or some other chipping material for the step itself. In a part-shade situation, wood risers and bark chipping for the steps would be more appropriate. Make sure that materials used in shade aren't going to create a slip hazard when wet.

Patios and seating areas

The traditional old cottage gardens never had seating areas as such – they didn't have the time to just sit around! The most you might find would have been a plank dropped across two wood rounds under a spreading fruit tree, or a wooden bench by the back door. In today's recreational society an outdoor living area tends to be a must! New houses usually come with patios, but even owners of older houses will have patios laid for entertaining purposes. Of course, the patio or seating area doesn't have to be adjacent to the back of the building, it could be further down the garden or even at the end. And, if your garden is large, you don't have to stop at just one seating area or seat.

Creating a cottage-style feeling around patios/sitting areas is very much down to the use of planting. Choose plants that will spill over the edges of the hard landscaping to informalize the area; have groups of pots with cottagey plantings or obelisks for climbers in large pots; use climbers and ramblers on the house or on a structure (pergola/trellising) surrounding the area; and possibly leave gaps in the hard landscaping to plant low creeping plants in.

Small patio with table and chairs surrounded by cottage flowers.

ASSESSING THE SITE

Knowing your soil type, garden aspect and the areas of sun or shade is vital if you wish to create a garden in which your plants will thrive. All these key elements will influence your choice of trees, shrubs and perennials. Buying the right plants will ensure healthy, impressive displays. *Don't fight nature* – work with your garden, and your garden will reward you. Working with your garden is possibly the hardest thing you'll have to do, and requires a strong will, particularly when out at nurseries and garden centres. Try not to buy 'must-have' plants on impulse! New introductions of plants often look stunning and are found under the bright flashy banner displaying a wonderful picture. But, before you are tempted, check that the plant will suit *your* garden.

I have known friends pick up some beautiful plants – only for them to be dead within the year! They return home with the 'prized' plant and then very often wander around the garden looking for a space to fit it in. Eventually, a small space is found, and the plant put in and watered. However, they didn't check the suitability of the plant for their garden; neither did they actually place the plant in the correct part of the garden – as it was pushed in where they could find space! It is preferable to know the requirements of your own garden and whether a plant will suit your particular conditions, and to buy accordingly. This method will result in a healthier and more floriferous garden.

Large patios require large showcase borders of cottage planting.

BETH CHATTO'S GARDEN

Beth Chatto was an advocate of 'right plant, right place' and she experimented to find the plants that best suited her garden's conditions – a damp garden and a dry garden. Realizing that gardeners couldn't always find the correct plants to suit the correct areas, she started a nursery to solve this problem. I would suggest that Beth Chatto's garden and nursery is a great place to start if you require plants for specific areas. Information regarding the garden is given in Appendix I.

Soil types

Although many plants will cope in a variety of soils, for plants to really thrive in your garden it is essential you know whether your soil is heavy or light, acid or alkaline. It is not difficult to identify your soil. Simply getting a handful should immediately give you a clue – if it feels sticky and heavy when wet, it will be clay; if it feels gritty and flows through your fingers, it's a light sandy soil. The best possible result is a soil between the two. This is a loamy soil, and will be slightly cohesive yet crumbly in the hand.

Another important factor is the pH of the soil. The bulk of plants are happy in a neutral soil; normally said to be pH7 or thereabouts – a little acid or a little alkaline is no problem. Soil testing kits are readily available from most nurseries or garden centres and come with an easy-to-read colour match chart. It is best if you take readings from more than just one area within a large garden, as you can often have bands of varying types. Look around your area as well to see which plants are growing well, as this often is a good indicator of the local soil type. If there are lots of rhododendrons, heathers and camellias around you, the soil will probably be acid. Chalky soils are generally alkaline, and as pinks prosper on them, they can be a good indicator of this type of soil. There are now websites available which will tell you the soil type in your area after putting in your postcode, but a more accurate evaluation will be gained by a soil test. After finding out the pH of your soil, work with it and put in plants that best suit it.

Long cottage-style border on heavy clay soil adjacent to the front drive.

Aspect

Another valuable piece of information is which way your garden faces. You don't really want to be planting sun-loving plants in a north-facing border! To assess which way your garden faces, either use a compass or work out how the sun moves across the garden, as it rises in the east and sets in the west.

Most gardeners want a lovely warm south-facing garden, as it has the greatest amount of light throughout the day. However, being south facing means the beds will be hot and therefore dry out fairly quickly in the summer. This is where choosing the correct plants for the situation matters. A north-facing garden or border will evidently get less sun and be colder. It requires a little more thought in terms of planting as fewer plants like this aspect within the garden. East-facing gardens (or areas within the garden) gain from the early morning sun, which makes them ideal for sitting out with a morning cup of tea, but unsuitable for early-flowering plants. Camellias for example, should not be planted in east-facing borders/walls, as cold frosty nights followed by bright sunny mornings result in the flowers being scorched. Finally, west-facing gardens that get the sun late in the day are ideal for parties, a seat for sitting out with a drink, and white flowers that illuminate as it gradually gets darker.

Also worth thinking about is the region of the country where your garden is, as different regions have different weather patterns and micro-climates. East Anglia has the least amount of rain, making it the driest part of the country; the south-west is wet and has little frost due to the Gulf Stream; the west is generally the wettest area; and the north of the country is colder than the south. These conditions will all affect the design of the garden and what can and can't be grown. For example, the east has very drying winds, but by using either hedges or trellis the wind can be filtered, thus improving the conditions for the plants.

Sun and shade

Finding out which parts of your garden will be in sun or shade matters, as this too, will affect your planting choices. Whether you have moved into a new garden or are developing an old one, you'll always have areas of sun and shade. Buying plants that suit the right situations is important as they will give you a healthy, flowery garden that will require less attention in terms of watering, staking and weeding.

Full sun positions – hot, dry areas
With south-facing gardens or areas in full sun, think carefully about the planting. Certain groups of plants will suit the baking summer heat better than others – use herbs, Mediterranean type flowers, silver and grey foliage plants, and plants that have adapted to hot sun. Cottage-style planting is an absolute bonus in sunny situations as the plants themselves are generally tightly packed and jostling for space. Due to this idea of 'never an inch wasted', the foliage overlaps and helps retain moisture underneath.

South-facing cottage border on light sandy soil at its height in July.

Gravel or scree areas in full sun also suit loose cottage-style planting, allowing plants to easily self-seed to create that informal look, but at the same time assist water retention. One stunning gravel garden that illustrates this idea and gives the visitor some wonderful plant combinations to consider, is the drought gravel garden created by Beth Chatto. Another good example of a dry garden has been created at RHS Hyde Hall, but if you don't live close enough to these, I'm sure you'll find some gardens with similar situations close to you.

Dry shade positions – under trees and hedges

This can be subdivided into two groups: partial shade and deep shade.

Dry shade is difficult to cope with, as roots from trees or hedges will take up a lot of the water. However, partial shade (under silver birch, rowan and fruit trees, for example) is certainly easier to deal with than deep shade that is found under trees like copper beech. It is worth making the most of the early spring under trees before the canopy has opened up.

In the early period of the spring plenty of light and rain can reach the plants under the branches. Early spring borders under trees look stunning, brightening up the garden and lifting the spirits at this time of year. A varied mix of spring bulbs, ground cover, perennials and annuals will ensure colour throughout the early part of the year.

Deep shade, on the other hand, is more difficult and options are more limited. There are some plants that will cope, but be wary: many can eventually become a nuisance if not kept in check – these being ivy, sweet woodruff, vinca and *Euphorbia amygdaloides* var. *robbiae* (known as 'Mrs Robb's Bonnet'). *See* Appendices II and III for lists of plants for dry shade and dry sun.

TIPS FOR COPING WITH A DRY GARDEN

- Plant out at the correct times of year – new plants should be planted in either spring or autumn. Don't buy and plant out in July and August if you can help it, as the plants will struggle, need constant watering and ultimately be weaker. Beware about buying plants and then going away on holiday – you'll return to dead or dying specimens.
- Choose drought-resistant plants that suit your soil.
- Reduce the drying effects of wind in your garden by subdividing it with dwarf hedges, trellis or screens.
- When planting out, dig a deeper hole than the pot requires, fill the hole back up to the correct 'pot depth' with compost, plant and water really well and then only when required. This will make the plants tougher and encourage the roots to grow downwards. Putting in a plant and watering continually will only encourage shallow root systems that will inevitably dry out quickly in long dry spells.
- If you do have plants that require more in the way of watering, group them together in *one bed* – this way you're not running around all over the garden with a watering-can. You could even incorporate a leak-hose system within the bed.
- If growing plants in pots/containers, be aware that they dry out quickly during hot weather. Always water well in the evenings when it is more beneficial. Don't use small pots – they will have a large surface area in comparison to the volume of compost inside the pot and will therefore dry out extremely quickly. Larger pots will require less watering, as they have a greater volume of compost to surface area ratio.

DESIGN

Any garden is a combination of hard landscaping (patios, paths, walls) and soft landscaping (the planting – trees, shrubs, perennials). A balance needs to be achieved to create a harmonious garden, and although in a cottage garden the emphasis is more on the creative planting style, some hard landscaping is essential. The amount of hard landscaping is down to the owner's preference and requirements. If a large entertaining area for eight to ten people is a must then there will be a greater area of hard materials than a garden that is devoted to just paths weaving through luscious plantings of cottage flowers.

If you are aiming for a cottage-style garden it doesn't really matter whether or not your garden has a large area of hard landscaping; it will all be dependent upon the use of the planting to soften the whole. However, if you are working on a new garden or area, ensure the design is sorted first.

The cottage style has a wonderful ability to suit any garden, large or small, traditional or modern; but is certainly ideal for smaller

DRY SHADE BORDER

Requirements: A spring border for the extremely dry shade area next to the entrance gates to a drive.

The area next to the entrance gates was believed to be a 'dead zone' where nothing would grow. Two huge conifers sat up against a long garden hedge that divided the front garden from the main road. This large corner area was bone-dry and dark, due to the hedge and the large low spreading conifer branches.

Plants require light, so the first job was to lift the canopy of the conifers by taking off some of the lower branches. The garden hedge height was also reduced. This made a massive difference and after adding some topsoil over the conifer roots, the new large bed was ready for planting. A grass path was laid around the back of the conifers for access, and finally the new border was planted up with plants that would cope with a very 'dry shade' position. The so-called 'dead zone' was transformed into a cottage-style spring border under the conifers – as can be seen in the photographs here.

Dry shade border under two large conifers with the lower branches taken off and the height of the hedge behind reduced.

The dry shade border three years on, with cottage plantings of columbines, hellebores, lamiums, epimediums, ferns, hostas and polemonium.

The dry border under the conifers with a view through to the feature pot in the corner.

The stunning *Brunnera* 'Jack Frost', a great dry shade plant, planted next to the trunk of one of the conifers.

Feature pot in the hedge corner immersed in cottage flowers, including epimediums, peonies, dicentra, ferns, columbines and hardy geraniums.

gardens, long and thin gardens, courtyards or even passages. With small gardens, dispense with the lawn and concentrate on the planting scheme.

Be very careful to *keep things in scale* in small plots – often owners will plant too large a tree into a small garden, not realizing the size it will eventually achieve. A large tree will overpower a small space, restrict the light level and take up a large amount of water. I have unfortunately seen tiny front gardens planted with a central tree (monkey puzzle, cherry tree or similar) which in a number of years has overwhelmed and dwarfed the garden and cut out light from the property. There are a few small trees which would be suitable, lilac being one that was traditionally grown in a cottage garden. In the same way, don't introduce an over-large piece of sculpture or feature that is out of scale with the size of the garden.

In small cottage gardens, make the most of every inch of space – utilize the whole plot. In Britain, with generally good-sized gardens we tend to waste a lot of space that could otherwise be used. Cottage gardeners never wasted space. Even areas of your plot that seem impossible to do anything with, can with a little thought be gardened.

Garden rooms

Garden rooms have become very popular in recent years, in part due to the gardens of Sissinghurst and Hidcote. Garden rooms were used throughout the Arts and Crafts gardens movement of the late nineteenth and early twentieth century to create separate areas for colour-schemed herbaceous borders, kitchen gardens, rock gardens, herb gardens, rose gardens and water gardens.

The idea of hedged rooms with an element of surprise creates an intriguing feel to a garden that many gardeners now wish to develop.

For old cottage gardens such ideas mattered little, as their main focus was being productive. Today, however, many of us wish to use 'garden rooms' to our advantage. The idea is particularly suitable for subdividing very long, narrow gardens, these often being the 'back' gardens of terraced houses in towns and cities. Using this technique alters the look of the garden, and instead of appearing exceedingly long and thin, changes into a series of smaller gardens which seemingly appear wider. It creates a feeling of excitement and interest, and not being able to see the whole garden at once makes a small garden feel larger. Large cottage gardens, too, can benefit from being subdivided into rooms which can then be treated in different ways – perhaps a colour-schemed room, a vegetable patch, a quiet corner, a cutting garden or a room of pots.

Margery Fish's lovely cottage garden at East Lambrook Manor in Somerset was created as a series of loosely defined linked areas which led from one to the other, each with exciting combinations of cottage flowers. These rooms included the Rock Garden, the 'Green' Garden, the Ditch Garden, the Sundial Garden, the Terrace Garden, and the White and Silver Garden.

Dividing up your garden into rooms can be achieved in different ways – walls, hedges, trellis or clever planting. Walls are expensive but can create permanent closed-in rooms and do offer the opportunity for 'greening' with either trained fruit trees or climbers. Hedges offer a wide choice of possibilities, both in terms of height and colour of the hedging material. Taller hedging can be used to create a room as a retreat, whereas lower or dwarf hedges can subdivide but allow further rooms to be glimpsed beyond. Subdivision with hedging creates a green backdrop for cottage

A stunning long garden room at Stillingfleet Lodge Gardens near York.

LONG AND THIN BACK GARDEN

Requirements: Back garden to have a cottage border closest to the house, a seating area for summer in the second room, and a low maintenance third room further down. No lawn.

The long thin back garden had the advantage of already being subdivided into three rooms with trellis and a hedge. In the first room all the grass was taken up, a path was constructed to lead down the garden, the trellis was painted and a cottage garden border planted up. The second room required a seating area in the corner for use in the summer and another path to continue down to the end room, which was to have gravel enclosing the existing fruit trees.

'Before' photo of the first garden room in this very long thin garden.

The first garden room partially completed; grass gone and brick edging ready for cobbles.

Cobble path complete, gravel next to the pond laid on weed-proof matting, and flower border dug over in readiness for planting up.

Cottage border planted up, with the trellis forming a background but allowing a glimpse through to the second garden room with a newly constructed patio for seating.

12M (40FT) SQUARE BACK GARDEN

Requirements: Large lawn for children, separate productive garden, greenhouse, cottage borders.

The back garden, which faced due south, was separated into two rooms by a diagonal path running down the garden. Trellis panels followed the path and created a screen with an archway through to a plot with vegetables, fruit trees, herbs and a greenhouse. A large lawn for children to play on is enclosed on three sides with cottage planting.

Large lawn surrounded by cottage-style planting with trellis panels diagonally across the garden, creating a further room.

The partially hidden productive area with vegetables, fruit trees, herbs and greenhouse.

'planting schemes' but also aids the plants by filtering any strong winds. Trellis panels are another wonderful material to use when creating rooms within a garden. Trellis has many advantages: it encloses a specific area yet allows a partial view through to the following room, it can be painted to tie in with other features, it can be used as frame for climbing plants, and also comes in a variety of designs (diamond or square). Trellis allows for partial separation of the garden, which means the whole garden isn't seen in one go, yet helps retain a feeling of space and openness. Like hedging, any form of trellis with climbers established on the framework will filter winds that blow through the garden.

Carefully designed planting can also divide gardens into rooms. A combination of evergreen shrubs, tall perennials and cottage flowers can create a green divide that allows a partial view through to the following area yet defines the present area. Tall perennials defined as 'see through' plants do much the same job as trellis, dividing up areas of the garden yet allowing a view through. Plants falling into this category include *Verbena bonariensis*, *Veronicastrum*, *Thalictrum*, and *Helenium*.

Use of circles

The use of circles in garden design is extremely useful and pleasing to the eye. Circles work particularly well in small gardens, creating a feeling of spaciousness. Wherever you stand in a circle, you will always have the diameter of the circle in every direction, and this tricks the eye into believing the space is 'larger' than it seems.

For longer gardens, interlocking or overlapping circles help maintain the open feeling but at the same time lead you down the garden. If the garden is slightly shorter, ensure the circle closest to the house is very much larger and the second circle smaller, as this creates perspective, which again makes the garden feel much larger than it actually is. Circles are also very effective in awkward or irregularly shaped areas, being particularly good in triangular plots, with the width of the circles again creating space and enhancing the design.

Grass circles benefit from being brick edged, as the edging maintains the shape and prevents the loss of the circumference. The bricks should be level with the soil so the mower can run over the bricks and cut the grass efficiently.

Marking out a circle in the garden is quite straightforward. All that's required is a short piece of a garden cane, a piece of twine or string and a can of spray marker paint. Push the cane firmly into the ground where you feel the centre should be and attach the twine. Decide on what radius you need and attach the twine around the paint marker can. Walk around in a circle, spraying the circumference as you go and making sure the twine remains taut. This should give a visible circle when complete.

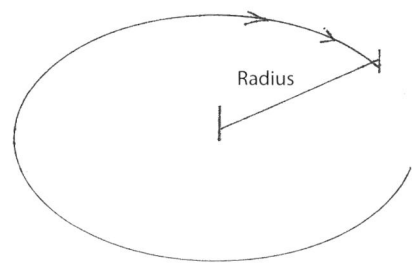

Diagram showing a circle and line of direction.

What was an awkwardly triangular-shaped soggy grass area has been redesigned as three interlocking circles. The area now has a sense of space with features within the circles to focus upon amongst the cottagey planting.

Creating a sense of space

With gardens getting progressively smaller, it is worthwhile knowing how you can make a small cottage garden seem larger. There are various design processes that will assist in this endeavour. As previously mentioned, circular designs create a spacious feel to a garden, and there are now plenty of circular patios that can be purchased at DIY centres.

If you are laying a patio in a small garden, use smaller sized slabs rather than large ones. Not only are they easier to handle, but the eye sees many more slabs, and this has the effect of tricking the eye into believing that because there are so many more, the area must be larger! If you wish you could use bricks or block paviours as an alternative, which would give the same result.

If a small garden is enclosed by fencing (most are), then painting the fence helps. A brown panel is dark and dull, and it does nothing to show off planting. If you paint the fence a green/blue or silver/grey colour, it lightens the interior of the garden and produces a good background to show off flowers.

Use of plants within a small garden is also important. Colours can be used to your advantage as our eyes adjust differently to certain colours, which in turn affects our perception of depth – *cool colours recede*, whereas *hot colours advance*. This knowledge can assist in making decisions on the composition within a garden, especially if the garden is small. Cool coloured flowers of blue, mauve and white should be planted on the periphery of any garden, and vitally in a small garden, as these colours will recede and make the garden appear larger than it actually is. This idea is a great design tool for small gardens and garden rooms, and in such areas, it might be worth creating a scheme using only 'cool' colours to give the whole garden a feeling of space.

Hot colours (red, orange and vivid yellow) on the other hand, advance, and give a feeling of the garden closing in. If hot colours are planted at the end of a garden, the distance will seem somewhat shorter. Gertrude Jekyll stated that blue/green flowers and foliage should be kept in the distance, and red or another strong colour placed in the foreground, as this created greater depth in the garden. To follow Jekyll's advice means in general, keeping hot colours in beds closer to the house, in borders up against the house wall, or in pots on the patio. Borders that move out into the garden should be graduated, with the warmer colours closer to the house and cooler colours nearer to the garden boundaries. This would result in a garden with greater spatial perspective. Therefore, keep your red-hot tulips crammed into pots either side of the door!

Case Study 2.5

SMALL CAMBRIDGE BACK GARDEN

Requirements: Cottage-style back garden with paved area for sitting out on. No lawn.

The garden is only 8m (26ft) long by 4.5m (15ft) wide, and to make it seem larger a number of ideas were put into practice. The fence had trellis along the top and was painted a silver/grey colour to show off the planting. All fences were wired so that climbers could be grown to green up the perimeter. The cottage-style planting was deliberately kept within the pastel range towards the bottom of the garden so that it looked to recede. The circular patio also creates a sense of spaciousness. A mirror was put up to add reflection of planting on the opposite side of the garden. The only 'hot' colour, the red rose, was placed close to the house so as not to interfere with the 'cooler' colours down the bottom, therefore helping to create perspective.

The colour scheme has been deliberately chosen to make the garden recede and seem larger.

The 'hot' red rose is kept close to the house and only seen when you step out into the garden.

The circular patio, the horizontal slatted back gate, the trellis and the pastel-themed planting all help to create a sense of spaciousness in the small garden.

Borrowed views

Creating borrowed views also helps make a small cottage garden feel larger. Borrowing a view from outside the garden, even if it's just the neighbour's, and drawing it in creates a sense of space. A borrowed view can be achieved in a number of ways: a simple wrought-iron gate, a window made in a clipped hedge or fence, or possibly the curved branch of a tree to create a frame.

Beds and borders

When designing beds or borders, create a mixture of both narrow and wide ones. Have large corner beds that can accommodate a small tree or large shrub. Large borders are superior to narrow ones and create the opportunity to design a good deep planting scheme that can be a mixture of shrubs, perennials and ground cover. Remember, cottage plants expand, clump up, spill over and cascade, taking up quite large amounts of space. Narrow borders don't accommodate cottage plants, so give the plants space to do their thing, even if it means cutting into the lawn to create a larger bed, or possibly dispensing with the lawn entirely!

Whilst on the subject of how quickly cottage plants expand from what seems a small clump in the ground, be aware of this fact when first planting up a border. Don't be tempted to place cottage plants too closely together just because the border seems huge when the plants first go in. A newly planted border will often look fairly bare, but three or four years down the line, these plants will have expanded to fill the border. If you squeeze in too many plants to begin with, the border will eventually get congested, and the clumps will require splitting or taking out. It is wiser to

The lovely large border in this cottage garden gives a great opportunity to have mixed planting with substantial patches of flowers.

A large cottage border under a Victoria plum tree with drifts of lupins.

The window has been deliberately positioned in the wall to give a 'borrowed view' through to another garden area.

plant at the correct spacing in the first instance, and fill any large gaps with annuals and biennials until the plants get established.

Large borders should be divided up with the odd large shrub or a piece of trellis to create hidden corners of surprise, perhaps with a pot, sculpture, a well-placed seat or water feature. Surprise is a lovely element within a garden and can even be engineered in a small space. The surprise need not always be an ornament; an effective group of plants, or one particular plant, can be placed to catch the attention either through an arch, around a corner or in the next garden room. Plants in pots work particularly well in this respect.

Plant triangles

Use plant triangles to improve a border. We all know that plants should be placed in a border with lower or ground cover plants at the front, moving up in height to tall perennials at the back. Plant triangles work along stretches within the border, and are based on the scalene triangle. A scalene triangle is a triangle with every side different, and is often used by flower arrangers to form the basis of a design. Beth Chatto was one of the first gardeners to realize this idea could be transferred into borders and her garden near Colchester is worth visiting to see this idea in practice. A plant triangle will improve the look of a border, as your eye will subconsciously follow the lines of the triangle and thus take in the whole planting picture. The method is simply a way of grouping plants to form a triangle, and one triangle can be arranged to overlap a second, to create continuity within the border.

FURTHER CASE STUDIES OF COTTAGE-STYLE GARDENS

I thought it would be appropriate to end this chapter with some case studies of gardens that I have created in the cottage garden style. I have focused more on small gardens, as in general, garden size has reduced considerably as land for housing is in such short supply. In each case, I have tried to show the 'before' and 'after' photographs. I hope these examples show that a cottage garden design is a viable style for small modern gardens.

Plant triangles

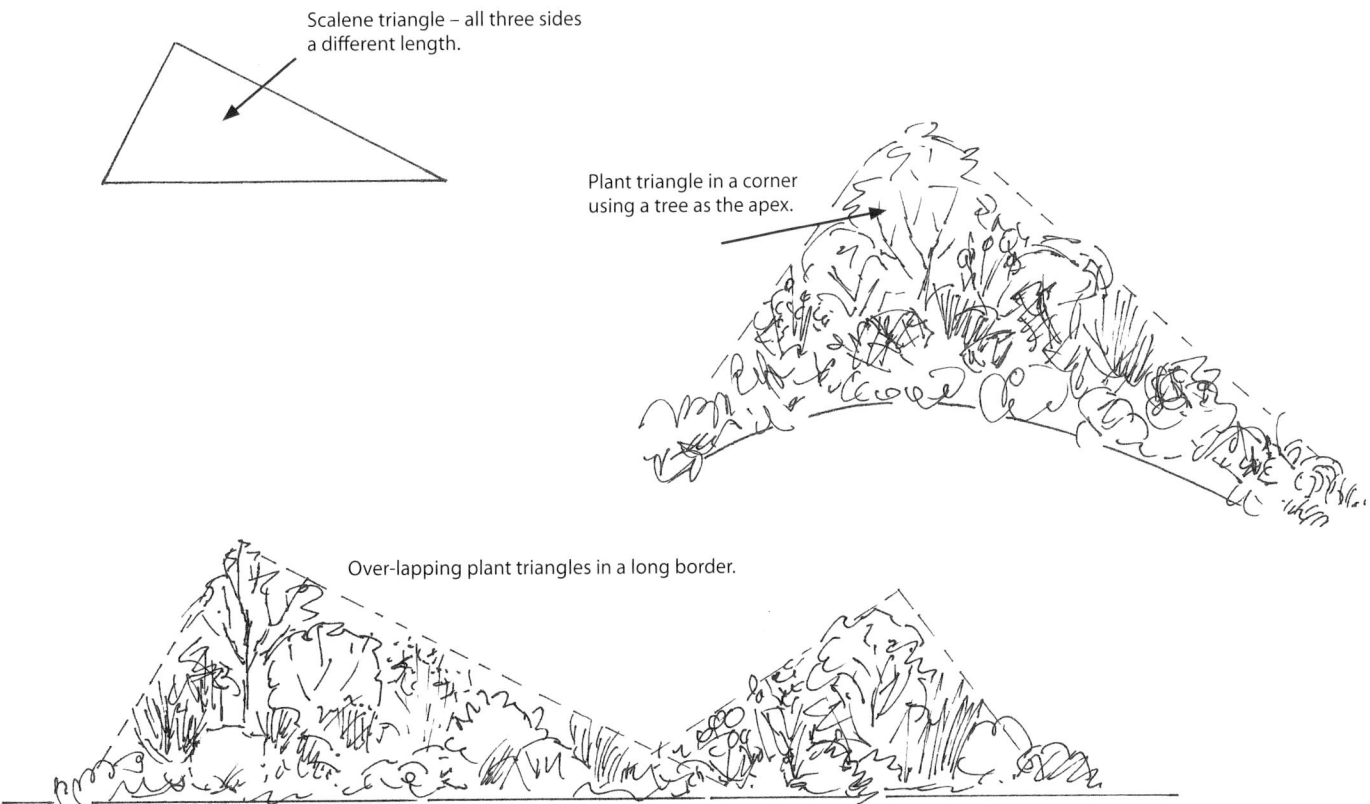

Scalene triangle – all three sides a different length.

Plant triangle in a corner using a tree as the apex.

Over-lapping plant triangles in a long border.

Case Study 2.6

MARGARET'S SMALL BACK GARDEN

Requirements: The very harsh slabbed garden was to be softened with plenty of cottage planting and some evergreen form (box hedges), having colour throughout the year and providing somewhere to sit.

To achieve the design, all the slabs had to come up, but many were put aside to be used again. The slabs could then be re-laid, the roll-top edging cemented in, and the borders dug over and filled with topsoil. The box hedges, *Amelanchier* tree, and cottage flowers were then added to finalize the design.

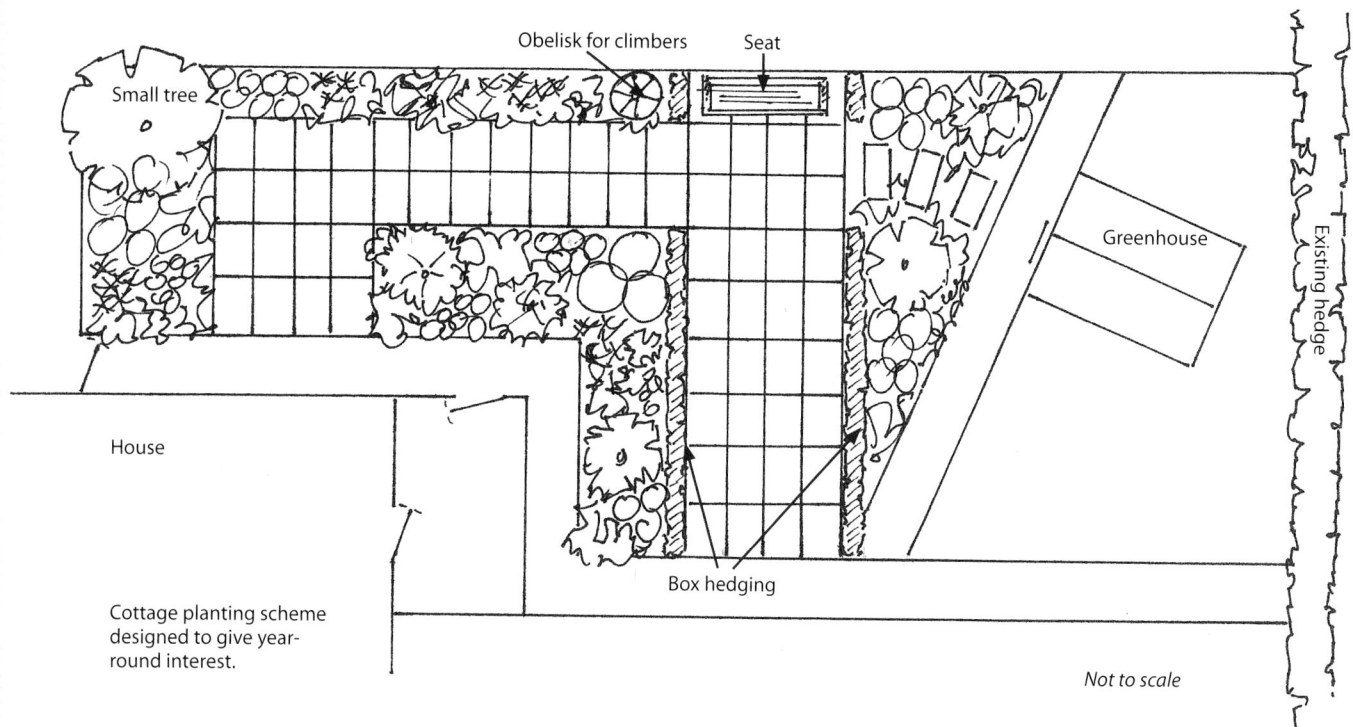

Garden plan for Margaret's small back garden.

'Before' photo showing the harsh, uniformly slabbed area prior to the cottage-style re-design.

The re-used slabs, seating and box hedging adding structure to the garden.

The borders planted up in cottage style.

View down to the end border with an *Amelanchier lamarckii* tree in the corner.

The borders two years after planting, with the flowers beginning to spill over the edges.

Case Study 2.7

Requirements: Change the gravel front area into cottage-style garden with easy access to the front door and side cupboard door. Colour throughout the year and evergreen structure in the form of dwarf box hedging. Borders to be retained by rope top edging.

The design for this small front garden was straightforward, with two borders running down either side and cottage planting to spill over in profusion. Aspect southwest facing and soil a good loam. The borders were planted up with a combination of bulbs, ground cover and perennials, making the most of every inch of space.

What was originally just a gravel area now has two borders planted up either side of a path.

The two front cottage borders after three years.

The left-hand side cottage planting – including *Allium cristophii*, *Paeonia* 'Duchess de Nemours', *Nigella damascena*, *Catananche caerulea*, *Erigeron karvinskianus*, *Convolvulus cneorum*, and the under-rated *Tellima grandiflora*.

The right-hand side border – including *Sisyrinchium striatum*, hardy geraniums, cornflowers, lupins, London Pride, eryngiums, alliums, peony, and *Astrantia major*.

Case Study 2.8

MOOR HOUSE COTTAGE GARDEN

Requirements: A cottage-style garden to wrap around a large Victorian house with a modern garage, old trees and large areas of lawn. A framework of shrubs, colour throughout the year and different seating areas.

The very large lawned garden surrounded the house and its attached conservatory at the back. The garden required substantial borders full of cottage plants to create a background, a better path from the drive to the back door and planting schemes to cope with either dry sun or dry shade (under the trees) as the soil was light and sandy.

Two lawns were retained, a large back lawn and a smaller front lawn. A wider path with a metal arch was constructed which allowed for flowers to spill over the edges in sweet abandonment. The arch was planted with clematis and an everlasting pea. Secondary paths next to the hedges and around the back of the large borders were laid, and herbaceous borders planted with large drifts of cottage plants.

The front lawn and cottage borders of The Moor House, Potterhanworth, Lincolnshire.

Large, curved cottage border between the roadside hedge and the two front bay windows.

Wide path with arch leading to the back door with the large back lawn surrounded by cottage planting.

End of the lawn behind the kitchen with a feature pot and gravel circle covering up a large manhole cover (accessed easily by pulling back fabric matting and gravel).

Chapter 3

Cottage Planting Style

USE OF COTTAGE FLOWERS

The use of flowers in cottage gardens of the past was simple but effective; there was no thought put into displaying them, it was more a case of practicality. Flowers were generally placed where they were needed; soapwort (*Saponaria officinalis*) close to the wash-house, herbs for the kitchen near to the back door, and scented flowers under the windows and over the doors. The flowers were admired by the cottagers, but were purely a pretty mixed tangle of colour and scents, there never being any set design nor any thought about colour schemes.

The modern cottage gardener, however, considers the design of the garden and the aesthetics of flower groupings to be an essential element within the garden. To this end, you might glean ideas from TV programmes, gardening magazines and by visiting other cottage gardens. Although still using the traditional old cottage flowers as a basis, intermingle newer modern varieties of plants, and have fun working with colour schemes, whilst at the same time retaining that romantic feel in the planting style. Be individualistic, as cottage gardens have always been a reflection of their owners. In times past, every cottager often had to work with the same range of plants as the neighbours, yet the resultant garden was always different. The plot size and shape, the soil, the aspect, and the likes and dislikes of the cottagers all had an effect upon the garden. Your cottage garden, too, is your own work of art and although gaining ideas from other sources, should reflect your own tastes and colour preferences.

Important planting suggestions for cottage gardens

- Try to have a few wide borders to give yourself the opportunity to bring together a variety of shrubs, perennials, annuals and ground cover to create height, frothiness, form, texture and large swathes of flowers.
- Don't have 'bitty' beds – use some large groupings or drifts to create real interest.
- Aim for a loose tangle of flowers with lovely flower combinations.
- Allow plants to brim over the edge in uneven groups to add informality and delight.
- Contrast plants one against the other – large leaves to bring out small, floaty flowers.
- Use plant 'incidents' to rest the eye on within the border.
- Graduate colour within the garden – hot colours nearer and cool colours further away.
- Have some good evergreen structure for year-round interest.
- Top up any gaps with annuals as the earlier plants die back.
- Find out which plants complement one another and keep a record.

A 'cool' combination of alliums, nigella, *Erigeron karvinskianus*, *Convolvulus cneorum*, *Gillenia trifoliata* and *Cephalaria gigantea* (giant scabious).

- Try for seasonal continuity – from early bulbs to late season flowers.
- Allow self-seeders and plants to naturally weave through the borders to help link the planting.
- Don't always follow the rules – if a tall plant has seeded at the front of the border, leave it and see how it looks before pulling it out! Climbers don't always have to climb; try letting a clematis ramble over the ground in amongst the other perennials – you might be surprised at the result!
- Use every inch of your garden – aim to have no bare ground. In doing so, you'll create a green tapestry with a diversity of cottage flowers that will retain moisture and keep down weeds.

Drifts of flowers

Drifts of flowers in cottage gardens are not new, although we now conscientiously contrive to drift flowers through the borders to create that cottagey feel to the garden. Previously, drifts of flowers were formed accidentally as flowers were allowed to self-seed about the garden creating large unplanned displays. We need only look to Mother Nature to see the wonderful effect of one plant in large drifts and how these drifts make us catch our breath – in the early spring the carpets of snowdrops, wood anemones or bluebells; the cow parsley drifting along the side of roads; and the great swathes of corn poppies in the fields. The sheer quantity makes the picture, and yet, when we go to the garden centre, we are content to buy just the one plant of a particular variety. According to old cottagers, when new plants were put in the garden, they were planted for the Trinity or the Seven Good Years of Plenty – in other words, in *threes* and *sevens*.

A clematis scrambling across a group of sedums, creating an interesting combination.

Drifts of *Allium cristophii* with dark purple bearded iris at Elton Hall Gardens, near Peterborough.

An informal drift of *Eucomis bicolor* in a sunny cottage border.

A large drift of variegated honesty in a part-shade cottage border.

Drifts or patches of the same flower give the garden a flow and harmony that can't be achieved by simply throwing in a mix of flowers, however good that mixture might be. A large drift in a border gives the eye 'time to pause' and take in the bigger picture, whereas a dotty border, although looking good at first glance, means the eye flits around, which reduces the border coherence and appeal.

I have often been told that drifts of plants are only suitable for long borders in large gardens, but I have to disagree. Even in small cottage gardens, just one or two drifts of the same plant can make a huge difference to the appeal of the garden and lift it out of the ordinary. One plant just doesn't have the same impact or effect as a group. In large cottage gardens, one can afford to be generous and plant in larger groupings, but in small gardens, threes, fives and sevens will suffice. Drifts or groups of plants look better if planted in *odd* numbers. Essentially don't be dotty – create some flowing drifts or groups to tie the cottage borders together. Sometimes the best way to create a beautiful cottage border is to have 'more of less'.

A good example of how drifts can be a better option is in the planting of hellebores. These attractive and long-flowering spring plants are attention grabbers, and when planted as single specimens look quite beautiful. However, if planted as a group, a transformation takes place as the flowers help lift one another, with delicate pink flowers showing up against rich almost black flowers, and white flowers helping to lift the delicate pinks. You only need to see a group of different coloured hellebores to realize the stunning effect that is created, as opposed to single specimens dotted around!

Pastel-coloured flowers (delicate pinks and light blues) have a tendency to fade into the background amongst other foliage and flowers, and it is therefore essential that these are planted in drifts to help give the flowers a greater emphasis within the border. For example, if you purchased a lovely delicate pink low-growing plant, it may well have looked the bees knees at the nursery where it was displayed en masse; however, once you get home and plant it in the border in amongst the other competing plants, it suddenly looks lost and insignificant. The solution is either to buy three plants at the nursery so as to form a good grouping and therefore a presence in the border; or alternatively, buy one plant, bulk it up in a spare piece of ground, and when large enough, split the clump and plant out as a group.

When it comes to 'hot' coloured plants (red, orange, yellow) one plant will easily suffice, as hot colours have impact and stand out dramatically. Should you be designing a 'hot coloured border' however, then groups of these colours create a more harmonious planting effect.

NORAH LINDSAY'S THOUGHTS ON DRIFTS

The secret to a successful herbaceous border is to have a profusion of hardy plants well placed in irregular groups or patches, all giving the impression of growing naturally and producing the effect of a happy and contented companionship.

And also –

There must be a constant variety in design, one group of plants showing off and enhancing the next, and a cunning juxtaposition of contrasts, achieved by planting in patches … the patches or plant colonies should be bold and well-defined, but of irregular outlines, and intimately blended so that there is no set appearance.

Ground cover

Ground cover has always played an important role in cottage gardens, helping to maintain moisture and keep weeds under control to a certain extent. But it actually does far more, filling in what could potentially be dead space under trees and shrubs, and creating a foil for other taller plants by giving them a contrasting base through which they can erupt.

Ground cover is extremely useful for sloping gardens as a stabilizer, where the mat-forming properties of the plant help stop erosion of the site. Evergreen ground cover is often the best option for this situation and contributes year-round interest.

Of course, the correct form of ground cover will be required to suit the situation, dependent upon soil type and sun or shade positions within the garden. Every garden, in fact, different areas of every garden, will have unique qualities which may well suit certain ground cover plants better than others. The only way to find out is to do a little research and then plant what you feel will suit. If the plant struggles then you might need to re-think your planting, and find something more suitable.

When planting ground cover don't be bitty! It is far more attractive as a large swathe of foliage that acts more effectively as a foil for other plants. Contrast can be obtained by using dark foliage ground cover combined with a secondary tier of light-coloured flowers.

Full sun

Alyssum saxatile	An old cottage favourite for walls and path edges, with grey-green foliage and masses of yellow flowers.
Campanula	A good number of mat-forming varieties, including C. carpatica, C. poscharskyana, and C. 'E.H. Frost'.
Cerastium tomentosum (snow-in-summer)	A vigorous spreader with narrow grey leaves and masses of white flowers in spring/summer.
Dianthus varieties	A good range of lovely flowers and leaf forms.
Erigeron karvinskianus	The Mexican daisy that flowers on and on!
Hardy geraniums	In particular G. renardii, G. 'Mavis Simpson', G. 'Rozanne'.
Helianthemum (rock roses)	Mat-forming silver-grey evergreens having a long flowering period.
Iberis sempervirens (candytuft)	An evergreen with clear white flowers in spring.
Nepeta (catmint)	A good selection with N. 'Six Hills Giant' being the largest.
Ophiopogon planiscapus 'Nigrescens'	This black grass has become a very popular ground cover making a great contrast with other plants.
Osteospermum (African daisies)	Not all varieties are hardy, but they are long-flowering plants for dry, full-sun positions.
Phlox subulata	A floriferous evergreen mat-forming plant for sun.
Saxifraga × urbium	A cottage favourite known as 'London Pride'.
Stachys byzantina (lamb's ears)	A beautiful silvery foliage plant with the variety 'Silver Carpet' a useful non-flowering variety and 'Macrantha' a superb flowering form.
Thymus varieties	A wide selection of bushy and creeping forms.

Part shade

Ajuga reptans	A tight-knit spreading ground cover with spikes of dark blue flowers in the spring. The dark-leaved varieties are particularly striking.
Alchemilla mollis	Will happily cope with most positions in the garden. Forming attractive clumps, the sulphur-yellow flowers will blend with anything.
Bergenia cordifolia (elephant's ears)	The large evergreen leaves form a carpet for the flowers to rise from in the early spring. The purple-leaved variety is particularly attractive.
Brunnera macrophylla 'Jack Frost'	'Jack Frost' is a great choice for part-shade, having an abundance of forget-me-not type blue flowers in April/May above stunning foliage.
Convallaria majalis (lily of the valley)	A favourite cottage ground cover, lily of the valley, does exceedingly well in dry shade and comes in a variety of forms.
Epimedium varieties	Forming tight spreading clumps, the heart-shaped patterned leaves form an almost year-round ground cover that has dainty flowers in spring.
Galium odoratum	Our native 'sweet woodruff' is valuable but can be rather invasive.
Lamium maculatum	The 'dead nettles' are very useful and attractive plants for dry areas, with Lamium 'Beacon Silver' a lovely variety with pink flowers.
Pachysandra terminalis	A great evergreen for under shrubs and on banks to help retain soil.
Persicaria affinis (knotweed)	The elongated mid-green leaves provide a good foil for the tall spiky pink flowers. 'Darjeeling Red' has both red and pink flowers.
Pulmonaria officinalis (soldiers and sailors)	This ancient medicinal herb doubles up as excellent ground cover for shade. The variety 'Sissinghurst White' has wonderfully bright flowers.
Veronica gentianoides	A ground cover much used by the author, with dark green mats of evergreen leaves and tall spires of pale blue flowers in the spring.
Viola odorata (sweet violet)	The cottage violet with semi-evergreen leaves spreads fairly rapidly. The purple-leaved form – labradorica – is slower and creates dark mats.

Dense shade

Epimedium × *versicolor* 'Sulphureum'	The yellow flowers of this epimedium float above clump-forming mats of foliage that copes with deep shade.
Euphorbia amygdaloides var. *robbiae*	Tall tough ground cover with lime-green flowers in early spring, but beware: it does have a tendency to spread once established.
Geranium nodosum	An evergreen dark-leaved geranium that copes well in dense shade yet still produces a mass of five-petalled blue flowers on loose clumps.
Pachysandra terminalis	As referred to above, creates good carpets of foliage in dense shaded areas, but not the variegated form.
Vinca minor (periwinkle)	A fast-growing plant with starry flowers for awkward positions. Flowering for long periods, there are over seventy varieties to choose from.

The striking foliage of *Brunnera* 'Jack Frost' makes excellent ground cover.

The old cottage favourite, lily of the valley, used for dry shade ground cover.

A profusion of delicate flowers of London Pride (*Saxifraga* × *urbium*) float above evergreen mats of foliage.

Use of evergreens

The old cottage gardens hit a high point in midsummer with glorious displays of flowers and masses of roses. In the winter, the gardens looked exceedingly bare, being devoid of the rich tapestry of flowers and herbs and having just a few meagre rows of vegetables. There were, however, a few traditional evergreen trees and plants to give the garden a modicum of structure, and at the same time, provide greenery for Christmas decorations. These evergreens were the old native British plants of holly, ivy, box and yew. There is no doubt that holly and ivy were the two most vital evergreens for the Christmas period, although rosemary was another early addition.

The modern cottage gardener is luckier, in that there is a far greater range of evergreens to call upon to plant for year-round structure. Evergreen plants offer the cottage gardener a green background for summer flowers and interest in winter. Even in a small cottage garden, one or two evergreens will give the design some architectural substance.

Variegated, and silver- or gold-leaved evergreens, give light and contrast to the garden, and many are good to grow for flower arrangements. Silver-leaved evergreens are particularly suited to sunny dry positions within the garden.

When choosing evergreen shrubs, check they are suitable for your soil (acid, neutral, alkaline), check they'll be happy in the position you're thinking of (sun/shade), and check the ultimate size they will grow to – remember, shrubs often become 'big'.

Table 3.2 provides some suggestions for evergreen shrubs; although not comprehensive, it will give you some ideas on which could possibly be suitable for the cottage garden.

TABLE 3.2: EVERGREEN SHRUBS

Small to medium evergreens	Medium to large evergreens	Silver-leaved shrubs
Berberis (compact forms)	Aucuba (spotted laurel)	Artemisia
Euonymus fortunei 'Emerald Gaiety'	Berberis	Brachyglottis 'Sunshine' (formerly Senecio)
Hebe (some varieties)	Ceanothus	Convolvulus cneorum
Hypericum	Choisya ternata	Lavandula
Phlomis fruticosa	Daphne odora	Santolina
Pieris japonica	Elaeagnus	
Sarcococca (sweet box)	Escallonia	
Skimmia japonica	Fatsia japonica	
Teucrium chamaedrys	Hebe (large)	
	Mahonia aquifolium	
	Olearia macrodonta (NZ holly)	
	Osmanthus × burkwoodii	
	Photinia fraseri 'Red Robin'	

Fatsia japonica 'Spider's Web' in this cottage border creates a structural evergreen presence.

Use of vertical plants

Height is vital in cottage gardens, but occasionally the garden is so small that a tree, arbour or pergola is just not a viable option. In narrow borders or in really small front gardens (particularly town or city gardens), tall vertical perennials come into their own. Vertical perennials take up little space yet provide structure, depth to the border, and flower. These wonderful back-of-the-border perennials will often effortlessly give a planting scheme another dimension in borders lacking in depth. Caution must be exercised when choosing the plants, as you don't want anything in small areas that is going to romp away and take over. The traditional tall cottage 'must haves' are delphiniums and lupins, but even these require a certain depth of border. Better verticals that take up minimal space yet give maximum flower are *Verbena bonariensis*, *Thalictrum*, *Verbascum*, *Crocosmia*, and – my particular favourite – *Veronicastrum virginicum*.

Climbers

Whereas evergreens provide the main framework within the garden, climbers provide a loose vertical flowering 'overcoat'. If chosen carefully, climbers can offer so much in a cottage garden, including an evergreen background, a vertical flowering wall and a scented area. The traditional cottage structures for climbers were rustic porches over the front door, cottage hedges and large old fruit trees. However, the scope is far wider for the modern cottage garden, which often uses arbours, archways, pergolas, fences, trelliswork and metal obelisks.

In terms of actual plants, roses and honeysuckles were originally the main climbing plants used, although the wild clematis (old man's beard) was often seen galloping along the cottage hedge. The variety of options available to the modern cottage gardener is vast, with a huge range of both deciduous and evergreen climbers available.

Elegant, tall *Thalictrum aquilegifolium* in a long cottage-style border.

Verbena bonariensis taking up very little space in this tiny front garden.

An everlasting pea gives good vertical height in a narrow border.

A rose and clematis combining to create flowery vertical height.

Gap fillers

As summer wears on, the early spring plants die back and leave unsightly holes in borders. To keep the cottagey feeling continuing, it is a good idea to fill these gaps with long flowering annuals that will maintain the flower power within the border into the autumn. My 'go-to' annual for this purpose is *Cosmos*, but there are many annuals worth considering for this purpose depending on your own preference. You could either grow some annuals from seed for this purpose or go and buy what you require from a nursery or garden centre. I always seem to manage to come across surplus annuals for sale at the end of people's drives – these usually being well grown extras that they don't need and are happy to part with cheaply!

Ideal fillers include:

- *Amaranthus* (love-lies-bleeding)
- *Centaurea* (annual cornflower)
- *Cosmos* (white or mixed)
- *Cosmos atrosanguineus* (chocolate-scented form)
- *Heliotropium* 'Cherry Pie' (scented like ripe cherries)
- *Osteospermum* (Cape daisies)
- *Nicotiana* (tobacco plant)

In addition, tender salvias are a great space filler, as they flower on and on into the late autumn. And for those who like it hot, then begonias, marigolds, nasturtiums and zinnias could well suit.

Edible plants as gap fillers shouldn't be overlooked, as they rightly fit with the cottage garden idea of companion planting, doing two jobs: contributing to the kitchen whilst filling the border gaps. Herbs such as basil, coriander or parsley could be pushed into spaces, as could 'cut-and-come-again' lettuce or the delightfully colourful ruby chard.

An alternative to planting in the borders is to have some pots of annuals or tender perennials which can be placed in the gaps, particularly in larger spaces. My suggestions for this purpose include chrysanthemums, dahlias, fuchsias, pelargoniums, nasturtiums and salvias. Variegated leaved and scented pelargoniums as gap fillers add a certain zing to the border.

REPEAT PLANTING

Also known as 'link' planting, this technique is frequently used in long herbaceous borders in many stately home gardens. Repetition produces a harmonious continuity within a border as your eye is drawn down the border by the use of either a repeated plant or a repeated group of the same flowers, thus linking the border together. Subconsciously, the brain ties the repeated pattern together, making the whole scheme feel more united and coherent, creating a rhythm and knitting a border together. In long wide herbaceous borders, a number of different plants in different positions are normally repeated – a tall perennial or distinctive shrub along the back, a medium height perennial (or drift) in the middle section, and an edging plant or ground cover repeated along the front.

Although seen mainly in stunning single or double herbaceous borders, this technique is easily transferred to the cottage garden where it can lift a bed or border, generate continuity and draw the eye. This technique is particularly useful for very long, narrow borders to help achieve some continuity in what would otherwise

Nepeta 'Six Hills Giant' repeated along this herbaceous border at Kelmarsh Hall, Northamptonshire.

The two drifts of the delicate blue spires of *Veronica gentianoides* tie the two opposite borders together.

be just a mixed border. For these straight, narrow borders good vertical perennials work best, taking up little space yet producing the desired effect.

Perennials worth considering for this purpose include:

- *Alcea* (hollyhock)
- *Campanula*
- *Echinacea*
- *Eupatorium*
- *Helenium*
- *Iris sibirica*
- *Liatris spicata*
- *Lupinus*
- *Sisyrinchium striatum*
- *Thalictrum*
- *Verbascum*
- *Verbena bonariensis*
- *Veronicastrum virginicum*

Clumps of white tulips have been repeated to draw the eye down this border at Coton Manor Gardens, Northamptonshire.

Allium senescens has been repeated along the edge to help bring the border together.

The stately *Salvia turkestanica* has been repeated in different areas to unify this garden room.

The repeated drifts of *Allium cristophii* create cohesion in this small front garden.

For borders with greater depth, you might like to consider repeating plants along the front or over the path, in which case *Alchemilla mollis*, catmints, dwarf lavenders, low growing hardy geraniums, origanums, heucheras and the wonderful Mexican daisy, *Erigeron karvinskianus*, would all be good options.

In larger cottage gardens that have been subdivided into garden rooms, it is useful to repeat a particular plant throughout the different rooms as it ensures a tying or linking together of the separate areas, creating a more coherent garden. The best plants to use for this type of repeat planting are either plants with striking foliage, silver-leaved plants, a repeated evergreen (box balls) or plants with long flowering periods.

The following plants would be suitable choices:

- *Alchemilla mollis*
- *Allium cristophii*
- *Artemisia*
- *Brunnera* 'Jack Frost'
- *Erigeron karvinskianus*
- *Heuchera* (any good leaved form)
- *Lavandula* 'Hidcote'
- *Stachys lanata* (lamb's ears)

Sometimes it need not be a plant that is repeated to create the desired effect. Repetition of a particular *colour* does exactly the same job and can be just as effective. For instance, repeating pale yellow flowers throughout a border, or a number of different plants with white flowers. Both would tie the border together beautifully.

PLANT INCIDENTS

With the recent explosion of a greater variety of wonderful foliage plants for the garden, the idea of a 'plant focal point' or 'plant incident' is much easier to achieve. The plantswoman Beth Chatto was of the opinion that an occasional bold-leaved plant was an essential element in any garden, acting as a focal point to rest the eye on. A plant like this will draw the eye and create a 'pause' which will then allow for the scene around it to be taken in. In her garden near Colchester, Beth Chatto used large clumps of hostas with their big attractive leaves to create her statement plant incidents. Not all of us can use hostas as they do best on moist fertile soil in light shade. However, any bold-leaved plant will work, particularly if the plant is either variegated or dark-leaved. *Bergenia cordifolia* 'Purpurea' is a good example, with its bold purple elephant's ears, as is *Melianthus major*, with its handsome glaucous evergreen leaves. Another good choice is *Fatsia japonica*, although this does get rather large, and therefore perhaps *Fatsia japonica variegata* would be a better choice for a small garden.

If large bold-leaved plants don't do it for you, there are alternatives. Big visual vertical perennials will do just as well. *Thalictrum* 'Elin' works exceptionally well, reaching a height of 2.5m (8ft) with eye-catching purple stems and wonderful blue-green foliage, all topped off with a cloud of lilac flowers. Two other good showstoppers include *Onopordum acanthium* (cotton thistle), a huge thistle reaching 2.5–4m (8–13ft), and *Crambe cordifolia* (giant sea kale), which erupts into a massive head of stunning white scented flowers over large leaves; both of these require dry sun.

Another option is to include plants that have either silver or steely-blue foliage. Both these colours 'catch' the eye and make

The large patches of pale yellow *Anthemis* 'Sauce Hollandaise' repeated in different areas tie the planting scheme together.

Eryngium × zabelii 'Big Blue' makes a stunning plant incident in a border.

The sea-holly *Eryngium giganteum* provides a wonderful point of interest in the border.

The striking silver cardoon creates a dramatic incident in this cottage garden.

it pause momentarily. Eryngiums (sea hollies) make spectacular plant incidents in the border, particularly *Eryngium giganteum*. Other wonderful silver plants that will create a presence include *Brunnera* 'Jack Frost', *Santolina chamaecyparissus* (cotton lavender), *Convolvulus cneorum, Caryopteris clandonensis,* and if you have the room, the magnificent *Cynara cardunculus* (cardoon).

DUAL-PURPOSE PLANTS

In the past, cottage garden plants invariably had more than one purpose. Not only did they have attractive flowers but provided medicinal cures, pest repellents, and – importantly – leaves, petals and seeds for use in cooking. We still grow many of these old cottage plants, but usually purely for their beauty rather than their other virtues. However, there are a few plants/herbs that are still grown not only for their attractiveness but also their valuable benefits. For instance, lavender, which has many virtues apart from

its obvious wonderful scent, foliage and flowers. Bees love lavender, but certain pests detest it, and it is a particularly useful pest repellent when dried and either hung in a wardrobe or kitchen, or made into lavender bags to be put in amongst clothes. Many other herbs, too, have dual properties, being delightfully scented with lovely flowers, but also being vital for their use in cooking.

For the modern cottage garden, where space is at a premium, having plants that can offer more than just flowers (however lovely) is a real asset to any border. Newer varieties of dual-purpose plants provide something rather different compared to the traditional uses. They offer a way to utilize every inch of the garden for a longer period of the year, create areas of interest even after flowering, or form a textured foliage background which later flowering plants can use to help showcase their appeal. These newer varieties of plants have interesting coloured or evergreen foliage, attractive seed heads or a stunning autumnal colour leaf change. These valuable plants can be used to create seasonal continuity within the garden.

Beautifully geometrically structured seed-heads of *Iberis* 'Masterpiece'.

Seed-heads of *Allium schubertii* stand out brilliantly against the dark-leaved dahlia.

Plants with seed heads

Plants with flowers followed by attractive seed heads create the opportunity for continued interest in a border after the flowers have finished; they should be considered for inclusion in areas that are mainly filled with spring flowers.

Alliums are a wonderful choice for dry, sunny borders, as their spectacular starry heads even when drained of their colour still retain a highly pleasing dried star-burst structure. They can be left to help tie borders together from spring through to late summer.

Honesty and nigella, two old cottage favourites, are both blessed with interesting seed heads. Honesty has marvellous oval-shaped seed heads that gradually turn translucent, adding light to borders towards the end of summer and having the bonus of being ideal for cutting. Nigella, on the other hand, has unusual puffed-up seed pods that stand erect after the delicate flowers have disappeared. Darker markings running down the pale-green sides of the immature seed heads make quite a statement intermingled in the border.

Similar to nigella, the annual opium poppy also has a striking seed head. Long grown in gardens, *Papaver somniferum* (the bread-seed poppy), has large light-mauve flowers with dark eyes on tall erect stems. The pot-like glaucous seed capsules create a strong presence in the border and can be dried for house decoration as well.

Another traditional cottage flower, the Martagon lily, which in June has the wonderful Turk's cap flowers ascending the stems, will, in late summer, have dried cup-like seed capsules which resemble narrow candelabras.

TIP FOR DRYING SEED HEADS

Seed heads wanted for drying from either poppies or nigella should be picked whilst still green but when the stems have begun to harden. They can then either be hung upside down in a bunch or put in tall glass jar to dry fully.

The electric-blue flowers of eryngiums (sea hollies) also retain their attractive upright spikiness once their blue flowers have faded. They often turn from blue to silver, and then from silver to a papery brown colour when dried in the sun. The variety called 'Miss Willmott's Ghost' is particularly good for structure.

Plants with hips and berries

Any border plant that has either berries or hips is dual purpose, not only bestowing a vibrant red or orange colour in the autumn, but also providing food for wild birds. Varieties of rose, if chosen with care, will guarantee that the 'queen of flowers' not only embellishes the summer garden with colour and fragrance, but will also give a display of vivid red rose hips in late summer and early autumn. Not all roses have large, colourful hips, so some research is worthwhile, but as long as you don't cut off all the dying flower heads during the summer, hips will always be produced – old species roses, rugosas, and ramblers and climbers will give a good display. The rose hips could also be used to make rose-hip syrup, should you wish.

The most traditional cottage trees for berries are the holly and rowan. Both are woven into cottage garden history having superstitions related to their position within the garden and their uses throughout the year. Holly trees are generally too big for most gardens nowadays and are rarely used for hedging; however, there are some smaller variegated varieties worth considering.

Sorbus aucuparia (rowan or mountain ash tree), although eventually growing fairly large, has lovely white flowers in spring, dense clusters of wonderful red berries in the autumn, and is a good tree for autumn colour with leaves turning either yellow or red/purple. This elegantly shaped tree is worth considering for a larger garden, being tolerant of any soil and most aspects. There are many varieties to choose from and the colour of the berries can be red, white or yellow.

Other worthwhile berried plants for the cottage garden include pyracantha and cotoneaster. Both will look terrific when laden with red or orange berries, but whereas pyracantha has long nasty thorns, cotoneaster is the better choice for safety and ease in pruning. Both can be used as a shrub, hedge or wall plant and are valuable not only as a flowering plant but to attract and feed birds.

Plants with autumn colour

In the late nineteenth century China opened up, and as a result, plant-hunters sent back large numbers of trees and shrubs that had the dual purpose of beautiful flowers in spring followed by stunning autumnal foliage colour. The greatest discoveries were the Japanese maples or acers. These trees, which vary in size, not

A magnificent display of showy *Rosa rugosa* hips.

only have interesting foliage throughout the year but turn stunning colours in the autumn. Most of the *Acer palmatum* varieties are hardy, and although preferring a cool, semi-shade position in the garden, will be just as happy in a large pot if no space is available.

My own favourite dual-purpose small tree for a cottage garden is *Amelanchier*. There are two main varieties available, both quite similar – *A. lamarckii* and *A. canadensis*. Probably the best variety available is *Amelanchier lamarckii* 'Ballerina'. These versatile small trees have many attributes, making them worthy of a place in every cottage garden, whether as a stand-alone specimen or as part of a larger border. In the spring the bare branches are literally covered in a snow of beautiful bright white flowers, leaves follow, and then berries are produced in June or July (hence the name Juneberry). Then in the autumn the tree has wonderful crimson-coloured leaves. Reaching only about 10m high (30ft), it will tolerate any soil in sun or part shade – what more could you wish for in a tree for a cottage garden?

Variegated and coloured foliage plants

Plants with variegated foliage, marbled foliage, silver foliage or dark purple/black foliage, also possess an important dual purpose: their flowers and the permanence of interest of their leaves. One particularly good early spring flowering foliage plant and a recent introduction to gardens is *Brunnera* 'Jack Frost'. It has airy delicate blue forget-me-not flowers which rise above the sparkling silver heart-shaped leaves which are veined with green. Once the flowers have finished, the beautiful clump of leaves shines on, offering an attractive ground cover for other cottage flowers to float over. There are two other forms which are also worth searching out: *Brunnera* 'Hadspen Cream' which has bright white margins to its green leaves, and *Brunnera* 'Looking Glass' which has bright silver leaves.

The dark purple foliage of *Physocarpus diabolo* creates a dramatic presence in this garden.

Heucheras are another group of clump-forming perennials that have marvellous foliage virtually all year, but also lovely floaty flowers that add to the cottagey feel. In recent times there has been an explosion of incredible colourful-leaved heucheras that are now essential foliage plants. It all started with a chance seedling at Kew Gardens of the glossy purple-leaved *Heuchera villosa* 'Palace Purple'. By the 1990s a plethora of richly marked leafed varieties had arrived on the scene, with the promise of evergreen foliage interest all year, and sprays of delicate flowers in early summer. There is now a massive range of heucheras in every conceivable colour giving you the opportunity to choose a plant that ties in with your border, and to act as a foil for other plants. They are also excellent feature plants for pots.

Plants with foliage other than green will make a statement in the border, and if placed correctly, act as a foil for other flowers. Silver-leaved plants are particularly useful, as they produce light, demand attention in the border and bring neighbouring flowers into sharp focus. Of course, they also flower, giving two aspects to silver-leaved plants or shrubs. Although requiring a well-drained soil and full sun, *Convolvulus cneorum* is probably the only bindweed you'll ever want to deliberately grow! It is a non-invasive dwarf evergreen shrub (60cm) with large white trumpet-like flowers in summer which cover the silky-haired metallic silver foliage. Grow this plant either at the front of a border where it can be used as a contrast plant, or in a pot as a feature plant.

Other silver plants worth considering include lavender, lamb's ears (*Stachys byzantina*), cotton lavender, artemisia, sea holly (*Eryngium*), the late-flowering shrub *Caryopteris clandonensis* and the tall glaucous-blue foliage of Russian sage (*Perovskia*).

Purple or dark-leaved foliage plants are exceedingly useful, as dark leaves draw the eye and create impact if planted as a one-off specimen, acting as a pause in the garden. They provide contrast with other plants and flowers, which can be effectively juxtaposed against them, or in the case of larger shrubs, with climbers growing through them. Dark purple leaves work particularly well with red and pink flowered plants. Possible perennials for the garden include dark-leaved geraniums, sedums, heucheras and dahlias; and shrubs worth considering are *Sambucus nigra* 'Black Lace', *Cotinus coggygria* 'Royal Purple' (smoke tree), *Physocarpus* 'Diabolo', *Berberis thunbergii atropurpurea* and the dark-leaved Japanese maples.

SEASONAL AREAS AND 'WOW' BORDERS

I always think it is advisable to group together flowers that bloom at the same time. It is impossible, and even undesirable, to have a garden in blossom all over, and groups of flower-beauty are all the more enjoyable for being more or less isolated by stretches of intervening greenery.

Gertrude Jekyll, *Wood and Garden* (1899)

In the first major cottage garden that I designed and planted up from scratch, I took on board what Gertrude Jekyll said about grouping seasonal flowers together for a more desirable effect. The spring borders of bulbs, ground cover and spring plants, were planted so as to flower together throughout the early months of

The 'July' border in School House cottage garden in Lincolnshire.

The seemingly chaotic mass of cottage flowers in the 'July' border.

the year (February to May). These borders were all deliberately wrapped around or placed up against the cottage on purpose, allowing me to see the wonderful spring combinations from the lounge, dining room and kitchen windows. This enabled me to make the most of all the lovely drifts of spring flowers without having to venture out of the house on cold, miserable spring days, and cheered me up inside the cottage. As these spring borders gradually finished and changed to stretches of mainly green foliage, other later flowering areas came into their own. These secondary groups of late spring/early summer flowers were designed to give colour further out in the cottage garden, along paths, under arches and around seating areas where one could stroll or sit with a cup of tea to enjoy the better light and sun. As Jekyll points out, these later areas of colour were now 'cheek by jowl' with the earlier spring beds, which now being mainly green foliage, emphasized the secondary borders and made them look more effective.

Within this cottage garden I also designed a June/July Room, where all the flowers were specifically chosen and arranged to flower within a limited time span, so as to create a 'wow' factor for a particular area of the garden. It took many years to get things right, as the soil was very sandy and free-draining and the whole area faced due south. It was exciting to test out different plants to find out whether they were drought tolerant, required little attention and fitted into the overall design.

I consciously chose and endeavoured to design a cottage garden where the flowers bloomed together at specific times in specific areas, and not have flowers blooming generally throughout the garden in a bitty, unrelated way. Of course, every cottage gardener is an individual, and as individuals we all have our own ideas, but I wanted to suggest here that border groupings that flower at the same time can create something special within a garden.

USE OF COLOUR

In old cottage gardens there was no conscious or deliberate gathering together of flowers in order to create particular colour combinations or schemes. Plants were simply pushed in randomly where there was available space and where they seemed to do best. However, many cottagers did often have a pretty mess of traditional or well-loved flowers in one area where they could be admired. As previously explained in Chapter 1, the cottage with the narrow strip close to the lane often had the flowers packed in beneath the front windows where colour and scent could be appreciated. Here, the heady mix of vibrant colours jostled with one another, helping to hold each other up, and creating a visual effect of differing heights, foliage and flowers. This picture of the little front cottage garden being a riot of colour has resulted in the term 'cottage garden mix'. One only needs to buy a packet of seed labelled 'Cottage Favourites Mixture' to find the modern equivalent today.

The modern cottage garden – without the need to grow vast quantities of vegetables, vigorous spreading medicinal or pot herbs, or large fruit trees – has now turned its attention to concentrating on colour combinations within the garden, a fun and enjoyable venture with the aim of improving the look of the garden. Some of course, still believe that a 'proper' cottage garden should purely be a mix of everything, but others prefer to give more thought to the design of the cottage garden and the arrangement of the flowers within it. This style of cottage gardening has become very popular and allows gardeners to have a more artistic approach to their borders. In part driven by the Chelsea Flower Show, the idea of colour schemes shows no sign of abating and gives many gardeners the opportunity to continually change and improve the visual aspect of their garden.

Luckily, for modern-day cottage gardeners, there is a far greater range of colours available than ever before, and the continual development of so many varieties opens up even greater scope to experiment and compose colour-coordinated borders or corners within the garden. Colour can be a very personal choice: some prefer pastel shades throughout the garden, whereas others prefer to embrace the 'hot' colours of red, yellow and orange. Some believe orange and pink together is a definite *no* in any border, but some are happy to place together whatever they feel works. Other factors that persuade gardeners towards certain colour combinations include: fashionable plants; visiting other gardens and seeing other perspectives on colour schemes; gleaning planting ideas from gardening programmes and magazines; and discovering which range of colours best suits their own garden. Garden visiting is now extremely popular, as it offers the ordinary gardener the opportunity to see at first hand what an artistic approach to borders can achieve. Probably the two most visited gardens in England are the National Trust properties of Sissinghurst Castle and Hidcote Manor, both of which have colour-schemed rooms and borders. As gardeners we often try to emulate the colour-coordinated schemes we admire, in the hope that we can achieve better plant associations within our own gardens. To enable the average gardener to improve plant compositions, it is worth knowing some of the basic principles relating to colour.

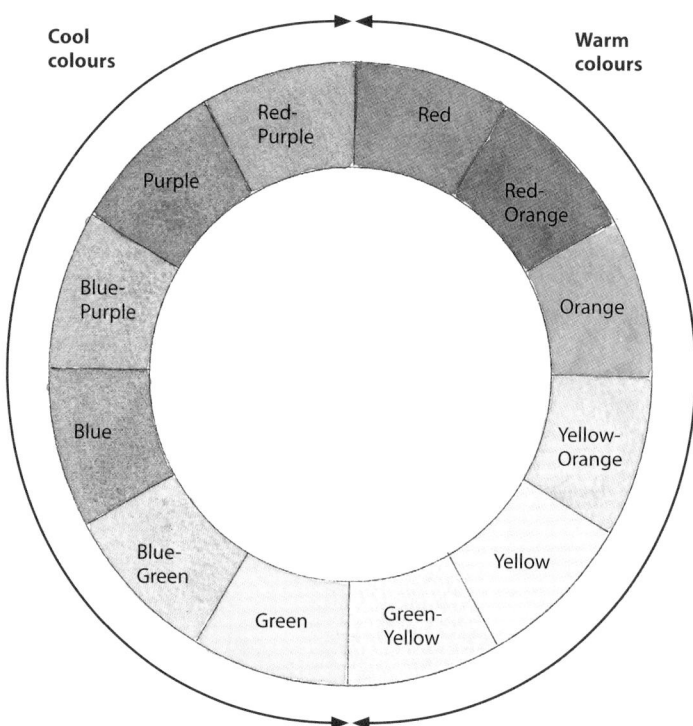

The colour wheel.

Colour composition

Gardens belonging to artists frequently showcase lovely seemingly sophisticated colour-schemed borders. They may well have an instinct for colour, but quite often the artists also have a good knowledge of colour theory. It was the artist Gertrude Jekyll who introduced the world to colour schemes within the garden, and she emphasized that designing a border was 'like painting a picture with flowers' – where the colours should blend with one another. Jekyll's planting schemes for Edwin Lutyens' garden designs rightly made her famous, launching her gardening career, but more importantly, they introduced to the world the possibilities of colour combinations in gardens for the first time ever.

Like all artists, Gertrude Jekyll had the advantage of knowing the relationship of colours from the artist's colour wheel, which illustrated 'hot' colours on one side and 'cool' colours on other.

Jekyll was taught about the use of colour whilst at art school and later transferred this knowledge to the garden, creating stunning colour-coordinated borders. Once Jekyll had opened the door on the use of colour schemes in garden rooms or herbaceous borders, many other garden designers quickly followed her example, and individual rooms showcasing particular colour themes became fashionable. The flood gates were opened, and colour schemes are now something we take for granted when we visit gardens. Jekyll's 1908 book *Colour in the Flower Garden* was a bestseller and is still the only book you'll ever need which explains the relationship of colours within the garden and how they are best put into practice.

Another great practitioner in the use of colour schemes was Norah Lindsay. Norah had a natural talent for composing large, long herbaceous borders, and although we don't design borders on the same scale as Norah Lindsay anymore, her colour theories are worth knowing. To quote Norah, 'An elaborate colour scheme should include all tints of the rainbow, but the colours should be kept within their own group, with delicate shading being preferred to violent contrasts.'

JEKYLL ON COLOUR SCHEMES

It is a curious thing that people will sometimes spoil some garden project for the sake of a word. For instance, a blue garden, for beauty's sake, may be hungering for a group of white lilies, or something of palest lemon-yellow, but it is a blue garden and there must be no flowers in it but blue flowers…. My own idea is that it should be beautiful first, and then just as blue as may be consistent with the best possible beauty.

Gertrude Jekyll, *Colour in the Flower Garden* (1908)

Harmonious and contrasting colours

The first major rule that can be applied to a garden from the colour wheel is that any two or three adjacent colours on the wheel will be in harmony with one another. These are called analogous colours, which simply means any colours that sit next to one another on the colour wheel blend beautifully, whether on the cool or warm (hot) side. For instance:

- Yellow and green/yellow
- Red and orange/red
- Red, red/purple and purple
- Blue, blue/purple and purple

The colour pink doesn't appear on the colour wheel, as it's a combination of red and violet, so you need to consider it in the red-violet range and use it as such. Pink blends particularly well with blue and purple, as well as with red, terracotta and violet.

Contrasting colours, also known as complementary or clashing colours, are those colours which appear opposite to one another on the colour wheel. They are always a combination of a hot colour and a cool colour, and give a brighter feel when used in gardens. Pairing two such opposite colours will make an attractive combination and create drama in a border – a good example being the combination of orange and blue.

An excellent pairing of blue nigella and purple alliums.

A harmonious inter-planting of dark- and light-flowered hardy geraniums.

A lovely late season colour combination of pink nerines and blue asters.

A wonderful mix of achilleas – there being no harsh yellows, oranges or vivid reds to spoil the harmonious grouping.

Background colour

A major consideration when planning a garden is the background colour of walls and fences, as these remain constant unless repainted. A house or cottage wall made of red brick will do nothing for red flowers, as they will disappear into the background, whereas white flowers, pale yellow flowers and silver foliage plants will stand out. If the wall is painted white, changing the background colour, then the flowers up against it will need to be more vibrant and white flowers should be excluded.

Similarly, the usual dark brown wooden panelled fence that is put up around the average garden will work brilliantly for lighter flowers – yellows, whites, pinks and light blues – but not at all well for darker flowers (dark blues, purples, blacks). Painting a fence changes the background and allows the gardener to reassess the relationship of the flowers against the fence. A white painted fence will be excellent for the darker coloured flowers but not at all for the white flowers! In my opinion, the best background colour for a fence is a blue-green or silver-grey coloured fence, as this works extremely well for all flower colours.

A stunning contrast of the steely-blue eryngium against the yellow button-centred anthemis.

A hot yellow achillea paired with a deep purple/blue salvia.

Green is a colour

When it comes to borders, the best background colour is that of nature – green. Gertrude Jekyll insisted that green is a colour which needs careful consideration. It is a restful and restorative colour for eyes, but of course comes in a vast range of differing shades which will require complementary planting. This is particularly important when using hedges as a background, with yew being a very dark dense green, privet a mid-green, and any variegated hedge a light green background.

One major area of green in large gardens is the lawn. Acting rather like a green carpet, a lawn can be one of the best foils to help emphasize borders. Clipped grass paths do the same job, creating not just a functional route, but a foil for the planting schemes used alongside.

When you purchase a new plant, take the opportunity to place the plant (still in its pot) up against different backgrounds to see how it looks. You can move it around the garden until you find the ideal position – with a good background and complementary planting around it.

Use of silver and grey foliage plants

Probably the most valuable colour in the cottage gardener's armoury is silver. Silver or grey foliage plants will add highlights to borders and garden rooms; they create a certain coolness in a scheme and help lift the surrounding planting. These colours combine exceedingly well with evergreen structure to create a

The painted fence creates the right background colour for the cottagey planting.

The silver artemisia acts as a brilliant foil for the dark-flowered dahlia.

TABLE 3.3: SOME SUGGESTIONS FOR COLOUR SCHEMES	
Scheme	**Flowers and foliage**
White border/ room	Whites, creams, silvers, greys
Yellow/gold border	Variegated plants, yellows, pale yellows, whites
Pastel border	Pinks, blues, whites, silvers, very pale yellows
Blue/purple border	Dark blues, purples, mauves, silvers, greys
Red/purple border	Deep reds, purples, dark foliage background plants, silvers
Ghost border	Silvers, greys, whites
Blue border	Blues, silvers, greys

background for all colour schemes, but harmonize particularly well with pastel schemes (blues, pinks, whites, mauves).

When delicate pink or blue flowers are placed against silver foliage it assists in enhancing the colours, making them stand out. Conversely, silver and greys will 'tone down' bright colours when placed against them. Silver and grey plants also work wonderfully as a contrast colour against dark colours, such as purples and rich reds. Their light quality can be used as a foil to show off dark flowers to the maximum and will create an amazing feature combination in a border.

The other wonderful use of silvers is for 'moonlight' rooms or borders. Together with bright white flowers, silvers and greys will begin to illuminate and glow as dusk approaches. Silvers provide light within a garden at night and can be combined with night-scented plants to create a specific area where a seat could be placed to enjoy the garden in the late evening.

I cannot summarize the use of silver any better than Norah Lindsay, who said, 'A bold planting scheme affords a harmony in shades where the delicate tones are predominant with swathes of silvery foliage as a foil to brilliant flower masses.'

Colour schemed borders and rooms

Possibly the most famous colour-schemed garden room in the world is the 'White Garden' at Sissinghurst. It has spawned many copies as enchanted gardeners try to emulate what Vita Sackville-West achieved. Vita hit the nail on the head when she wrote about her grey, green and white garden:

Provided one doesn't run the idea to death, and provided one has enough room, it is interesting to make a one-colour garden. It is something more than merely interesting. It is great fun and endlessly amusing as an experiment, capable of perennial improvement, as you take away the things that don't satisfy you, and replace them by something better. A grey, green, white and silver garden looks so cool on a summer evening.

As Vita says, colour-schemed borders or rooms are fun and immensely interesting to create, and they don't need to be on a large scale either – a cool bed around a seating area, a 'hot spot' to enliven a dark corner, a narrow border running alongside a path, or if you wish, a separate colour-schemed garden room.

For larger cottage gardens, having either a garden 'room' or a particular area limited to a specific colour scheme helps break up that 'sameness' within the garden, giving a different feel as you move through the garden.

Single-coloured borders can be effective in both smaller and larger cottage gardens, creating a monochromatic look. Here, you are relying on the harmonious tones of one colour, which can give a stunning appearance within the garden. For maximum effect, I would suggest that the colour range be reduced and the background foliage and texture worked upon to help underpin the planting.

For areas where you intend to sit out in the warmth of the evening and catch the last rays of the sun, you could follow Vita's idea and go for white flowers and silver/grey foliage plants as a basis. White flowers actually become luminous at dusk and create an elegant light of their own. Add some silver and grey plants which have their own ambience, and lastly, some night-scented plants to enthrall your sense of smell. It is no coincidence that many white flowers are highly scented so as to attract moths, and this will work in your favour to help create a wonderfully ethereal evening spot in the garden.

However, care must be taken with white gardens, as great mass plantings of white flowers often create too vivid a contrast with the surrounding planting. Instead, intersperse the white flowers as highlights amongst greens, silvers and greys, as Vita did.

I have always found that it's a good idea to keep a notebook when creating a colour-schemed border so that each year both good combinations and utter failures can be noted down. This helps you to remember what 'needs to be altered' in order to improve the scheme the following year.

The structural box hedging emphasizes the flowers in the 'White Garden' at Kelmarsh Hall.

Pastel schemes – 'cool' colours

The pastel range of colours (whites, pinks, blues, purples, pale yellows, silvers, greys) can be brought together to create a cooling, calming area within the garden. A pastel scheme is particularly appropriate for full sun and dry soil aspects or areas of the garden, and the Mediterranean plants are extremely suitable as a basis for such a scheme, as these plants often have silver/grey foliage to combat the hot sun.

I have always preferred pastel schemes for my designs. It is a personal preference, but I feel these shades work exceedingly well in small cottage gardens, making the garden a restful oasis and creating a feeling of space. Pale yellows add hints of highlights amongst the paler colours, and deeper reds and purples can also be incorporated and add dark contrasting colours. However, bright yellows tend to ruin such schemes, being too harsh, grabbing attention and taking away from the overall feel of what you are trying to achieve. Silver and grey foliage plants can be used as highlighters in preference to hot yellows, as they exude a lovely brightness without the harshness.

Hot border schemes

In general, the 'hotter' range of colours come into play more during mid-late summer and running into autumn. Colours that fall into this category include reds, vivid yellows and oranges. The most obvious example of a 'hot' red is the bedding pelargonium used extensively in parks and large containers in town centres and seaside resorts.

The hot range of colours is ideal for late flowering schemes, when these colours are more predominant and often long lasting, not being fazed by the late summer heat. The following plants

A 'cool' border of blues, pinks and whites at Stillingfleet Lodge Gardens, near York.

Part of the well-designed 'hot' herbaceous borders at Stillingfleet Lodge Gardens.

JULY BORDER IN A LARGE COTTAGE GARDEN

The cottage border has been designed as a pastel colour scheme of blues, pinks, whites and pale yellows. Not only is the border colour-schemed, but every plant has been carefully chosen to flower in June/July to create a 'feature' border, with the terracotta achilleas and purple-leaved sedum adding a touch of much needed contrast within the border. In addition, all the plants were required to be drought tolerant as the front garden of the cottage faces due south and the soil is extremely dry and sandy (the soil runs through the fingers if a handful is scooped up!). The planting design shows the plants chosen for this particular scheme.

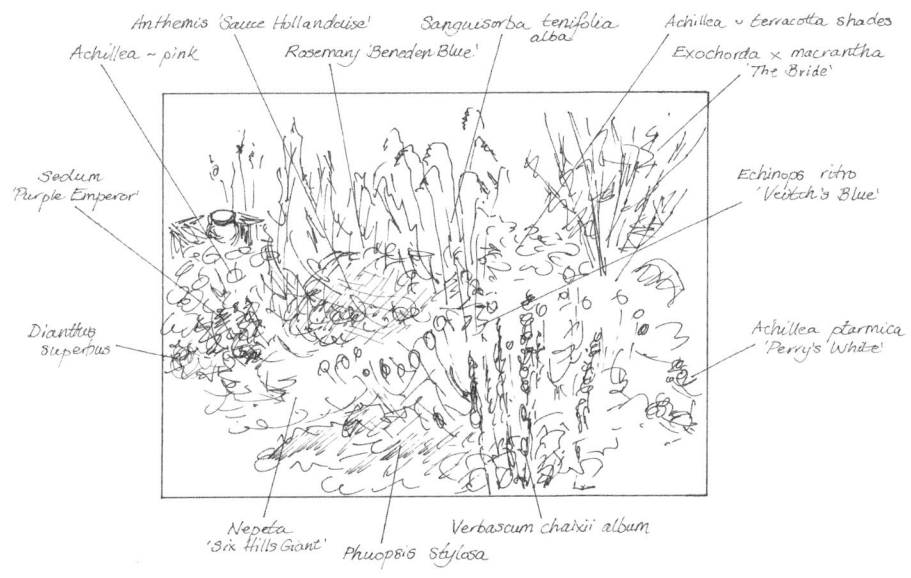

Planting design for a July cottage border.

The pastel colour schemed border at School House cottage garden in July.

Case Study 3.4

THE RED BORDERS AT PARCEVALL HALL

The Arts and Crafts style gardens of Parcevall Hall near Skipton were designed as a series of terrace rooms, at the bottom of which are the highly evocative red borders. These 'hot' borders are at their peak in late August and September, being enclosed by neatly clipped hedges, which display the planting scheme beautifully. The two photographs show the borders at their best in late August.

One side of the double herbaceous 'red' borders at Parcevall Hall in Wharfedale.

A stunning combination of 'hot' colours, including a deep pink astilbe, purple hazel, *Crocosmia lucifer*, *Monarda didyma* (bergamot) and *Gaillardia*.

MARIGOLD COTTAGE HOT BORDER

The 'hot' border at Marigold Cottage was specifically designed to give late season colour and create a feature to light up in a slightly shady area of the garden. The colour scheme is predominately yellow and red, with just a hint of pink and orange. Important structural foliage in the form of fennel and globe artichoke adds vital contrast and height in the centre of the border.

Planting design for Marigold Cottage's 'hot' border.

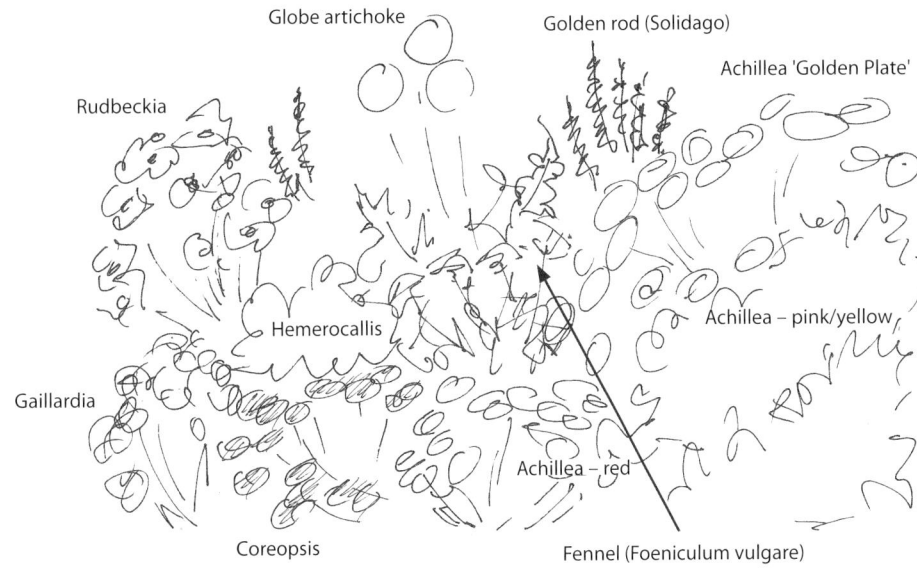

The 'hot' border at Marigold Cottage garden in Sutton-on-Sea.

Chapter 4

Cottage Flowers

At first, the emphasis of the cottage garden was dictated by the need for a productive plot, and plants were only grown if they had a purpose – beauty was a bonus. As time passed, many new plants arrived in England, and like everyone else, the cottager was always pleased to acquire something different. With very few possessions to speak of, these new acquisitions became 'treasured' flowers that were passed down from generation to generation, eventually becoming what we now consider traditional cottage flowers.

The modern cottage garden takes a different approach to its predecessor, as modern-day society has the luxury of time to garden, time to relax in the garden and time to admire the garden. As a result, today's cottage-style garden is far more reliant upon charming borders full of colourful flowers rather than a patch of cabbages and herbs.

At the beginning of the evolution of the cottage garden, the native flowers would have constituted the greatest quantity of plants grown; and then as monasteries acquired plants from Europe these filtered down to the cottager. Later still, plants from wealthy gentlemen's gardens (where some cottagers worked) found their way into cottage gardens; these admired flowers in one cottager's garden quickly passed to others within the village, thus spreading around the local area. Eventually, in the nineteenth century, the nursery trade assisted in a more widespread distribution of new hybrids and varieties from China, some of which also quickly became popular in cottage gardens.

Because of the lack of time to tend to plants, cottage flowers have always had to be hardy, easy to grow and self-seed, and be resilient to having pieces chopped off a clump at random. The plants had no choice but to thrive on neglect, as the vegetables were more important to the cottager. So, the traditional cottage flowers have always been tough, generally disease resistant and able to cope with little or no attention. For today's busy lifestyle, these attributes make the old cottage flowers extremely valuable as the backbone of any garden.

Which flowers should be grown in the modern cottage garden? Every gardener has their own ideas: some wish to stick rigidly to the older genuine varieties of roses and flowers; others wish to be more flexible and bolder, using both old favourites and new fashionable plants. You need not restrict yourself to what you might consider traditional cottage flowers. Just like those old cottagers, gardeners today love new introductions or unusual varieties on offer, and there is now a vast array of excellent plants to choose from. Assuming that your plant choice suits your situation, you should feel free to plant newer varieties that take your fancy, so long as they retain that cottagey appeal in the border. In fact, most modern varieties also have the advantage of greater disease resistance, longer flowering periods and standing without support. A modern cottage garden designed with a clever mixture of native, traditional and newer hybrids will give continual colour and scent throughout the whole year.

This chapter outlines a selected number of favourites that fall into three categories – native, traditional and modern – cottage flowers that should be considered essential to any cottage-style garden.

A cottage border with blue delphiniums, anthemis, eryngiums, a dark-leafed hardy geranium and a clump of white *Salvia turkestanica*.

NATIVE COTTAGE FLOWERS

Many native flowers became the earliest cottage favourites. Foxgloves, violets, primroses, cowslips and honeysuckles, to mention just a few, have always been present in the cottage garden. Many probably self-seeded from woods or meadows and were simply left to be admired, whilst others were found to be extremely useful and were deliberately dug up and transplanted into the garden. A sensible cottager would take note of where plants grew in the wild and try to replicate the position within the garden: a woodland plant being planted in shade, a meadow plant in a sunny corner. After generations of being grown in the garden, the original purpose of a native plant was often forgotten or perhaps not required, but because it had always been grown in the garden, it had acquired the position of a much-loved flower.

Alchemilla vulgaris – lady's mantle
Common names: dew cup, duck's foot, woman's best friend.

The variety sold today is not our native form, but the larger leaved and flowered variety called *Alchemilla mollis*. Lady's mantle was known for its medicinal properties in earlier times, but is now used widely as a pleasing cottagey ground cover. Its beautifully scallop-shaped leaves and sulphur-yellow flowers will informalize paths, edges, walls and patios. Although it is worth growing just for the shimmering dew drops that sit in the leaf centres first thing in the morning, the flowers seem to naturally blend with other plants, making it an invaluable addition in any cottage garden. It is easy, accommodating and suitable for any position or soil type; and although it has a habit of spreading, it is not difficult to keep in check.

Aquilegia vulgaris – columbine
Common names: granny's bonnets, doves around a dish, granny jump out of bed.

These delightfully promiscuous flowers are another old cottage favourite. The spurred flowers rise above the delicate foliage in late spring or early summer, and come in a great range of colours, in both single and double forms. Preferring a part-shade position, they are very easy to grow and are a great combination plant with early ground cover.

Our native columbines are blue, purple, pink and white; the vibrant hot colours and bigger spurred varieties of *Aquilegia canadensis* being introductions from North America. However, whichever variety you use, these floaty flowers create that crucial cottage feel, and the plants will freely self-seed throughout your borders.

White columbines (*Aquilegia*) or – as cottagers called them – 'doves around a dish'.

Alchemilla mollis with the morning dew on its leaves.

A delightful double-flowered columbine seedling.

Campanula varieties – bellflower

The nettle-leaved bellflower, *Campanula trachelium*, is native in the woods in Kent and can be found on the Pilgrims' Way to Canterbury. This wild form was the original 'Canterbury bell' which was associated with the medieval pilgrims, whose horses wore bells. Today, however, the name 'Canterbury bell' refers to the biennial bellflower *Campanula medium*, which was introduced *c.*1590.

Flowering from late spring through to midsummer, these flowers are perfect for the informality of the cottage garden. Native bellflowers such as *Campanula trachelium* or *Campanula glomerata* (clustered bellflower) are still popular; however, *Campanula persicifolia* is also ideally suited, and the variety 'Chettle Charm' is a stunner. *Campanula carpatica* is a low clump-forming bellflower with a long flowering period that is best suited for the front of the border, containers and pots, or cascading over walls and edges.

Centaurea varieties – cornflower

Common names: blew-bottle, ragged sailor, bachelor's buttons, hurt sickle.

The cornflower family is very large, with both annual and perennial varieties. The traditional annual blue cornflower, *Centaurea cyanus*, was once a weed and a nuisance in the corn fields as it quickly blunted the sickles at harvest time. Although grown in wild-flower areas within gardens, this cornflower has generally been superseded by the perennial varieties developed from *Centaurea montana*. Cornflowers love poor soil and appreciate a sunny position. Having a long flowering period (May to September) they are ideal for cottage borders, wilder areas or even containers. Particularly good varieties include *Centaurea montana* 'Amethyst in Snow' and *Centaurea* 'John Coutts'.

The large white flowers of *Centaurea cheiranthifolia*.

A mixed drift of *Campanula persicifolia*.

A clump of the long-flowering *Centaurea* 'John Coutts'.

Convallaria 'Albostriata' one of best variegated forms of lily of the valley.

The white form of our native foxglove, *Digitalis alba*, which is good for part-shade positions.

TIP

Foxgloves self-seed profusely. This is actually a bonus; let the plants seed around and intermingle within the border, then in the spring pull up any seedlings that aren't required, and simply leave the ones in the border which create a drift of flowers.

Convallaria majalis – lily of the valley
Common names: May bells, Our Lady's tears.

A native of dry woodland, the plant is happiest in shady poor soil positions, and will thrive under a hedge where it can run freely. Highly perfumed, the pendant milk-white spring flowers are lovely, and the plant quick to establish. The Victorians loved to have pots of the plant to scent the house, but cottagers believed it was extremely unlucky to bring the flowers indoors. My own favourites are 'Hardwick Hall', a larger form with a silver-white edge to the leaves; and the variegated form, 'Albostriata', which adds a touch of elegance to any shady border.

Digitalis purpurea – foxglove
Common names: witches' gloves, bloody fingers, fairy bells.

This native biennial is still an immensely popular cottage plant. The name 'foxglove' can be traced back to the Saxons who believed the plant was deliberately given to the fox by wicked fairies, enabling the cunning fox to put his paws inside the flowers and then tip-toe silently into the hen house! My own favourite is the white form, *Digitalis alba*, which I find most useful to light up and give structure in dry shade. Like the common purple form, it adds a stately presence to the back of any border. All foxgloves prefer semi-shade positions but will happily grow in any soil. There is also a perennial variety worth considering, called *Digitalis lutea*. Although not growing as tall as the ordinary foxglove, it too, is happy in shade and tolerant of all soils. This variety has glossy narrow leaves with primrose yellow flowers and forms good clumps which just need cutting back at the end of the year.

Lonicera periclymenum – honeysuckle
Common name: woodbine.

Found in English woods, this useful plant was quickly transferred to the garden. A classic cottage plant, it has remained a firm favourite through to the present day, its heady scent on hot summer evenings wafting in through open windows or infusing the air around an arbour.

Honeysuckles, being woodland plants, prefer cool shade for their roots and, if possible, a west-facing position. There is an extensive variety of honeysuckles to choose from nowadays, and even a good winter-flowering choice, *Lonicera fragrantissima*. Honeysuckles come in both deciduous and evergreen varieties and are generally happy in any soil, although they always fare better planted in the ground than pots. They are ideal for wildlife: birds will nest in the foliage and enjoy the red berries in the autumn, and moths will be drawn to the nectar in the evenings. If you wish, you could grow a honeysuckle over the cottage door, as in the past; this provides the owner with 'good luck' and apparently keeps any evil from entering over the threshold.

Primula vulgaris – primrose

Common names: darling of May, first rose of spring, Easter rose.

This much-loved pale-yellow flower is a harbinger of spring; the common name 'primrose' comes from the Latin *prima rosa,* meaning the 'first rose of spring'. It was Gertrude Jekyll's favourite woodland flower and she planted large drifts under the hazelnuts in her garden at Munstead Wood. The primrose has been a fashionable flower for centuries, whether planted in the garden of the manor house or the poor cottager's plot, bringing joy to all in the early part of spring.

Having a long association with woods, elves and fairies, primroses have enjoyed the shade of the cottage hedge since Saxon times. A must-have cottage flower, primroses have a knack of finding their own place to prosper within the garden. To keep clumps looking good they should be lifted and split every few years. The common primrose is a delight in the garden, but there are also some striking double varieties worth looking out for.

Viola odorata – violet

Common names: sweet violet, wood violet, shoes and stockings.

The name 'sweet violet' speaks for itself, and poets wrote lyrically about the unrivalled scent of the flower, which they considered intoxicating but brief. Easily finding their way underneath the old cottage hedge or in other shady spots, violets spread rapidly, and were always a common sight in old gardens.

The typical single blue flower has diversified, and colours now range from dark blue, through mauve to pink and white. Seemingly not as popular now as in the past, possibly due to their propensity to spread too much, they are still valuable ground cover in areas of shade. *Viola labradorica* is an interesting form which although still scented has its blue flowers show-cased against dark purple leaves.

Viola tricolor – heartsease pansy

Common names: jump up and kiss me, Cupid's delight, love in idleness, three faces in a hood.

This bright little viola has been a garden favourite for centuries, and once established will seed around, often flowering from May to October.

The flower has always been linked to love, and in the Elizabethan period we know that the juice from the flowers was used as a love potion. Ladies believed that if this juice was smeared on their lips it would make them irresistible to any man! Apparently, if offered to a friend who had lost the 'love of her life' – the plant would *ease the heart*. Shakespeare made use of this plant, which he called 'love in idleness' in *A Midsummer Night's Dream*. It was collected by Puck to drop into Titania's eyes to make the fairy queen fall in love with an ass: 'on sleeping eyelids laid will make man or woman madly dote upon the first live creature that it sees.'

Our native primrose – one of the most loved cottage flowers.

The pretty purple-leaved violet, *Viola labradorica*.

Heartsease pansy contrasting wonderfully with *Ballota pseudodictamnus*.

Two good forms to look out for are *Viola hispida* 'Jackanapes' and *Viola* 'Bowles Black'. *Viola* 'Jackanapes' was bred by Gertrude Jekyll and named after her pet monkey! This is a lovely viola with bright yellow lower petals and two reddish-brown upper petals, whereas 'Bowles Black' has incredibly dark, velvety flowers.

All violas are clump forming and can spill over to informalize the front of borders or paths. They look splendid cascading over pots, planters, troughs or hanging baskets. They also have the benefit of a long flowering period, which can be extended by continual dead heading during the year. Although often grown as annuals, violas are actually perennial, and will easily earn their keep in the cottage garden growing in any reasonable soil in shade or sun. The flowers are edible (unlike the large-flowered pansies) and will certainly liven up any summer salad, should you wish to try.

Elegant spires of hollyhocks against an old stone wall.

TRADITIONAL COTTAGE FLOWERS

Many of the flowers considered to be traditional cottage plants simply started life as 'new' introductions. Throughout the medieval period 'useful' (herbs) or highly symbolic plants were regularly added to the monastery or castle herbers, and from there it was but a short step to the cottager's plot. Because many of the plants were of use, they were quickly assimilated into all gardens, and in addition, often escaped and naturalized in the countryside. In the Tudor period the first exotics started to arrive, these being plants grown purely for their beauty rather than just their herbal qualities. These fascinating new arrivals from Europe, Central Asia and the New World changed the garden from a purely herb plot to a show garden. Eventually filtering down to the cottage garden, by the mid-nineteenth century many of these so-called new exotics had been around for so long (some hundreds of years), that they had rightly acquired the term 'traditional cottage flowers'.

Alcea rosea – hollyhock

If there's one plant that is associated with the cottage garden more than any others, this is it! It's believed the Crusaders discovered and brought back this tall, single-flowered, sun-loving plant from the Holy Land as a wound herb. Placed in the castle physic bed, it quickly spread and became established in the cottage garden. Its common name is a combination of the Saxon 'hoc' being their name for a 'mallow' (as the leaves looked mallow-like) and 'holy' due to where it originated; essentially a mallow from the Holy Land.

By the end of the nineteenth century, hollyhock rust had arrived. Hollyhock rust is a fungal disease that severely affects the leaves, making the whole plant look blotchy and ugly. The hollyhock not only looks unsightly but will usually die quite quickly. With no easy method of controlling the disease, the plant started to lose popularity rapidly. This problem is still very evident today and has resulted in the plant being treated as a biennial, with gardeners not wishing to hang onto disease-ridden hollyhocks. However, the hollyhock is in fact a perennial, and was originally simply left in old cottage gardens to form a huge clump. Despite its tendency to develop rust, it is still a wonderful plant for the cottage garden in either full sun or part shade, and the disease can be managed by taking off leaves and spraying.

Plants will rocket skywards to give spectacular vertical structure, having either single or double flowers throughout the summer. If, however, you hanker after a more rust-resistant variety, choose the fig-leaved hollyhocks.

Aster novae-angliae and *Aster novi-belgii* –
Michaelmas daisies
Common name: starwort.

'Aster' comes from the Greek meaning 'star' referring to the flowers. The first aster grown in England was probably *Aster amellus* from Italy, known as blue starwort. However, asters didn't become popular until new varieties arrived from America in the seventeenth century, first from New England and then from the Dutch settlement of New Amsterdam (now New York). During the Victorian period, the gardener William Robinson couldn't speak more highly of them, and they became popular in all gardens. Flowering around St Michael's Day (29th September) they provide much-needed late season colour. These hardy perennials clump up quickly, will tolerate either sun or part-shade, generally don't require staking, and provide sprays of cut flowers. The only downside is powdery mildew on certain varieties. There are different things you can do to help combat mildew: plant in full sun, plant in a good windy position for air circulation, and make sure the soil is well-drained. However, you must also water regularly in dry spells, as being alternately dry and then wet puts the plants under stress and encourages mildew. The New England asters (*novae-angliae*) have a greater resistance to mildew and *Aster × frikartii* varieties (developed in the 1920s) are good, non-invasive compact types.

Astrantia major – **masterwort**
Common names: Hattie's pincushion, melancholy gentleman.

An understated hardy perennial, *Astrantia* makes a wonderful combination plant that sits well together with more striking flowers. It is particularly useful for underplanting roses, as they both appreciate the same slightly heavy, moist soil. The long-lasting shaggy pincushion flowers make it a plant often grown by flower arrangers. Easy to grow in sun or part-shade, division is best done in early spring or late autumn.

The delicate whitish-pink flowers are common, but there are now some stunning deep-red varieties available. Ones to look out for are: *Astrantia* 'Shaggy', *Astrantia* 'Ruby Wedding', and *Astrantia* 'Sunningdale Variegated'.

A group of asters in Hill Close Gardens, Warwick.

A CHANGE OF NAME FOR ASTERS

There has been a recent name change for all North American asters which is just filtering through to nurseries and garden centres. Unfortunately, these asters have been saddled with the new mouthful of *Symphyotrichum*. If you find asters at a garden centre with this difficult-to-pronounce name, be assured they are still asters! And, to make life difficult, asters from Europe and Asia are still called asters.

Astrantia major (Hattie's pincushion) combined with a blue salvia.

A lovely pink form of *Astrantia major*.

The highly scented *Dianthus* 'Mrs Sinkins'.

A clump of beautiful single snowdrops.

A clump of the wonderfully marked snowdrop *Galanthus* 'Trimlet'.

Dianthus varieties – cottage pinks

Common names: gillyflower, coronation, sops in wine, clove pink.

Pinks first came to prominence in the Elizabethan period, and although there were different varieties, often the names given to the flowers seemed to be interchangeable. The most popular of all early pinks were 'clove-scented'. The French *girofler* (meaning 'smelling of cloves') gave the English the term 'gillyflower', and these highly scented flowers were often added to mulled wine, which resulted in the name 'sops in wine'.

Dianthus plumarius, known as the 'garden pink' or 'cottage pink', being native to Austria and Hungary, was probably introduced by the Normans. Having a mat-forming habit, it was used as a fragrant edging plant running along the path to the front door.

The pink became one of the first 'florist flowers', and passionate gardeners bred new varieties of single, double or laced pinks. Many of these old varieties are still available and worth searching out, such as: 'Bridal Veil', a double white dating back to the 1700s; 'Dad's Favourite', an eighteenth-century maroon laced pink; and 'Mrs Sinkins', a classic highly scented double-white cottage pink raised by Mr Sinkins (Master of Slough Workhouse) *c*.1868, which like many traditional cottage flowers is actually Victorian.

Pinks love a full-sun position and although preferring the soil slightly chalky, will be happy in most soils. In the right spot they require little attention yet reward the gardener abundantly. They do have a habit of getting straggly, so propagate a few cuttings in late summer in readiness for when the main plant looks tired.

Galanthus nivalis – snowdrop

Common names: Candlemas bells, February fair maids.

Brought to Britain by the early monks from across the channel, these elegant white flowers have naturalized throughout the English countryside and are the earliest of the bulbs to cheer up the cottage garden during the cold, dark, short spring days. They love partial shade positions but will happily cope with sun. Let clumps develop, then split them after flowering (called 'in the green') to create your own natural drifts. Make sure they can be appreciated by placing the bulbs in the lawn or the front of borders close to the house.

Dahlia varieties

The first dahlia in Europe reached the royal gardens of Madrid in 1790, and the Marchioness of Bute sent some to England in 1798, but they failed. In 1804 the dahlia was re-introduced to Britain, and according to the famous garden writer John Claudius Loudon, by the 1830s, had become one of the most fashionable flowers in the country. Twenty years after this, over 700 named varieties were available to the Victorians, who created special dahlia gardens purely for their display. The plants filtered down to the cottage garden in the late nineteenth century due to their value for late season colour, having already waned in popularity in the gardens of the aristocracy by this time.

Dahlia 'Bishop of Llandaff', grown by Fred Treseden in Cardiff and first shown in 1928, can be given the accolade for bringing dahlias back into fashion in the early twentieth century. The semi-double red flowers stand out against the dark, virtually black foliage. Since then, there have been many more dark foliage dahlias, and a more recent stunner is *Dahlia* 'Twynings After Eight' having single creamy-white flowers.

Well-drained sunny cottage borders are ideally suited to dahlias and their inclusion in borders will amply repay a gardener with continuous flowers in the latter part of the year. For gardens with a heavy soil, dahlias can happily be grown in pots. Firmly back in favour in recent years, there are various distinct groups: single, cactus, semi-cactus, pompom, ball, anemone, waterlily and collarette.

Dahlias will continue flowering until the first frosts, which makes them extremely valuable to the cottage gardener; but always stake dahlias just as the foliage is starting to rise, otherwise their large heads will fall about and possibly even snap off. Staking is easy: use three or four wooden stakes (25cm square) which are 1m (3ft) high and place in the ground around the emerging foliage. As the stems put on growth, tie them onto the stakes with twine.

Should you lift and store dahlias? This is entirely up to you; but if the dahlias are planted in free-draining soil, you can simply cut down and cover with a mound of compost or mulch as a protection for the winter.

Delphinium hybrids

The marvellous stately delphiniums that grace borders and are thought of as indispensable in any cottage garden were in fact developed in the nineteenth and twentieth centuries. Considered a classic cottage flower now, these fabulous dense flower spikes only started making an appearance after Victor Lemoine, a great nurseryman in France, began to hybridize *D. elatum* in the 1850s. Then in the twentieth century the 'Pacific Giants' arrived from the USA. These delphiniums literally reached new heights, in shades ranging from blue, violet and pink through to white; and often with a central eye, or 'bees', as they are called. These stunners will give

Dahlia 'Ms Kennedy' – a vivid orange pompom variety.

The highly elegant *Dahlia* 'Honka Fragile'.

height at the back or in the middle of cottage borders in summer and often relate to other vertical stemmed flowers. Preferring a rich soil in sun and a more sheltered position, these flowers are wonderfully rewarding; but not coming true from seed, it is best to take root cuttings if you wish to enlarge your group.

In the Tudor period all delphiniums were called 'larkspur', but the two are slightly different: the larkspur, *Consolida ambigua*, is an annual that is far shorter and certainly not as showy. However, this is still a lovely flower to drift through and let self-seed in the middle of the cottage border.

The silver flower heads of *Eryngium giganteum*, also known as 'Miss Willmott's Ghost'.

The soft and incredibly beautiful flowers of *Eryngium alpinum*.

The dark-eyed magenta flowers of sun loving *Geranium psilostemon*.

Eryngium – sea holly

The sea holly is a beautiful plant for mid to late summer exuberance. Loving hot, dry and full sun positions, they will happily tolerate poor soil conditions and still create spectacular sprays of silver-blue flowers on erect stems. Their advantages over many other perennials include their steely-blue foliage, striking flowers of spiny bracts surrounding a central cone head, a long-lasting flowering period and attractiveness to bees. Grown only in a limited way until recent years, there are now a great many varieties now available to gardeners.

One of first to become widely grown was *Eryngium giganteum*, or the giant sea-holly. This was due to its connection to the famous gardener Miss Ellen Willmott, who always carried seeds of her favourite plant in her pockets and made sure she left some wherever she went! It quickly acquired the name 'Miss Willmott's Ghost' and is still one of best sea hollies to grow. The foliage starts off green but turns a tremendous steely-silver with large, silver-white heads. It dries well and should be left in the garden to continue to give structure throughout the remainder of the year after flowering.

Other useful varieties include *Eryngium bourgatii* 'Picos Blue', with an intense blue cone; *Eryngium alpinum*, a deeply cut-leafed sea holly with a feathery cluster around the cone; and *Eryngium planum*, with spiny silver-blue foliage and many small cone heads.

Hardy geraniums

Britain has various native geraniums which are called 'cranesbills' due to their beak-like seed capsules, and these would have been the first geraniums grown in the old cottage gardens. The magenta-flowered 'bloody cranesbill', *Geranium sanguineum*, which was common in the north of England, was used as a wound herb (hence the name) and would probably have been transplanted from the grassland or sand dunes for its healing property. On the other hand, the 'meadow cranesbill', *Geranium pratense*, has no herbal value, but the attractive violet flower possibly self-seeded into gardens from nearby meadows.

However, there is now a huge range of hardy geraniums available for the modern cottage garden in every conceivable colour and size, and for every possible position, from dense shade to full sun. Geraniums fit the criteria for a good cottage plant: totally hardy, easy to grow and divide, needing no real attention, often with a long flowering period, great for underplanting and a wonderful plant for casually spilling over edges, paths, pots, walls or borders. In addition, many have interesting foliage – some big and bold, some finely cut. And there are also purple-leaved varieties which add contrast to the border.

Name	Description	Height
Geranium nodosum	Clump-forming evergreen with blue flowers – an excellent choice for dry shade.	30cm (1ft)
Geranium nodosum 'Clos de Coudray'	As above but has purple flowers with white edges.	30cm (1ft)
Geranium phaeum 'Samobor'	A particularly good form of the 'dusky cranesbill' with striking dark patches on the leaves. Shade. Any soil.	60cm (2ft)
Geranium 'Brookside'	Long flowering, clear mid-blue flowers early to mid summer. Responds well to being cut back to produce repeat flowers.	60cm (2ft)
Geranium versicolor	A low clump-forming geranium with well-marked foliage and delicate lace-like markings on the flowers.	25cm (10in)
Geranium 'Victor Reiter'	A stunning dark purple foliage geranium with contrasting mid-blue flowers.	40cm (16in)
Geranium 'Rozanne'	Voted the nation's favourite geranium, it has large clear blue flowers with a white centre, and a long flowering period.	60cm (2ft)
Geranium renardii	Best in full sun, this geranium has mounds of soft evergreen sage-like foliage and attractively veined flowers.	35cm (14in)
Geranium 'Ann Folkard'	A vigorous spreading geranium having magenta flowers with a dark central eye over unusual striking yellow foliage.	60cm (2ft)
Geranium clarkei 'Kashmir White'	Finely cut mid-green loose foliage with stunning large veined white flowers.	40cm (16in)

A clump of the slightly more unusual *Geranium nodosum* 'Clos de Coudray'.

The elegant flower of *Geranium* 'Stixwould Lilac'.

Helleborus species – hellebores

Hellebores have become extremely collectible in recent years and are a great addition to the modern cottage garden. The lovely large-cupped flowers on stiff erect stems are one of the first indicators of spring and are a pure delight combined with an underplanting of snowdrops.

Our native plant *Helleborus foetidus* or the 'stinking hellebore', which gets its name from the smell of the seed heads, has attractive foliage and small pale green flowers. It is short-lived and has a habit of self-seeding prolifically all over the garden. The earliest flowering variety is *Helleborus niger* or the Christmas rose, which was a plant used by apothecaries for its curative properties.

However, the hellebores that have become the real favourites in gardens are *Helleborus orientalis* known as the Lenten rose. Generally flowering around Lent, they were introduced from Asia Minor in the mid-nineteenth century. Since then, constant hybridization has produced a large range of glorious colours to choose from – clear whites, pale pinks, buttercup yellow, deep reds, slate greys and even black. Particularly striking are the white and pink speckled-flowered hellebores. Double-flowered hellebores have become very sought-after, but for something really unusual, look out for the anemone-centred varieties.

Being a woodland edge plant, hellebores thrive in part-shade, although they will tolerate sun. A rich, retentive soil is ideal, but if you can't give them these requirements then dig in some manure to help improve their situation. Hellebores also look good in pots or containers but must have a rich organic potting compost.

Hellebores deserve a place in the cottage garden due to their extremely long flowering period, often from January through to April or May; they are also wonderful partner plants for other spring-flowering bulbs and flowers. It is important to cut the hellebore foliage down to about 25mm (1in) above the ground in late November as this prevents any disease being passed on from the previous year's leaves to the newly emerging ones the following spring. This technique has another advantage: the newly emerging flowers in the spring will stand out clearly and not have to compete with a mass of unsightly foliage! The flowers will throw out many seedlings around the garden if they are happy, and could give you some unusual and surprising results, but be wary of moving or splitting hellebores, as they resent this intrusion!

One of my favourite pleasures is to collect a variety of hellebore flower-heads and float them in a large shallow glass bowl. This allows the flowers to be seen at their best, as in the garden situation they hang down to protect the pollen from adverse conditions. This will provide a stunning centrepiece for the coffee table.

A spring border full of mixed *Helleborus orientalis*.

Hellebore flowers shown off by floating in a bowl.

PARTNERS FOR HELLEBORES

When hellebores flower in the early part of the year there are a number of early spring bulbs and plants which associate well with them. The classic partnership is probably underplanting hellebores with a drift of snowdrops, and if you have some dark or black flowered forms then a carpet of white will show up the dark colours brilliantly.

However, other plants that would combine well include primulas, ferns, pulmonarias, erythroniums, muscari (particularly the white form) and *Chionodoxa* 'Pink Giant' (which is a favourite of mine).

Lupinus – 'Russell lupins'

Lupins provide a brief but splendid high point in the cottage border, with their attention-grabbing columns of big, bright flowers. However, this has not always been the case, as lupins only became popular garden plants after George Russell improved upon what was available in the early twentieth century. He set himself the task of developing better varieties on his allotment from 1911 onwards. In January 1938 these new lupins were offered for sale for the first time, and took the gardening world by storm! His large floriferous plants in incredible colours graced all gardens and looked perfect in the middle of cottage borders.

Lupins are still hugely popular and a great addition to the cottage garden, but unfortunately their flowering is all too brief. A second flowering can be achieved by immediately cutting the plants down to the ground after the first flowering has finished – an action which also prevents mildew. Being a short-lived biennial, once flowering is totally finished, it is best to remove the plants and replace them with 'fillers' (perhaps cosmos). Young plants (propagated from earlier cuttings) can then be planted back into position in the autumn in readiness for the following year.

Thalictrum – meadow rue

Britain has a native form of the meadow rue, *Thalictrum flavum*, which has yellow flowers on tall stems in summer. But the modern varieties generally grown for their stunning fluffy flowers in today's cottage gardens are *Thalictrum aquilegiifolium* (French meadow rue) and *Thalictrum delavayi* (Chinese meadow rue). Adding good vertical structure to borders, these plants have bags of cottagey appeal, and are suitable for either part-shade or sun in a retentive soil. Many of the newer varieties have showy purple stems, which contrast artfully with the typical mauve flowers and the aquilegia-like foliage. Generally growing to a height of 1.2–1.5m (4–5ft) they are best placed at the back of the border and make a wonderful partner for foxgloves which flower at the same time. *Thalictrum delavayi* has larger, more impressive lilac flowers with white centres and is definitely worth seeking out.

A large drift of blue and purple lupins in a Lincolnshire cottage garden.

A drift of white- and lilac-flowered *Thalictrum aquilegiifolium*.

RECOMMENDATIONS FOR THALICTRUMS

- *Thalictrum aquilegiifolium* – usual tall, lilac-flowered variety.
- *Thalictrum aquilegiifolium* 'White Cloud' – a superb clear white.
- *Thalictrum aquilegiifolium* 'Thundercloud' – a newer, deeper purple variety.
- *Thalictrum* 'Black Stockings' – deep purple-black stems with purple flowers.
- *Thalictrum delavayi* – large delicate stunning mauvy flowers with long anthers.

- *Thalictrum delavayi* 'Hewitt's Double' – clouds of lilac gypsophila-like flowers; best as a group.
- *Thalictrum flavum* subsp. *glaucum* – soft yellow flowers above striking silver-blue foliage.
- *Thalictrum* 'Elin' – a cross between *flavum glaucum* and *rochebrunianum*, giving the tallest available thalictrum with large lavender-mauve flowers on glaucous blue foliage, up to 2.5m (7–8ft).

Japanese anemones

The plant-hunter Robert Fortune first came across this native Chinese plant growing in a graveyard in Shanghai, and subsequently introduced it to Britain in 1849. Flowering from late summer through to early autumn, just when everything else is starting to fade, it made these plants popular in every English garden. Like all typical cottage flowers, it was found to be easy to grow and required little attention once established.

Happy in sun or shade, the ordinary pink-flowered form prefers a well-drained soil. Once it has a foothold it can become a little invasive but is easily tackled and pushed back into place when necessary. There are now many large cupped-flower varieties to choose from, coming in different shades of pink or white. Generally flowering in August and September (although there are some earlier flowering forms) they reach 120cm (4ft) and have no need to be staked. A good single white form is *Anemone* 'Honorine Jobert' and a common semi-double white is *Anemone* 'Whirlwind'. Japanese anemones are good partner plants for asters.

Veronicastrum virginicum

Also known as 'Culver's root', this tall perennial has architectural stems with ascending circles of pointed leaves topped off with long, elegant veronica-like flowers in various colours. Hailing from its native Virginia, the plant doesn't require any staking, stands up to wind, is non-invasive and clump forming, easy to prune, has no pest or disease problems, and bees love it. It also has that essential cottage garden 'feel', which makes it a good choice to join other mid-border plants that flower in July and August.

RECOMMENDED VERONICASTRUMS

- *Veronicastrum virginicum* 'Apollo' – a good mid-blue flower reaching 1.2m (4ft).
- *Veronicastrum* 'Pointed Finger' – the blue flowers bend over and point in all directions.
- *Veronicastrum album* – an excellent pure white form, height 1.5m (5ft).
- *Veronicastrum roseum* – a pale pink form.
- *Veronicastrum* 'Fascination' – a darker blue form with flowers that flatten off at the tip.
- *Veronicastrum* 'Lavendelturm' – a lovely lavender-blue flowered form, height 2m (6ft).

Veronicastrum 'Apollo' paired with *Verbascum chaixii* 'Album'.

Veronicastrum 'Pointed Finger', a tall, fascinating variety, contrasting with the vivid red flowers of *Sanguisorba stipulata*.

Recent additions

There are many other plants which have entered the cottage garden in recent centuries and become favourites due to having those qualities which tie in with the blousy feel of a cottage garden. Too numerous to discuss at length, here are some suggestions to investigate for your own cottage garden: *Verbena bonariensis*, *Heuchera*, *Echinacea*, *Helianthemum*, *Eupatorium*, *Hylotelephium* (sedum), *Penstemon*, *Crocosmia*, *Phlox*, *Cosmos*, *Verbascum*, *Buddleia* and late-flowering *Salvia*.

SEASONAL FLOWERS

Spring

Spring is the long-awaited joy after the bleak winter, and with midsummer, is one of the two main flowering periods of the cottage garden. Each day brings a new delight in the garden, as forgotten favourites re-appear and flower, and the borders start to fill with drifts of bulbs. Trees and shrubs too, start to blossom in the modern-style cottage garden.

A cottage garden should be inter-planted for continuous seasonal colour, so that as certain flowers finish and fade, others come through to provide the next series of highlights. Bulbs, perennials, annuals and biennials can be used to create flowering combinations in the border to catch the eye. This might take some time to achieve as you experiment and find out what works well and what doesn't. Different soils and situations also play a part, but there is a vast range of spring plants to choose from, and every garden will be able to accommodate a fine selection of early flowers.

Winter aconites and pearl-white snowdrops give the promise of the oncoming spring and look natural in drifts in part-shade under trees. Quickly joining them are other shade lovers including the long-flowering hellebores, primroses, anemones, violets, columbines, pulmonarias, dicentras and epimediums. Three particularly good, but rather invasive ground covers for dry shade in spring include sweet woodruff, wild garlic and periwinkle, and if you have either a wild or small wooded area, they are worth considering. In the case of periwinkle, *Vinca major* or *Vinca minor*, there are a number of attractive but less invasive forms.

Epimediums are really worthwhile ground cover plants, with a number of varieties tolerating dry shade conditions extremely well. Tough attractive heart-shaped leaves make tight mats that act as a base for later flowering plants, and in some varieties have the bonus of autumnal colour. In early spring, wonderful delicate flowers – often with long, four-cornered spurs – dance above the ground and newly forming leaves. These spreading, yet non-invasive perennials, have become popular in the last few years as new hybrids with larger and brighter flowers have been produced.

The beautifully marked leaves of *Epimedium rubrum* make excellent ground cover.

The bright spring flowers of the clump-forming *Epimedium* × *warleyense*.

Spring flowers for sunnier areas in the cottage garden include alyssum and aubrieta, both of which are happy in rockeries, borders, path edges or hanging gracefully from natural stone walls. Perennial candytuft, *Iberis sempervirens,* is another excellent edging plant for sunny spots, having short evergreen foliage with

TABLE 4.3: RECOMMENDED VARIETIES OF EPIMEDIUM	
Name	Description
Epimedium × versicolor 'Sulphureum'	Primrose yellow flowers above well marked leaves.
Epimedium × rubrum	Vivid red flowers with white centre petals, red patterned leaves, good autumn foliage colour.
Epimedium 'Fröhnleiten'	Strong grower with bright yellow flowers for sun/shade.
Epimedium × warleyense	Taller variety with glossy leaves and vivid orange and yellow flowers. Excellent for dry shade.
Epimedium 'Amber Queen'	Lovely large bronze/orange winged flowers for part-shade/sun and needing a richer soil.
Epimedium pubigerum (hairy barrenwort)	Small evergreen clump-forming epimedium with shiny heart-shaped leaves and clusters of small white flowers.
Epimedium 'Lilafee'	A large lilac flowered variety for sun or part-shade, requiring a richer soil.

extremely white round clusters of flowers – a particularly good variety is 'Masterpiece', which is a taller, more erect form, with a long flowering period. Other traditional edging includes London Pride, forget-me-nots, bergenias (elephant's ears) and *Veronica gentianoides*.

For sunny borders are doronicums, wallflowers and *Pulsatilla vulgaris*, a native of Britain that warrants a position in the cottage garden due to its enchanting large purple bell-like flowers and silky seed heads. And, for the middle or back of the spring border, there's honesty, sweet rocket, alliums and tall bearded iris.

Spring bulbs

Bulbs are ideally suited to the cottage garden and can be planted to come up through perennials, thus using every inch of space. Placed in drifts within the border, bulbs complement spring ground cover. Much like spring flowers, some bulbs prefer shade and will be wonderful companions for flowers in dappled light under trees; other bulbs like open full sun positions where they can appreciate the spring warmth.

The obvious spring bulbs are daffodils, or Lent lilies, and to obtain the correct cottagey effect avoid planting in rows. Cast them over the ground to get a natural look and simply plant to

The highly scented *Narcissus* 'Pheasant's Eye' or Poet's narcissus.

The early flowering multi-petalled *Narcissus* 'Rip van Winkle'.

the required depth wherever they land. There is a huge choice of modern varieties, but if you're looking for something traditional, then the pheasant's eye narcissus, *Narcissus poeticus recurvus*, is a good choice; or perhaps the intriguing double form for the front of the border, *Narcissus* 'Rip van Winkle'.

Naturalizing bulbs for the cottage garden include the reliable *Muscari* (grape hyacinth), *Scilla* and *Chionodoxa*. All love sun and well-drained soil, and will carpet the ground in early spring, lifting the spirits and providing a backcloth for other early plants. *Scilla* and *Chionodoxa* are sometimes difficult to tell apart. Both have blue six-petalled starry flowers, but the *Scilla* has vivid blue flowers that hang their heads, whereas the softer blue flowers of the *Chionodoxa* look upwards. A striking variety of *Chionodoxa* to grow is the larger flowered *C.* 'Pink Giant'.

Other spring bulbs which create impact are the Crown Imperials, *Fritillaria imperialis*. These stately plants were first introduced to Britain in the sixteenth century and were quickly acquired by every gentleman of taste. It didn't take them long to filter down into the cottage garden, and they were among the few plants that were grown for no other reason than to look spectacular. The crowning head came in yellow or orange, and gave some height to the sunny well-drained cottage border. Unfortunately, they not only give a stately presence but exude a wicked smell! Even in the sixteenth century it was believed they smelt of foxes, so best not to place too close to the back door!

Arriving from Turkey at about the same time as Crown Imperials were the first tulips. Hugely popular in all gardens today, they were originally so expensive that only the very wealthy could afford them. It is a different story today now that the Dutch have developed and propagated great quantities which can satisfy the growing demand. The colour range is immense, and if your garden soil isn't suitable, then pots of tulips are an ideal solution. A mass of tulips in an attractive pot can act as an eye-catcher or centrepiece. Alternatively, pots could be placed either side of the front door to make an entrance statement. Tulips are best grouped together for impact, and of late the fashion has been to have tulips erupting out from a mass of light blue forget-me-nots.

Summer

As late spring overlaps the early summer, a host of traditional cottage plants weave a tapestry of colour over newly emerged foliage. These include such glorious flowers as astrantias, campanulas, alchemilla, foxgloves, hardy geraniums, alliums, cornflowers, peonies, irises (bearded and *siberica* types), London Pride and pink cow parsley.

These early summer flowers are quickly replaced by other cottage treasures such as *Sisyrinchium striatum*, verbascums,

later-flowering hardy geraniums, peonies, pinks, lavenders, bright marigolds, tall delphiniums, salvias, tradescantias, heucheras, a host of herbs, lilies, achilleas, hollyhocks, the silver- and grey-leaved plants of stachys, artemisia and cotton lavender; and of course, more than anything else, the 'queen of flowers' – the rose.

In late summer other flowers take to the stage, such as sunflowers, echinacea, everlasting peas, phlox and nepetas; and added to these are perennials that flower in the late summer and continue on into autumn, which include penstemons, dahlias, asters, crocosmias, salvias and agapanthus. A perennial that is seen everywhere nowadays, due to its extensive use at the Chelsea Flower Show in recent years, is *Verbena bonariensis*. This attention-grabbing plant has tall, stiff, architecturally vertical stems with flattened heads of vivid lavender-purple flowers, which last for long periods. Its qualities, which include longevity of flowering, bright coloured flowers, adaptability to most soils and positions, and ease of self-seeding, make it a winner for any garden.

Russian sage, *Perovskia atriplicifolia*, is a good all-purpose perennial for the cottage garden. A cloud of fluffy tubular flowers float at a height of 90cm (3ft) above the glaucous-blue serrated foliage and add a silvery sheen to the border. The variety 'Blue

PINK COW PARSLEY – *CHAEOPHYLLUM HIRSUTUM* 'ROSEUM'

Unlike the tall creamy-white heads of the common roadside parsley, this particular variety is non-invasive. A good plant for mid-border with delicate umbels of light pink which float gracefully above a finely cut foliage.

A stunning drift of non-invasive pink cow parsley, *Chaerophyllum hirsutum* 'Roseum'.

Spire' is excellent. The leaves are highly pungent when crushed – smelling like Vick's VapoRub, according to my children!

The remarkable clear blue *Salvia patens* (gentian sage), which arrived from Mexico in 1838, will add late season exuberance to any cottage border or pot. It is best treated as an annual, although can be over wintered if you have a greenhouse. The variety 'Cambridge Blue' is a particularly good light blue variety.

A late-flowering plant, seemingly rarely grown, is *Calamintha nepeta* 'Blue Cloud'. This wonderfully loose, low bushy perennial has highly aromatic foliage, particularly when brushed against, and masses of light blue lipped flowers. Loving a full sun, well-drained position, and only reaching 60cm (2ft) at the most, it is loved by butterflies and bees.

Late-season flowers of Michaelmas daisies, dahlia, nerines and persicaria.

Autumn/winter

Late season flowers were few and far between in old cottage gardens. It is only recently that we have a greater choice of possible solutions to extending the season. New arrivals from China in the nineteenth century and an explosion of newly developed varieties from nurseries have massively improved the situation.

Asters (starworts) were probably the first of the late flowers to be taken in and loved by cottagers. They just do their own thing, spreading around and flowering profusely on long wiry stems without support – an ideal cottage plant.

Other groups of late season flowerers include salvias, crocosmias, sedums (now *Hylotelephium*), chrysanthemums and Japanese anemones. And there are often still dahlias, heleniums, rudbeckias and eupatoriums in flower. A brilliant late true-blue flower can be found on the tall, elegant *Salvia uliginosa* – certainly worth the space.

Distinctive plants associated with late summer/autumn are the *Kniphofias* (red-hot pokers). This truly exotic looking plant with loo-brush type flowers, is not to everyone's liking, but has the advantage of a very long flowering season (April – November) and loving dry, full sun positions. The common form *Kniphofia uvaria*, which has the well-known fiery twin-coloured flowers, rockets up to 2m (6ft). They are particularly good for coastal gardens and partner tall late-season perennials, such as heleniums, extremely well.

Autumn bulbs

Bulbs for gardens at this time of year certainly aren't as numerous as in the spring, but there are a few to brighten up the shorter days of the autumn. Coming originally from South Africa, nerines are the bright pink flowers that are seen in many gardens throughout September. Naked ladies (autumn crocus) which enjoy being naturalized in grass or drifted under trees, have large lilac or pink flowers that shoot up out of the ground without any clothes (no leaves). Two other bulbs that enjoy a shady spot and love to spread under trees, are the autumn cyclamen – *Cyclamen hederifolium* – and its relation, *C. coum*.

The stunning long-flowering *Salvia* 'Amistad' – ideal for late-season colour.

Kniphofia 'Timothy', a late-flowering dwarf form ideal for small cottage gardens.

Grasses

A mention must be given to ornamental grasses which seem to have become so very popular in recent years. Although not exactly traditional cottage flowers, they have a feel about them that seems to blend in with the style of planting that sums up cottage gardens. Late autumn/winter is when grasses shine in the garden as their seed heads waft gently in the breeze.

SCENT

The most highly esteemed flowers in the cottage garden have always been the ones with scent. In the past when 'foul aires' were commonplace, due to privies and unwashed bodily smells, any scent that delighted the nose was a valuable commodity. Cottagers appreciated roses and honeysuckles climbing over the cottage and beds of scented plants under the windows, so that the perfume could gently waft into the cottage both day and night.

Roses

Roses are an obvious traditional choice for scent in the cottage garden and highly versatile. As in the past, roses can be grown up over the cottage, or up through a good strong tree, or simply allowed to ramble or climb over a rustic porch, arbour or pergola. Fragrant shrub roses can be placed within sunny borders, where they can look their best, and be positioned for ease of picking and gaining the perfume as you pass by. The old-fashioned roses normally have the greatest fragrance, but often require support for their large heads. There are some modern varieties that have managed to combine old-fashioned elegance and scent on a more robust plant, which sometimes has more than just the one period of flowering.

FRANCIS BACON

In his essay 'Of Gardens', Bacon writes in 1625 that there is '... nothing more fit for delight, than to know what be flowers and plants that do best perfume the air.' Sir Francis then goes on to list: 'damask and red roses, musk roses, the Sweet Briar, wallflowers (to be placed under the window), pinks and clove gillyflowers, violets and honeysuckles.'

Garden pinks

The *Dianthus* family of plants was renowned and valued in the Elizabethan period for its scent. The clove-scented pink or gillyflower became an essential knot garden plant, and the carnation a vital scented flower for pots. The biennial Sweet Williams (*D. barbatus*) were also loved by the Elizabethans and soon found their way into the cottage garden, where the big upright clustered heads of frilly flowers with a pepper-like scent enthralled the summer border.

The great age of development for the pink was the nineteenth century, when hundreds of different varieties appeared, although not all could claim a good fragrance. One, though, has remained a firm favourite, that being *Dianthus* 'Mrs Sinkins', which has an intoxicating scent to its shaggy white flowers. Possibly more difficult to find are *Dianthus* 'Fimbriata', a seventeenth-century pink; and *Dianthus* 'Inchmery', a pink eighteenth-century variety. Often evoking a memory of Grandma's garden, pinks come in single and double forms, and in a huge array of colour combinations. They do best on very free-draining limey or neutral soils in full sun.

Sweet peas

Out of a genus of 100 species of pea, only one, *Lathyrus odoratus*, has any perfume. This annual pea discovered by the monk Father Cupani on Sicily in 1697, and said to be first called 'sweet pea' by the poet Keats in 1817, was absent from the cottage garden until its development in the late nineteenth century by Henry Eckford. In 1900 Henry showed 130 new varieties at the Crystal Palace Sweet Pea Exhibition, all with a stunning scent. In 1908, the first frilled-petal sweet peas were discovered by Countess Spencer's head gardener at Althorp Park, and not long after, a Cambridge grocer called Mr Unwin found a wavy form in his garden and named it 'Gladys Unwin' after one of his daughters.

Scented pots

Few cottage gardens would be without the weed from Egypt which arrived in the mid-eighteenth century and was named *mignonette* by the French, meaning 'little darling'. Also called 'sweet reseda' it quickly became a must-have pot plant in both France and England due to its incredible scent which helped mask the offending smells indoors. The tiny pale-yellow annual flowers will last the summer if you plant successional sowings, and whether you grow it in a pot by the back door or in a bed close to the house, a packet of seed is worth the investment.

A further highly scented cottage plant which made an impact in the Victorian garden as a bedding and pot plant, is *Heliotrope* 'Cherry Pie'. Coming originally from Peru, the plant is grown as a half-hardy annual for its unusual scent, like 'cherries baked in a pie'. The clusters of deep purple flowers above large dark green leaves look superb in pots on the patio.

Another rather unusually scented annual for pots is *Cosmos astrosanguineus* or 'chocolate cosmos'. Hailing from Mexico, the attractive dark maroon flowers really do smell like chocolate. Requiring full sun, like all cosmos, it is best to dead-head frequently, to prolong the flowering period.

Evening scent

Many of the most fragrant flowers are those relying upon their pollination by moths. What these flowers lack in terms of size or colour, they more than make up for with perfume. For any gardener wishing to enjoy the garden in the evening, these night-scented cottage flowers are best gathered around a seating area, placed under windows, or planted by paths so that the fragrance will gladden the mind. Below is a list of flowers that could be grown to add a delightful evening scent:

- *Hesperis matronalis* – sweet rocket, dame's rocket, dame's violet.
  Delightfully pronounced evening scent, with flowers ranging from purple through to lilac and white. Growing to 90cm (3ft), this attractive biennial will freely naturalize by seed if simply left to its own devices. Leave a few flower heads to seed if tidying up the scruffy heads.

- *Oenothera biennis* – evening primrose.
  The fragrant yellow flowers scent the evening air from June to September, with each flower only lasting 24 hours. Self-seeding biennial. Height 1.2m (4ft).
- *Matthiola longipetala* – night-scented stock, evening stock. Easy to grow lilac-purple flowered annual that exudes a delicious fragrance. Height 30cm (1ft).
- *Nicotiana sylvestris* – tobacco plant.
  Preferring a good soil and light shade, plant as a group where the rich perfume can be appreciated. Long flowering – July to September. *N. alata* is also excellent. Height 1.5m (5ft).
- *Phlox paniculata* – common garden phlox.
  A cottage favourite, the tall perennial garden phlox comes in a range of colours – pink, white, purple and red. Preferring a moister position in sun or part shade, the showy flowers are great for cutting. Powdery mildew can be an issue; to help combat this, give the plants plenty of air and space, mulch the roots in summer and always water at the roots. Height 1m (3ft).
- *Crambe cordifolia*
  A spectacular perennial sea kale with branching stems that hold a huge cloud of white flowers in summer. Plant in a sheltered spot close to a seat for the evening fragrance to pervade the air. Height 2.5m (8ft).
- *Lonicera periclymenum* – common honeysuckle.
  Honeysuckles give out their delicious intoxicating scent at dusk, and our native variety is still the best for fragrance. Grow a honeysuckle over a porch or arbour, plant it up through a large fruit tree or train it over a pergola. No cottage garden is complete without a honeysuckle.

Scented climbers

Roses and honeysuckles have always been the traditional fragrant cottage climbers, but there are other choices worth considering. Jasmines are popular, and all have the interesting star-shaped flowers, but beware: the winter jasmine, although a good looker, doesn't have a scent. In contrast, *Jasminum officinale*, the common jasmine or poet's jasmine, has a sweet possibly musky scent if given a warm sunny position or a structure to climb over. Other later-flowering fragrant jasmines include *Jasminum beesianum*, which has reddish-pink flowers, and *Jasminum × stephanense* with paler pink flowers. The 'star jasmine' from China, *Trachelospermum jasminoides*, although not truly a jasmine, has become more widely available and is certainly a desirable evergreen climber. Its flowers are

A lilac form of *Hesperis matronalis* (sweet rocket) flowering together with *Camassia leichtlinii alba* and *Iris sibirica*.

A wonderfully scented form of garden phlox.

highly scented and occasionally followed by bean pods. Although not completely hardy, it will be happy on a sunny sheltered fence or structure and has the bonus in autumn of the leaves turning a wonderful deep-red colour.

For spring fragrance and flower power you can't beat wisteria. All wisterias are scented, some with a hint of perfume, some rather overpowering. The newer *Wisteria floribunda* cultivars are all guaranteed to have good scent, but to achieve this you need to ensure the plant flowers well every year, and therefore you should cut back every January/early February to two or three flowering spurs.

There are three vigorous but pleasantly scented clematis for the modern cottage garden. The very common, very fast-growing *Clematis montana* varieties give off a slight almondy scent in the spring, and can be particularly useful for covering fences, pergolas, old sheds and buildings. The evergreen *Clematis armandii* with its elliptical leathery leaves, also has good fragrant white flowers, and is best grown near either the front or back door so that the scent is appreciated during comings and goings in the evenings. For summer through to early autumn fragrance the choice should be *Clematis* × *triternata* 'Rubromarginata' – a terrific clematis with highly attractive white-centred star-like flowers with vivid red spurs. Masses of flowers emit a beautiful heavy scent, and it is a perfect partner for a trellis or pergola eventually reaching 6m (19–20ft). Don't be put off by its vigorous nature as it is easy to cope with, being cut back to 30cm (1ft) above the ground either in late winter or early spring to prevent a tangled mess.

The attractive and highly scented flowers of *Clematis armandii*.

Scented shrubs

The largest scented plant in old cottage gardens was the lilac, and it is still probably a valuable option even today, with many smaller but highly scented varieties available. However, if you have the space there are some other attractive shrubs worth thinking about:

- *Choisya ternata*, or Mexican orange blossom, is a popular medium-sized shrub for gardens, having evergreen palmate leaves and star-like white scented flowers.
- *Osmanthus delavayi* is another evergreen shrub to add background structure to the garden. Slow growing with small deep-green leaves and masses of tubular, highly scented white flowers. Best placed near to a seat.
- *Viburnum* × *bodnantense* 'Dawn' is a large deciduous shrub for the back of the border with vividly scented pink flowers on the bare stems from autumn through to early spring.
- *Philadelphus* or mock orange, is a useful shrub for early summer scent, with large white cupped flowers having an 'orange blossom' fragrance to them. The variety 'Belle Étoile' is a good compact shrub for smaller cottage gardens.

- *Sarcococca* or Christmas box, is definitely worth the space in your garden. A dark-leaved evergreen shrub, it produces the most deliciously fragrant tiny white flowers from December to March. Place either in the ground or a pot near the front door to lift your spirits during cold, bleak winter days. *Sarcococca hookeriana* is a compact form, whereas *Sarcococca confusa* is larger and looser.
- *Daphne mezereum*, a shade-loving small shrub, was probably the first to be cultivated in gardens. All varieties are highly fragrant, and will be just as happy in pots as in the ground so long as the roots are kept cool. Being slow growing they are ideal for small cottage gardens.

Scented bulbs

In the spring, the two major bulbs that scent the garden, and of course the house when placed in a vase, are daffodils and hyacinths. The majority of daffodils really don't have much scent but there are some that have a beautiful perfume; these include the varieties 'Thalia', 'Geranium' and 'Actaea'. Daffodils look and smell wonderful cast around the garden in drifts.

The hyacinth, which arrived in the sixteenth century, has remained a firm friend to the cottager due to its amazing fragrance. They quickly became a florist flower, usually grown in pots for winter into spring, and this guaranteed their continued presence on the cottage windowsill. They flower far earlier indoors than out, so it's possible to have two bites at the cherry, and have both indoor and outdoor hyacinths, where they are best in groups near the back door.

Once the summer arrives, the flowering bulb that comes into its own is the lily. The lily has always been the rival to the rose, with the Madonna lily (*Lilium candidum*) being revered for centuries, having the twin virtues of a sweet scent and purity of the colour white. Possibly the oldest grown lily in Britain due to its association with the Virgin Mary, this plant also became a cottage favourite, with its large, perfumed flowers scenting the July garden. A great clump would often grow in the cottage garden, as unlike today, cottagers didn't move plants around; this ensured the lily's survival, as they resent disturbance. In the Elizabethan period the more exotic Martagon or Turk's cap lily (*L. martagon*) arrived and eventually found its place in the cottage garden, but this lily has little scent.

In the early twentieth century, the 'regal lily' was discovered in China by the plant-hunter Ernest Wilson. An intense perfume comes from the stunningly large glowing white trumpets with vibrant yellow throats and strong pinkish-purple lines along the outside. Flowering in July/August these make a good feature pot plant for a sunny spot or well-drained border position.

TRADITIONAL HERBS

Flora Thompson, writing about village life in *Lark Rise to Candleford* (1945), tells us that the herb patch included thyme, parsley and sage for cooking; rosemary to flavour lard; lavender to scent clothes; and peppermint, camomile, tansy, balm and rue for physic (healing).

Herbs are still highly popular, but in general we only grow a few essential culinary herbs for the kitchen, or scented dwarf herb hedges for their foliage and flowers in the summer. Herbs are extremely worthwhile additions to any cottage garden and can be grown in a number of different ways, but they must be planted in a good sunny position on sandy or very free-draining soil, with only mint enjoying a moist soil. Herbs can be distributed throughout the garden in amongst the other cottage flowers, their foliage adding contrast and scent deterring pests; or they can be grouped together in one area, which has the advantage that the herbs will all be enjoying the same ideal situation of dry sun. It is believed that the poorer the soil, the more concentrated the flavour of the herb.

Herbs in the walled garden at Kelmarsh Hall, Northamptonshire.

Herbs were often planted in a patch close to the back door of the cottage for ease of picking, and this is still a worthwhile consideration, particularly as most back doors come from the kitchen. Another possibility is creating a formal herb garden. A brick herb wheel or a knot garden with box hedging and a central sundial are both extremely attractive options. Where space really is at a premium, a group of pots, troughs or even a windowsill might be more appropriate. Plastic or wooden troughs could even be placed on brackets and attached outside the kitchen window, making picking a joy!

Large traditional herbs

Rosmarinus officinalis – **rosemary**
Height: 1.5m (5–6ft).

Although loving the salty air of the coast, rosemary is quite at home in any sunny, well-drained spot in the garden. More than any other herb, it prefers being planted against a sunny wall, where it receives maximum heat. It has many attributes, both culinary and medicinal, and is loved by bees. Being an evergreen, it brings some background structure to the garden, and is available for use in the kitchen all year round. It is also happy in a large pot and requires little in the way of maintenance, except for a trim after flowering to keep it in check.

The ordinary form can get big and straggly, but there are other varieties available, and even prostrate forms. Two better upright varieties include 'Miss Jessop's Upright' and the large flowered 'Benenden Blue'.

Lavandula angustifolia – **old English lavender**
Height: 60cm (2ft).

No cottage garden was ever without rosemary or lavender. Washing could be thrown over the lavender bush or hedge to dry and scent it; and dried lavender heads were essential for placing in muslin bags to push under pillows, between linen and in the pockets of clothes. Another plant for bees, the dwarf varieties are ideal for smaller gardens and pots. The following lavenders are worth considering:

- *L.* 'Munstead' – introduced by Gertrude Jekyll, a good dwarf variety for hedges and knots.
- *L. stoechas* – French lavender, having distinctive bracts on the top of the flower, attractive but tender.
- *L.* × *intermedia* – known as the 'cottage garden lavender'. 'Grosso' is an excellent variety for cutting.

Lavandula stoechas (French or tufted lavender), a wonderfully aromatic dwarf shrub for dry sun positions in the cottage garden.

- *L.* × *intermedia* 'Edelweiss' – a white form, also ideal for cutting.
- *L.* 'Hidcote' – a wonderful compact variety with plenty of stunning purple flowers.

Hyssopus officinalis – hyssop

Height: 60cm (2ft).

An evergreen bush with fragrant blue flowers that lends itself to clipping and is a good border plant. Although introduced in the medieval period, it is not especially popular today. Also available in white- and pink-flowered varieties; the cut flowers (fully open) are good for vases. The leaves can be used in salads.

Salvia officinalis – sage

Height: 60–90cm (2–3ft).

Said to give long life to those who use it, it has been recommended as a remedy for a whole host of complaints in the past, and certainly seems to work as a gargle for sore throats. Nowadays, its main virtue is for cooking, and although the ordinary common sage is probably best, the attractive purple or variegated sages can also be used. Sage tends to get woody quickly, and it is worth taking a few cuttings in order to replace the old plant every few years.

Laurus nobilis – bay

Height: 7.5m (22ft).

There is no denying that a bay is going to get large and will need a sheltered site and space in a garden. Bay trees are also hardier in the ground, but a better option is probably a pot-grown tree. Standard bay trees in pots are readily available and could give evergreen structural height as part of a group of pots, as a stand-alone feature or as a centrepiece in a more formal herb garden.

Essential culinary herbs

In general, all of the following herbs can be grown in the garden, within the vegetable patch, in pots on the patio, or even on the windowsill. Keep close at hand for ease of picking when required.

Allium schoenoprasum – chives

Height: 20cm (8in).

Used widely as edging along cottage paths. Both leaves and flower heads are good for salads.

Anethum graveolens – dill

Height: 60–90cm (2–3ft).

A good aid to digestion from early times – used for soups and fish dishes.

Borago officinalis – borage

Height: up to 60cm (2ft).

A very old herb, although not much used today. A good bee plant, the flowers can be used as edible decoration on salads. Best grown where it can be allowed to self-seed every year.

Petroselinum crispum – parsley

Height: 15cm (6in).

Recorded in 1440 by Jon the Gardener, this herb has constantly been used in Britain, mainly in parsley sauce, that wonderful accompaniment for the goose. Said to be difficult to germinate, try pouring boiling water into the seed drill before sowing. There are two types of parsley grown: curly and flat-leaved (having a more robust flavour).

Thymus – thyme

There are two groups: creeping thymes and bushy thymes. The low-growing prostrate form, *Thymus serpyllus* (meaning 'serpent-like' and referring to its habit), is best for pushing between cracks in paths to be trodden on. The thymes used for cooking are the bushy forms, *Thymus vulgaris* (common or garden) and *Thymus citriodorus* (lemon thyme). These more upright varieties are used for soup, stuffings, and chicken and fish dishes.

Ocimum basilicum – basil

Height: 30cm (1ft).

Tender annual which needs full sun and shelter from wind. A perfect combination plant for tomatoes and for making pesto. Pinch off any flower buds to keep the foliage looking good. Leaves can be frozen or dried.

Coriandrum sativum – coriander

Height: 50cm (20in).

Used in a great many dishes, this fast-growing annual has a more pungent flavour. Plant in sun or part-shade, and make successional sowings throughout the year until late autumn.

Mentha – mint

Height: 60cm (2ft).

There are several excellent types of mint, depending on your requirements. All mints prefer a slightly moist soil in sun or part-shade. A useful herb but not good in the border as the roots run like mad! In small cottage gardens it is best planted in a large pot, which confines it yet makes it easy to cut for cooking. For a healthy plant, lift out, split and repot yearly in fresh compost.

The following varieties are worth growing:

- *Mentha spicata* (spearmint) is a good choice if you wish to grow just one variety. It is ideal for making mint sauce, mint tea and useful in soups and salads.
- *Mentha × piperita* (peppermint) has a stronger flavour and is a better choice for sweet making.
- *Mentha suaveolens* (apple mint) is mild and lovely in summer drinks.
- *Mentha × piperita* 'Chocolate' tastes rather like dark chocolate mints and is less invasive than other varieties.

Origanum – marjoram

There is much confusion over origanum and marjoram, but all plants are actually part of the origanum family and love a hot dry position within the cottage garden. Depending on what you prefer cooking, will help you make the right choice of herb:

- *Origanum vulgare* (wild marjoram) is the variety used extensively in Italy and Greece, and is referred to as 'oregano' having a stronger taste which is ideal for pizzas, pastas and sauces.
- *Origanum majorana* (sweet marjoram) is a milder tasting form that is generally used in most cooking to give a good background flavour.
- *Origanum onites* (pot marjoram) has smaller leaves and goes well with onions, garlic and for dishes requiring a *bouquet garni*.

You could of course, if keen on cooking, have one of each in the garden!

The large clump of chives next to the cottage path not only creates interest at the front of the border, but they are extremely useful for the kitchen.

Chapter 5

Companion Planting

Companion planting is a method of 'growing plants together for mutual benefit'. It was developed over the centuries in the cottage garden where it was found that plants could be useful to one another and help protect vegetables from pests, diseases and weeds. Space was always highly valued in the cottage garden and therefore vegetables, herbs and flowers were often planted in every available inch of soil. Flowers were often allowed to self-seed, useful herbs allowed to run through borders, wildflowers were left to their own devices and climbers allowed to scramble up through the fruit trees. This natural method of gardening yielded results that were observed and noted by the cottagers – less pest damage to vegetables, an increased yield, improved storage qualities for fruit and fewer weeds in a particular area. Any effective combination of plants was noted, used in subsequent years, and passed on to the next generation.

The practice of simply growing different plants together in a limited area brings benefits. The combination of plants covering the ground makes it far more difficult for weeds to get a foothold and at the same time preserves water. Mixing plants up also works wonders for attracting beneficial insects, assists in disguising the scent of vegetables and helps to lessen plants' susceptibility to disease. Growing a variety of plants together works well, as different plants make differing demands upon the soil; for instance, deep rooted plants thrive next to shallow-rooted ground cover. The seemingly chaotic mixture of the cottage garden in the past with flowers grown in amongst the vegetables was possibly

accidental, but, more often than not, it was a deliberate setting out of the plants that would benefit one another. Unfortunately, in the average garden today we tend to create very distinct, separate areas – the lawn and flower garden, the vegetable patch, the herb garden, the fruit orchard – whereas a better policy would be to mix up flowers, herbs and vegetables.

Early English gardening books mention some of the early discoveries made relating to plants that benefit one another in the garden. Thomas Tusser in *One Hundred Good Points of Husbandry* (1577) tells us:

> The gooseberry, raspberry and roses all three;
> With strawberries under them truly agree.

In the same year, the garden writer Thomas Hill in his book *The Gardener's Labyrinth*, mentions that 'broad beans should be grown between early potatoes, early and late peas to be grown together, and strawberry runners should be planted between rows of onions'. It seems onions were often grown with the alpine strawberries in the Elizabethan period as the pungent smell of the onions was believed to prevent pest damage. It is now recognized that onions or garlic grown near strawberries prevents fungal diseases.

William Langham, in his book *The Garden of Health* (1579), relates quite a different effect of companion planting, the fact that when certain plants are placed near to each other the scent improves – 'lilies and roses planted together will both smell the pleasanter'.

Unlike us, the early cottagers didn't have the advantage of a garden centre or high street shop that sold an array of products for every conceivable garden problem. They were forced to find

A perfect cottage garden combination of a climbing red rose intertwined with a stunning deep-purple-flowered clematis.

ways to cope with pests and diseases in a natural way; they had no choice, and therefore companion planting became a vital element of the cottage garden. Even today, many of the older generation or allotment gardeners use tried-and-tested methods of protecting vegetables or fruit, homemade remedies and sprays for tackling pest and disease problems, and the use of companion plants. This results in no detrimental effect on wildlife whilst maintaining the balance of nature.

COMPANION PLANTING IN THE GARDEN

Cottage gardening and companion planting go hand in hand, and although a great proportion of the companion planting ideas apply mainly to vegetables and fruit, it is also extremely valuable for the modern cottage garden in terms of helping prevent pests and disease on trees, shrubs, flowers and roses. Companion planting will make a garden healthier, with plants helping one another to prosper, and giving the gardener fewer plant problems and hopefully longer flowering periods.

Using cottage garden style companion planting will enable you to garden without the use of off-the-shelf products to deal with pests and disease to a great extent. Companion planting is a slower but kinder method of gardening, and although it won't eradicate all your problems immediately, it should mean you end up with a safer garden that is wildlife friendly.

Plant diversity – mixing things up for mutual benefit

In the modern cottage garden, the greatest proportion of the garden is devoted and designed around flowers, with possibly the odd pot or two of herbs, and a few, if any, vegetables. This is in total contrast to the old cottage gardens, which were essentially vegetable gardens with some herbs and flowers grown where they had space. The supermarket may have taken away the need to grow vegetables and herbs, but there is still a great deal of pleasure in doing so, having the advantages of knowing exactly where your food has come from, how fresh it is and that chemicals haven't been used. And there is nothing to beat fresh homegrown vegetables for taste.

If you feel you wish to grow some herbs and vegetables, 'diversity' is the key to reducing pests and disease within the garden. Simply growing everything together – vegetables, flowers and herbs all mixed up creates the best possible environment for a balanced garden. With vegetables and flowers intermingled, great blocks of the same vegetable are avoided, thus the modern problem of monoculture is dispensed with, resulting in greater disease resistance and the reduction of pests.

An old cottage 'husband and wife' team of lily of the valley and Solomon's seal. Two plants companion planted like this were thought to benefit one another.

A vegetable patch with traditional hollyhocks adding height and helping to screen the greenhouse behind in a Norfolk cottage garden.

For larger cottage-style gardens, growing some vegetables is relatively easy, as an area can be set aside specifically for their production. In this case, small fruit trees, soft fruit bushes (raspberries, gooseberries, currants) and any permanent vegetables or herbs, like rosemary, rhubarb or asparagus can be laid out systematically to suit the soil conditions. All the other required vegetables can then be planted and rotated as needs be. To assist with the reduction of pests and diseases companion planting methods can then be utilized using herbs and flowers deliberately grown amongst the vegetables. This will not only make the vegetable patch look colourful and cottagey but will be highly beneficial.

In smaller cottage-style gardens, which are the norm nowadays, a few raised beds are the best solution. Raised beds are not a new idea; they were used throughout the medieval period as a way of getting a better crop from a small, concentrated area. Raised beds have many advantages where space is at a premium. The fertility within the bed can be raised to a higher level with manure or compost and the depth of friable soil giving root crops the best possible start in life. The soil won't be compacted either, as the beds should be just wide enough to work upon from both sides; and as there is no path, crops can be packed in tightly to use every inch of space, making it exceedingly difficult for weeds to grow.

In terms of size, beds should be about 1m (3ft) wide and whatever depth you feel works for you. As with all vegetable plots, companion planting should be practised within the raised beds. Marigolds, borage, parsley, coriander, ornamental alliums or other companions will enhance the beds and do a 'power of good' at the same time.

There is a third method of growing vegetables which I feel works exceptionally well. It is a good solution for gardens of newly built houses where the plot is extremely small, but also for long, thin gardens of old town houses where there is hardly any space. The answer is to do as the old cottagers did, and simply grow the vegetables in amongst the flowers. This method is highly effective in terms of reducing pests and diseases, as the patches of vegetables hidden amongst the flowers make it exceedingly difficult for the pests to locate the scent from their favourite vegetable. Similarly, surrounding vegetables with herbs and flowers helps attract beneficial insects which are both predators and pollinators, making this method both rewarding and attractive, and giving a higher probability of a better yield. No chemical sprays are required, so you end up with a balanced garden that is entirely wildlife friendly. The method is simple and satisfying; for example, you could grow mixed lettuce varieties in a patch at the front of a border, a patch of leeks in the middle and a pretty, rustic tripod of runner beans towards the back of the border to create height.

Vegetables and herbs growing side-by-side with flowers in this cottage border.

Raised beds, particularly for small cottage gardens, have many assets. Watering, feeding, weeding and pest control are easier to maintain, the soil isn't compacted, the drainage improved and soil chosen specifically to suit the vegetables.

A yellow rose, valerian, herbs and vegetables growing together at the front of this cottage in the village of Hauxton, Cambridgeshire.

Rhubarb grown in a cottage border amongst hardy geraniums and verbascums, the large leaves creating a plant incident and anchoring the corner next to the path.

- Grow rhubarb in the border as a large foliage plant. Crop the stems in the early part of the year, then allow the big leaves to be a focal point against which floaty flowers can provide contrast.
- Use the wonderful colourful 'cut and come again' chard as a patch towards the front of a border.
- Have an asparagus hedge to subdivide the garden into rooms. The asparagus can be eaten early in the season and then allowed to create an unusual ferny hedge to separate areas.
- Grow a circle of leeks, which will have wonderful repellent properties within their area. Their blue-green foliage could be used as a contrast with other plants. Perhaps let a few leeks flower, as their heads are stunning and will astonish visitors.
- Grow squashes up over a pergola or an arch. Squashes love to climb and can be encouraged to do so over structures within the garden, creating an attractive feature and keeping the fruits from getting dirty. Butternut squashes are an ideal choice.
- Grow some outdoor tomatoes in a border with marigolds. They don't need to be in a line – perhaps grow them in a wavy line or a circle.
- Runner beans have exceedingly attractive flowers and can be companion planted in many ways. They were originally called 'arbour beans' being grown over arbours to cover them with dense foliage and flowers – the beans originally being ignored! You too, could grow them over an arbour, pergola, trellis or arch.

This asparagus hedge acts as a feathery screen subdividing this part of the garden into two rooms, once the asparagus has been cropped for the kitchen in the late spring.

Squashes can be grown up rustic tripods, or over pergolas and arches in cottage gardens, similar to these gourds at Helmingham Hall gardens.

Lettuce plants are worthwhile planting into gaps amongst flowers, as it disguises the scent of the crops resulting in fewer pests.

- Strawberries could be used as edging along paths, possibly with their favourite companion, chives. It makes for easy picking in season.
- If you have a compost heap or two, you could plant your squashes, courgettes or pumpkins in the top of the compost heap. All these vegetables are extremely greedy feeders and will benefit from the decomposing compost whilst not competing with other vegetables. It makes picking easier and helps disguise the unsightly compost heap at the same time!

Flowers, herbs and vegetables mix well together, and to do so produces a garden closer to the old traditional cottage garden. More importantly, it maintains a balanced garden that is beneficial to wildlife and provides good crops that don't require spraying.

Companion plants for roses

A cottage garden is never without roses, but roses often come with problems. Roses should always be underplanted; this creates moisture-retentive ground cover, looks attractive and extends the flowering season in rose beds, assists in preventing pests and diseases, and possibly even improves the scent of the roses.

Alliums are particularly useful as companions for roses as they help protect against blackspot and aphids. When it comes to roses, garlic is the 'king' of the companion plants. However, you may well not want your roses underplanted with garlic, so other options include chives, late-flowering garlic chives and all varieties of ornamental alliums. Ornamental alliums can be planted to come up around the roses, and the choice is now extensive, with tall spherical headed varieties or shorter ground cover ones. The only problem with the taller early flowering alliums is that the foliage at the base is messy and quite ugly, which means a second ground cover plant is often required.

One solution is the interesting *Allium senescens* subsp. *glaucum*, a ground cover allium sometimes known as the 'corkscrew onion' due to the beautiful glaucous blue foliage twisting in tight curls and unfolding as the plant comes into flower. Dense clumps of round lilac-coloured heads flower in late summer and reach about 15cm (6in) and are then frequented by butterflies and bees.

Alliums are known to improve the scent of roses, but if you're not intending to use them as companion plants, there are other methods which will still give you an enhanced scent. Fertilize the soil underneath the roses with onion skins (usually thrown away) from the kitchen or make up a liquid onion fertilizer, which will do the same job. Likewise, parsley will improve the scent of roses if underplanted.

Lavenders are another good companion for roses. Some years ago, I underplanted a neighbour's long row of red roses along his drive with *Lavender* 'Hidcote'. The rose bushes were initially covered with blackspot and greenfly but within two years all trace of blackspot and greenfly had disappeared. It doesn't have to be the variety 'Hidcote' as all lavenders work just as well; however, dwarf varieties are probably preferable.

Salvias are another good choice for roses and there is a huge variety to choose from – some flowering from early summer right through to late autumn. Salvias not only attract pollinating insects but help keep any plants within their vicinity clear of blackspot and mildew.

Other effective rose companions are marigolds, lupins and mignonette (*Reseda odorata*). A 'bad' companion for roses is box hedging. Roses dislike competition for their roots and unfortunately box is a hugely greedy feeder!

TO MAKE AN ONION FERTILIZER

Take about 3 handfuls of onion skins (peelings) and add to about 1 litre of water. Allow this to soak for 24 hours, then strain off the skins. Use under roses to help with pests, diseases, and the improvement of the rose scent.

A patch of dwarf evergreen *Allium senescens*.

Red roses running up one side of the drive to the bungalow have been underplanted with a hedge of *Lavender* 'Hidcote', which effectively deals with pests and diseases.

Companion planting for support

In old cottage gardens every part of the garden was utilized, and wishing to make the most of vertical space, any natural structures like hedges and fruit trees were used as structural companions for climbers. Common sights in old cottage gardens would include a honeysuckle scrambling up over the front porch, a native clematis (old man's beard) cascading over great stretches of the hawthorn hedge, or a large gnarled old fruit tree dripping with masses of scented roses.

In the modern cottage garden, we too can utilize that valuable extra vertical space. By companion planting climbers up through trees or shrubs you'll be making the most out of the space and giving yourself the opportunity of creating some wonderful combinations with foliage and flowers.

Unfortunately, the common hedge that surrounds today's modern garden is the conifer hedge, the roots of which exude toxins, making it impossible for most plants to survive at its base. Ideal companion hedges include the old 'mixed', privet or hawthorn hedge, where climbers such as honeysuckles, roses and clematis will happily use the enclosing garden structure. If you are lucky enough to have a beautiful dark yew hedge, then the 'flame nasturtium' (*Tropaeolum speciosum*), sometimes known as the 'Scottish flame flower', is a lovely climbing companion. It is a perennial nasturtium that can reach 3m (10ft) and prefers shady positions and acidic soil, but it is worth growing for its deep green foliage over which appear vivid red flowers.

Smaller evergreen hedges for subdividing the garden, such as box, do have companion options. Plant flowers which have a tendency to bend or flop down in heavy rain or wind, against clipped dwarf hedges, as the hedge will then not only provide structure within the garden, but structural support for the flowers, allowing them to be seen at their best.

Shrubs are a recent introduction into gardens with many wonderful varieties now available. Original cottage gardens didn't have shrubs, since space was always at a premium. However, with the modern cottage garden being designed as a flower garden, shrubs have become more important, and can be used like hedges as companions for climbers. Shrubs, like the old cottage hedge, provide climbers with the availability of cool roots at their base and a frame with access to sun at the top. Spring-flowering shrubs are crying out for a companion climber for colour in the summer. And why stop there? Have two climbers that flower at different times scrambling through the same shrub to maximize its structural potential. Be careful though, and make the 'right match', as you don't want a climber to overwhelm a shrub. Evergreen climbers can often be a problem, robbing shrubs of light. Match smaller shrubs to less vigorous climbers and only use rampant climbers in large trees. Plant any climber a small distance away from the shrub and on the shady side to ensure there is no competition for

The olearia shrub is used as a support for the large-flowered *Clematis* 'Jackmanii' – with the two plants deliberately planted so as to flower at the same time.

The large white heads of *Leucanthemum × superbum* 'Phyllis Smith' are adequately supported by being partially grown up through the stiff-stemmed hebe.

Eucalyptus gunnii used as a climbing frame, its wonderful glaucous foliage being the perfect foil for its companion climber, *Clematis purpurea plena elegans*.

The dwarf box hedges, clipped to a height of 30cm (1ft), help support the taller cottage flowers that would otherwise get beaten down in inclement weather or wind.

nutrients. Provide some guidance by way of a cane into the shrub and the climber will happily grow away and perform wonderfully.

Large vertical perennials will not only make a statement in the garden, but again, can be companion planted with a climber, so long as it isn't too vigorous. Use a good upright plant and a late season climber, which will give the perennial time enough to grow into a solid structure before the climber takes off. Gertrude Jekyll proposed this very idea at Hestercombe garden, where she wanted the giant Scottish thistle (*Onopordum acanthium*), which reaches 3m (10ft) and has huge spiky silver leaves with great purple this-tle-type flowers, to have the everlasting pea (*Lathyrus latifolius*) with its deep pink flowers to use the thistle as a climbing frame.

Fruit trees too, are obvious companions for climbers in the cottage garden. As the trees flower in the early spring and fruit in the autumn, it leaves a gap when the tree's structure can be utilized whilst the fruit is developing. This gap can be filled by flowering companion climbers. Roses should be the first choice, as they can scramble through the tree and provide a rich abundance of scented flowers in June and July. Be aware that rambling roses are vigorous and get very large, and are therefore not good companions for small fruit trees. Climbing roses are far better suited to fruit trees, as are the classic cottage climbers of honeysuckle or clematis. You could also consider annuals such as the 'morning glory' (*Ipomoea purpurea*) or 'black-eyed Susan' (*Thunbergia alata*). There is often an opportunity to grow more than one climber through larger fruit trees (old apple trees in particular), so having both a rose and later-flowering clematis climbing together creates a viable companion planting solution for continuous flower.

Almost all climbers need some form of support, particularly in windy areas, making companion planting an ideal solution. The combinations of climbers for growing up through a support are vast; however, some examples are given below:

- A late-flowering clematis with delicate white or blue flowers paired with a dark-leaved shrub such as purple hazel, physo-carpus or the purple smoke bush – the light flowers will stand out brilliantly as the clematis scrambles up through the shrub.
- A scented honeysuckle or clematis climbing up through an apple or pear tree. The less vigorous forms of *Clematis montana* would be ideal, as these need very little attention/pruning.
- An autumn-flowering clematis using a climbing rose as a support (whether on a wall or trained through a tree), which will ensure continuous flowering into the latter part of the year after the rose has finished. Consider *Clematis tangutica* 'Bill MacKenzie' or *Clematis* 'Anita'.
- A summer-flowering clematis or annual climber using an earlier flowering wisteria as support. The Chilean glory vine (*Eccremocarpus scaber*) would be a good companion as it likes the same aspects as wisteria.
- The stately scotch thistle (*Onopordum acanthium*), with its stunning silver foliage and large vertical outward growing stems, pairs beautifully with rich red-coloured summer-flow-ering clematis, such as *Clematis* 'Night Veil', *C.* 'Étoile Violette' or *C.* 'Rouge Cardinal'.

As well as good companions, there are of course some bad companions which will overwhelm and ultimately be very detrimental to the supporting plant. Rambling roses have already been mentioned, but other vigorous climbers totally unsuitable for small trees or shrubs include the hop (*Humulus lupulus*) and its golden form 'Aureus' (best on a trellis or arbour) and Russian vine or 'mile a minute vine' (*Fallopia baldschuanica*), which will simply suffocate the supporting plant.

Underplanting in borders

Underplanting is a form of companion planting. The main reason for underplanting is often aesthetic but has the other advantages of moisture retention and weed suppression. This has always been a common feature in cottage gardens where space was at a premium and therefore never wasted. Growing one plant beneath another uses every available inch of soil, but at the same time creating the two benefits mentioned above. There are ground cover companions for every situation in the garden – full sun, part shade, very dry shade, or even, extremely moist positions.

A favourite cottage plant often used for underplanting hellebores is snowdrops. I have always found that the bright white snowdrops work particularly well with the dark-flowered hellebore varieties. The stunning black hellebores are extremely fashionable nowadays but don't stand out in the early part of the year on dark, wet soil. However, underplanted with a drift of snowdrops, the dark flowers show up beautifully.

There are of course many worthwhile ground cover companions, not just for hellebores, but to plant under trees, shrubs, hedges and other taller perennials, but be wary: some are more invasive than others.

For dry shade positions: epimediums, lesser periwinkle (*Vinca minor*), lily of the valley, dead nettles (*Lamium maculatum* varieties), some low spreading hardy geraniums and sweet woodruff (*Galium odoratum*) are all good companions where there is reduced light and little moisture available. But keep an eye on the 'sweet woodruff' as it will eventually take over if not attended to!

Where the soil is more accommodating and the light level better, try *Alchemilla mollis*, *Ajuga reptans*, *Veronica gentianoides*, London Pride and again some of the low-growing or mound-forming hardy geraniums.

For full sun positions, particularly in dry sandy soils, low spreading thymes are excellent, as is *Erigeron karvinskianus* (Mexican fleabane) with mats of lovely white and pink daisies that flower from May through to the first frosts. As always, there are some hardy geraniums which are ideal for this situation, with *Geranium* 'Ann Folkard' and *Geranium* 'Mavis Simpson' being reliable in sunny spots.

A drift of *Epimedium rubrum* used as ground cover.

The gold-edged variety of lily of the valley 'Hardwick Hall'.

A stunning variegated form of lily of the valley.

The bright evergreen variegated variety of London Pride.

Companion planting to hide unsightly foliage

Geoff Hamilton once said, 'When Wordsworth's heart filled with pleasure at a crowd of golden daffodils, it's a fair bet he didn't see them two weeks later'. He was quite correct. Daffodils evoke much-needed pleasure at the beginning of spring, but we hate to see the awful foliage as soon as the flowers have finished. The long lasting but unsightly foliage is of course required to make food for the bulb for the following year and must be left. This leaves the gardener with a dilemma: when can the leaves be cut down, and if not, how can they be disguised? Daffodil leaves should neither be cut off nor tied up into knots, as it prevents food reserves required for next year's flowering being built up. Companion planting is the answer, and if spring bulbs are complemented with the right ground cover it negates the unsightly foliage problem.

When first planting a drift of daffodils, scatter them casually on the ground and plant where they land. Then choose an appropriate companion ground cover, whose foliage will rise-up around the bulbs as they start to flower, and so be at a good enough height to disguise the dying daffodil foliage. With daffodils, larger hardy geraniums work particularly well.

Ornamental alliums have a similar problem, with their leaves yellowing and curling over at the base of the bulbs even before the flower heads have fully opened. Therefore, these too, can be companion planted with a ground cover perennial. Again, hardy geraniums are exceptionally useful, but *Alchemilla mollis*, London Pride, *Erigeron karvinskianus*, heucheras or epimediums are all options; and there are also plenty of other alternatives.

Alchemilla mollis – one of the most useful cottage flowers.

The urn on a plinth acts as a central feature in this cottage garden, having *Allium cristophii* growing up through a companion planting of *Geranium cantabrigiense* which assists in hiding the unsightly foliage of the alliums.

A drift of early daffodils companion planted with *Geranium* 'Thurstonianum', which will eventually disguise the unsightly foliage of the bulbs once the flowers have finished.

This companion planting technique for bulbs is also a viable method for erythroniums (dog's tooth violets), colchicums (naked ladies), bluebells and any other bulbs you wish to consider. It works for pot-grown bulbs as well, and in fact creates more interest within the pot with the underplanting. One of my favourite combinations was a dark-leaved heuchera in a pot planted with five alliums that rose above the foliage.

I have tried this technique on a number of early-flowering bulbs and Table 5.1 provides a few suggestions.

TABLE 5.1: COMPANIONS TO HIDE UNSIGHTLY FOLIAGE

Common name	Botanical name
Daffodils with taller hardy geraniums	*Geranium* 'Thurstonianum' *Geranium* 'Sherwood' *Geranium phaeum* 'Samobor'
Ornamental alliums planted with…	*Alchemilla mollis* *Heuchera* 'Palace Purple' *Stachys byzantina* 'Silver Carpet' *Geranium sanguineum striatum* *Geranium cantabrigiense* *Origanum* varieties
Colchicums planted with…	*Geranium nodosum* *Lamium maculatum* 'Beacon Silver' *Epimedium versicolor* or *E. rubrum* *Ajuga reptans* 'Catlin's Giant'

Geranium 'Samobor' with its wonderfully marked leaves.

The aptly named *Stachys* 'Silver Carpet' or lamb's ears.

The stunningly marked heart-shaped leaves of *Epimedium rubrum*.

But alliums aren't just essential companions for vegetables. They are extremely useful in the fight against blight, rust, mildew and aphids on other plants. As already mentioned, they are exceedingly useful as companions for roses; but roses apart, ornamental alliums are good companion plants for all other plants and worth growing in the borders. They are even thought to help repel moles and rabbits!

Other plants that repel pests

Many plants have an ability to disguise the smell of other surrounding plants and therefore protect them from pest attack, but certain plants have such a vivid, pungent smell that they repel pests. In general, many herbs have repellent qualities and are ideal companions for both the border and vegetable plot, but some may be invasive and will require regular attention to ensure they don't take over! Feverfew, for example, does have useful insect repellent properties and is highly useful intermingled with the vegetables, but will spread rapidly if simply left to its own devices. On the other hand, lavender (which is a beautiful flowering shrub in its own right) has similar attributes as a companion plant, making it ideal for the garden. Rather more difficult to place in the vegetable plot, it is best planted as a lavender hedge to help divide up the plot, yet still deliver its repellent virtues.

Another excellent plant for either vegetable patch or borders are asters, which also deter most insects. You could possibly grow your asters in both areas if space allows, leaving the asters in the borders to flower, whilst using the asters in the vegetable plot for cut flowers. Chrysanthemums, too, are plants generally grown as a row in the vegetable patch for cutting but are just as at home in the garden border for late season flower. Chrysanthemums contain a natural insecticide (pyrethrin), which deters pests.

More recently, it has been found that dahlias have similar effects to marigolds, in that their roots help repel nematodes. Add to this the fact that their bright long-flowering heads attract predators, and you have a group of wonderful plants for either growing in borders or for cutting purposes amongst the vegetables.

Nasturtiums (*Tropaeolum majus*) are wonderful annuals for both garden and vegetable patch with an ability to repel whitefly in the greenhouse and deter bugs if inter-planted amongst squashes. Although nasturtiums repel whitefly, they themselves attract other aphids (blackfly), but this is not a bad thing, as these aphids are then drawn away from the other delicious offerings in the greenhouse. Such a crowd of aphids inevitably draws in the predators, which then consume great quantities of the pests. Nasturtiums can also be used as a 'cabbage white caterpillar trap'

Dahlias deliberately grown next to runner beans, as recent research has shown that dahlias aid vegetables in a similar way to marigolds. Of course, they also provide wonderful cut flowers.

TABLE 5.3: PLANTS WITH REPELLENT QUALITIES

Common name	Latin name	Prevents
Basil	*Ocimum basilicum*	Repels a variety of different pests.
Catmint	*Nepeta cataria*	Deters flea beetles, weevils and ants.
Celery	*Apium graveolens*	Deters cabbage white butterflies.
Chives	*Allium schoenoprasum*	Prevents blackspot on roses and benefits fruit trees.
Dill	*Anethum graveolens*	Repels aphids and spider mites.
Garlic	*Allium sativum*	Repels a host of insects and pests.
Hyssop	*Hyssopus officinalis*	Repels flea beetles and insects.
Leek	*Allium ampeloprasum*	Repels carrot root fly and other pests.
Marigold	*Tagetes and Calendula*	Repels soil-borne pests and diseases.
Nasturtium	*Tropaeolum majus*	Repels aphids.
Onion	*Allium cepa*	Deters carrot fly.
Radish	*Raphanus sativus*	Repels cucumber beetle and root flies.
Rosemary	*Rosmarinus officinalis*	Deters beetles, moths, flies, a good all-rounder.
Rue	*Ruta graveolens*	Deters beetles and fleas.
Sage	*Salvia officinalis*	Deters moths and maggots.
Tansy	*Tanacetum vulgare*	Repels invasive insects.
Thyme	*Thymus vulgare*	Repels whitefly.
Tomato	*Lycopersicon* varieties	Repels whitefly on cabbage.
Wormwood	*Artemisia absinthium*	Deters insects, slugs, snails and mice.

if planted around cabbages in the vegetable plot. This is because the butterflies would rather lay their eggs on the nasturtiums than brassicas. Once you find clusters of caterpillars, you can pick off all the leaves covered with them and then throw them with confidence on the compost heap – as caterpillars apparently don't go looking for new host plants and will die!

Plants that attract predators

The greater the diversity of flowers in the garden, the higher the number of predators that will be tempted in. This is effectively what a cottage garden is – a diversity of fruit trees, climbers, flowers, herbs, vegetables and ground cover. In general, predators are attracted by plants high in nectar, many of these being herbs. The fabulous predators that should be invited into the garden are ladybirds, hoverflies and lacewings.

Ladybirds
The lovely ladybird is a carnivorous beetle which feeds almost completely on aphids. Hundreds of eggs are laid by the adult ladybird in the midst of aphid colonies, so that when the larvae hatch, their food is at hand. Ladybird larvae will happily consume thousands of aphids. Living for up to three years, ladybirds appreciate shelter over winter, and this can be provided in different ways. According to the Woodland Trust, pine cones placed together with some dried leaves in the gaps create a wonderful winter hotel. However, ladybirds can often be found clustered together in box plants, so box hedges or balls could be considered in the design of your garden as an aid to welcoming in these beneficial predators.

Hoverflies
This clever insect has fashioned itself to look like a wasp so as not to be eaten by birds, and the adult hoverflies feed on nectar and pollen, with their larvae being voracious consumers of aphids and other garden pests. Hoverflies are therefore beneficial in both pest control and pollination.

Lacewings
These insects are extremely easy to identify, with their long lacy transparent wings over a green body. Both adult and larvae are massive consumers of aphids.

There are certain plants that attract these amazing predators, and it is best if they are companion planted with plants that regularly suffer from aphids. As a rule of thumb, any yellow- or orange-flowered plants seem to be the best at attracting predators and pollinators.

Looking through the picket gates into the circular vegetable garden at Wild Rose Cottage in Lode, Cambridgeshire. The box hedging provides structure and a wonderful home for over-wintering ladybirds.

TABLE 5.4: PLANTS THAT ATTRACT PREDATORS

Plant name	Predator
Ajuga	Ladybirds
Alyssum	Ladybirds and hoverflies
Angelica	Lacewings
Cosmos	Lacewings and hoverflies
Dill	Lacewings and hoverflies
Fennel	Ladybirds and lacewings
Lemon balm	Hoverflies
Marigolds	Hoverflies
Penstemon	Ladybirds
Sunflower	Hoverflies
Tansy	Ladybirds
Yarrow	Ladybirds, lacewings and hoverflies

THE USE OF HERBS

Since cottage gardening began, herbs have played a vital role, being used for much more than just cooking. Herbs were continually used for salads, medicine, dyes, strewing, perfumes, but also as companion plants in amongst the vegetables. Being easy to grow and needing little attention, resistant to pests and diseases, attracting bees and other beneficial insects, and curing all common country ailments, it is little wonder so many English herbals were written on the virtues of herbs.

Gardeners still love herbs, but in general it is more for their scent or use in the kitchen. Who could be without chives, rosemary, parsley or sage? But an important characteristic is often overlooked: herbs aid other plants in their vicinity. All vegetables are aided by aromatic herbs, but herbs should not only be grown in the vegetable patch; nor, if possible, should they be confined to a specific herb garden if you wish to take advantage of their companion properties. A formal herb garden is a lovely addition to any garden, but for effective pest control it is far better to spread the herbs around the garden.

Herbs include a wide range of plants, some being shrubs such as rosemary and lavender, whilst others are perennials, short-lived perennials or annuals. Apart from one or two, most herbs enjoy hot, dry, free-draining positions within the garden. Even today, many herbs are still used for their incredible medicinal properties, but generally in the modern cottage garden they are planted for look, scent and more than anything else, culinary purposes. There is nothing that beats collecting a few fresh herbs from your own garden when cooking. In addition, their scent, and their attractiveness to pollinators means herbs are a must-have in any garden. But it is their benefits as companion plants that make them so worthwhile distributing throughout the whole garden. Although you'll need to consider where they look best in your garden plan, try not to cluster too many herbs together in one area – the greater the distribution, the healthier your garden will be.

Herb hedges, whether planted around the vegetable patch, along a garden path or at the front of a long border, not only look highly attractive but are extremely useful in terms of companion planting – either assisting in repelling pests or attracting beneficial insects, and in many cases, both. Good hedging herbs worth considering are hyssop, rosemary, wall germander, thyme and lavender.

In the old cottage gardens, the path to the front door was frequently edged with just one plant. The most common edgings were double daisies, London Pride, pinks and marigolds. Marigolds, as previously mentioned, are exceedingly good companions and they would have not only looked pretty but been of great benefit. Other companion herbs useful as path edgings could include

A cottage border backing onto the vegetable and fruit patches containing various herbs including lavender, achillea and feverfew.

chives, parsley, rocket, garlic chives or summer savory (annual).

Specific patches or drifts of a particular herb will pass on their benefits of companion planting and simultaneously enhance the border. One lovely mid-border herb with a good long flowering period is *Achillea* (yarrow), which can now be purchased in a huge variety of wonderful colours. There is an opportunity here to pick and choose a variety of coloured achilleas to blend in with a particular border theme. Reds, terracottas, pinks and whites are a great combination; but you could have a 'hot' border and use various yellows and oranges – the choice and fun in designing the combinations is highly rewarding.

Various annual herbs are valuable assets in the borders as well. Allow the plants to self-seed, and then the following spring 'pull up' the ones you don't require, simply leaving the ones which will create a cottagey drift. This category includes marigolds and borage.

Silver- or grey-leaved herbs are extremely useful in gardens, being both a good repellent and a contrast plant. The White Garden at Sissinghurst makes great use of silver plants to tie the garden together and bring a lightness to the planting. Silver-leaved artemisias are worthwhile companions in sunny parts of any garden, and not just white-themed borders. Their strongly pungent leaves help to repel aphids in the vicinity and their leaf colour can be a brilliant companion in terms of design. Cool silver foliage herbs can be used as 'a contrast' when planted next to pink, dark blue or purplish flowers, helping the flowers to really stand out. Purple-leaved plants also contrast exceedingly well against silver.

Tonic plants

Yarrow and foxglove are known as tonic plants, this term referring to the effect these plants have on others within their vicinity – a 'tonic' for others!

Yarrow (*Achillea* varieties) increases the scents of nearby plants, fights off pests, and attracts all the vital beneficial insects. It is a tonic for the soil, returning many nutrients back into the area where it is planted.

Foxglove, a favourite cottage plant, also aids plants in the surrounding area. It was always grown under fruit trees in the old cottage gardens as it was found to improve the storage qualities of the fruit. This quality has since been proven, and it is now believed to improve the storage qualities of potatoes as well (if grown close by). Like yarrow, foxglove stimulates the growth of nearby plants and helps them build up resistance to diseases. Foxgloves are also one of the few plants that survive next to conifer hedges, and as most people know, are wonderful bee plants.

A fabulous drift of the 'tonic' plant yarrow. Long revered as a medicinal herb, yarrow (*Achillea*) is one of the best companion border plants for dry gardens.

Beneficial herbs

Borage – *Borago officinalis*
This pretty annual herb attracts hoverflies (good predators), whilst its leaves, which have a slight cucumber taste, can be used in salads, and the edible star-like flowers dropped into ice-cube trays.

If grown with strawberries, borage is believed to improve their taste and size, as mentioned by William Coles in *The Art of Simpling* (1656): 'Among strawberries sow here and there some Borage seed and you shall find the strawberries under those leaves farre more larger than their fellowes'.

Chives – *Allium schoenoprasum*
Not just useful for the kitchen, but a lovely plant for the front border or the vegetable plot. Chives are worth growing under roses to help tackle blackspot and inter-planted amongst carrots to deter carrot root fly. Planted under apple trees, they are believed to prevent scab. A homemade chive tea spray is a wonderful addition to the gardener's armoury and can be used to deal with scab or as an effective deterrent against powdery mildew on gooseberries.

Although the flowers of chives are thought of as 'pink' in colour, there is a good range, with some a pale pink, some mauve-pink and also the lovely white chives.

Chives, loved by cooks and bees, is a valuable companion plant in the garden. It is particularly useful planted under apple trees to deal with scab, and under roses to help eliminate blackspot.

Hyssop – *Hyssopus officinalis*
Often overlooked, hyssop is a good companion for all vegetables and if planted with cabbages will help deter cabbage whites. Its long flowering period (June–September) makes it useful in the border too, where it is adored by bees and butterflies. Hyssop is a great addition in the kitchen, being used for soups, stews, fish, meat and salads; and if planted under grapevines is believed to increase the yield.

Lavender – *Lavandula* varieties
Who could be without lavender? Lavender has a long history with English gardens for its many uses – being used dried for strewing, in wardrobes to deter moths, and hung from kitchen beams to deter flies. In the cottage garden, old English lavender made a good hedge to dry the washing on, scenting the clothes beautifully at the same time.

Lavender has always provided many medicinal and household uses, but as a companion plant its greatest virtue is its effect upon roses, protecting them against blackspot and greenfly. The best lavender varieties for roses are the dwarf lavenders such as *Lavender* 'Hidcote', although all lavenders will achieve the same results. Lavender, if planted in a sunny, dry position, will help repel pests (including rabbits), attract beneficial insects (bees), improve soil nutrients, and contribute its wonderful scent and flowers to the cottage border.

Marjoram – *Origanum* varieties

Marjoram acts as a stimulant to the growth of all plants in the vicinity. It can be planted anywhere in the garden and has many culinary attributes. Any edible plant near to marjoram is said to acquire a slightly better taste.

Parsley – *Petroselinum crispum*

Parsley benefits roses and tomatoes, and in the case of roses, helps increase their scent. An edging of curly parsley is not only useful but looks extremely attractive.

Rosemary – *Rosmarinus officinalis*

Although its common name remains the same, rosemary has after recent research been reclassified as *Salvia rosmarinus*. Rosemary was usually grown by the cottage door to make it easy to pick for the pot, but in addition, was believed to protect the cottage from evil. Noted for its beautiful blue flowers, its main use has always been culinary; however, like all herbs, other plants in the vicinity of a rosemary bush will thrive. Being a large evergreen shrub makes it difficult to place in the vegetable patch where crops are rotated, but branches can easily be cut off and used as the companion pieces placed alongside newly planted vegetables to ward off pests.

Sage – *Salvia officinalis*

These aromatic-leaved shrubs are still popular in cottage gardens, but require a very dry, sunny site. Sage is an extremely good companion for cabbages, but unfortunately, like rosemary, requires a fixed position in the garden. To circumvent this problem, simply pick off a handful of leaves, which you can then scatter between the rows of cabbage. Purple sage is an attractive form which is still useful in the kitchen but is ideal for contrasting colour schemes in the borders.

Summer savory – *Satureja hortensis*

This annual is worth sowing, being a wonderful companion for onions and beans. It is a useful repellent against blackfly on all varieties of beans and attracts many beneficial insect pollinators. Bees adore the flowers, which last from late spring all through the summer. In the kitchen, this culinary herb will happily team up with fish or meat but (as in the garden) is best with beans! It will look good in a flower border, a pot or the vegetable patch.

Thyme – *Thymus vulgaris*

A much-used culinary herb that looks perfect at the front of sunny borders as an edging plant, or in a pot, or as a dwarf hedge in the garden. Creeping thymes will be of no use when it comes to companion planting, but bushy thymes work well with tomatoes and any of the brassica family, repelling most problem pests. A thyme hedge would be a welcome addition between rows of strawberries, which benefit greatly from its presence. Roses too, underplanted with bushes of thyme reap the benefit of fewer pests and better growth. *Thymus* 'Silver Posie', with its attractive variegated foliage, is both useful and ornamental and an excellent choice as a companion plant.

THE FENNEL PROBLEM

Fennel is one plant that is the exception to the rule that all herbs are good companions, with the old country rhyme promoting this viewpoint: 'Sow fennel, sow trouble.' Although an attractive plant which is useful for cooking (seeds and foliage), used as a tea to calm nerves, and with stunning seed heads for flower arrangements; it has a detrimental effect on the growth of both vegetables and flowers nearby. Beans and tomatoes should be kept well away!

Some ideas for herbs in the garden

Unlike the old cottage gardens where most plants were considered herbs, our viewpoint has somewhat altered, and we tend to grow just ornamental or culinary varieties of herbs. Even these though, are extremely beneficial to the garden as companions. Generally, most herbs appreciate a sunny position and well-drained, light soil. Poor soils actually improve the scent and culinary properties of herbs. If you are gardening on heavy, retentive soil, the best option is to grow herbs in pots or raised beds, which makes harvesting easier but does limit their companion planting properties.

Rosemary, lavender and sage are large, shrubby herbs which can be used as feature herbs within the garden. All are happy if planted up against the cottage/house wall near the back door but are equally at home as centrepieces in a border. Lavender is particularly versatile either as an individual specimen with its lovely flowers half-hanging over a path, or as part of a scheme in the border, or as a hedge to take the eye along a particular path.

Silver- and grey-foliage herbs have a twofold use. Firstly, they can be used to create a highlight to focus upon within the border, or to juxtapose a secondary plant colour against. Secondly, the foliage also contains properties that make these herbs good companions for assisting with disease resistance and pest control. Attractive silver-foliage herbs include artemisias, lavenders, sages and yarrows.

The purple comfrey not only contrasts well with the pink poker-like flowers of the *Persicaria bistorta* 'Superba' but is a wonderful companion for the compost heap. The leaves contain nitrogen, phosphorus and potassium, and if added to the heap aid decomposition.

Companion planted sweetcorn and courgettes in the vegetable patch at Wild Rose Cottage, Lode. The courgette leaves preserve moisture and give shade to the sweetcorn roots.

VEGETABLE COMPANIONS FOR VEGETABLES

Over the centuries it has been discovered that certain vegetables perform better if planted with others, and conversely, certain vegetables seem to dislike being planted near others. A wonderful example of good vegetable companions was discovered when the English first arrived in America. The Native American tribes companion planted what were called the 'three sisters' – maize (corn), beans and squash. They constructed many flattened-off mounds, each for a small cluster of the three crops, which could be tended from all sides. A small group of maize was planted in the centre, and when this had reached about 15cm (6in), climbing beans and squash were planted alternately in a circle around the maize. The crops benefited each other, the maize providing a structure for the beans to climb up, and the spreading large-leaved squashes covering the ground preventing weed growth and retaining moisture.

In the same way that certain herbs or flowers should be companion planted to repel pests and diseases or attract predators and pollinators, it is good to know which vegetables should or shouldn't be grown together. For example, if you grow cabbages with outdoor tomatoes, the scent from the tomatoes should help repel the cabbage white butterflies – which love to lay their eggs on cabbages.

There are different vegetables that enjoy being a companion to another particular vegetable so it shouldn't be too difficult to plan the plot each year.

FRUIT COMPANIONS

Like vegetables, fruit trees and soft fruit bushes also appreciate companions. In today's cottage garden we don't usually have the space to grow full-sized fruit trees, but modern equivalents grown on dwarf rootstock are widely available, and respond in the same way to companion planting as their larger counterparts.

Possibly one of the oldest companion planting discoveries was that of foxgloves. It was noticed that if they grew under apple and pear trees, the picked fruit had better storage qualities. Apples, pears, plums, gages and cherries were commonplace in the cottage gardens, and in general, companion planted in an effort to improve their yields and obtain pest-free fruit. Growing different plants beneath trees benefits them in many ways – preserving moisture, suppressing weeds, improving the soil, bringing in pollinators, attracting predators and keeping pests off the all-important fruit.

For apple trees, the best companion is chives, as it is thought to protect the tree against scab, as well as attract beneficial insects. Nasturtiums have long been used to attract the aphids off fruit trees and yet cover the ground and look attractive at the same time – perhaps even helping to discourage codling moth. Hyssop and lavender too, are attractive yet helpful companions to all fruit trees. Yet another excellent companion is comfrey, but many gardeners will know it has an invasive habit. However, a form of Russian comfrey developed at Ryton Organic Centre by Lawrence Hills and called *Symphytum × uplandicum* 'Bocking 14' is a sterile variety which won't seed. Comfrey planted around fruit trees can be cut back in the autumn and the leaves left as a mulch for the tree.

TIP FOR PLANTING BRASSICAS

When planting out any brassica, chop up some rhubarb leaves and place in the bottom of each planting hole to help deter cabbage root fly.

TABLE 5.5: VEGETABLE/FRUIT COMPANIONS

Vegetable	Good companions	Bad companions
Asparagus	Basil, dill, strawberries, parsley, tomatoes	Onion
Beans	Beet, cabbage, carrot, corn, potatoes, strawberries, tomatoes, lettuce	Chives, fennel, onion
Beetroot	Cabbage, lettuce, onion	Runner beans
Broccoli	Beans, celery, dill, nasturtium, onion, potatoes, sage	Lettuce, tomatoes
Brussels sprouts	Beans, celery, hyssop, nasturtium, potatoes, rosemary, sage	Strawberries
Cabbage	Beans, beet, celery, dill, onion, rosemary, sage, peas	Strawberries
Carrot	Onions, leek, peas, radish, rosemary, sage, tomatoes	Dill
Cauliflower	Beans, beet, celery, dill, hyssop, nasturtium, onion, potatoes, sage	Strawberries, tomatoes
Celery	Beans, cabbage, leek, onion, tomatoes	
Chard	Beans, cabbage, onion	Cucumber, sweetcorn
Courgette	Beans, sweetcorn, nasturtium, onion, radish	Cucumber, potatoes
Cucumber	Beans, celery, lettuce, onion, peas, radish, tomatoes	
Garlic	Beetroot, carrot, tomatoes	Peas
Leek	Carrot, celery	Broad beans, broccoli
Lettuce	Beet, cabbage, carrot, radish, strawberries	
Onion	Beet, cabbage, carrot, lettuce, potatoes, strawberries, summer savory	Beans, peas
Pea	Beans, carrot, cucumber, lettuce, radish, spinach, turnip	Onion
Potato	Broad beans, cabbage, lettuce, marigold, onion	Squash, sunflower, tomatoes
Pumpkin	Beans, sweetcorn, nasturtium, radish	Potatoes
Radish	Beans, cabbage, cauliflower, courgette, cucumber, lettuce, peas, tomatoes	Hyssop
Runner beans	Cucumber, lettuce	Beet, onion
Spinach	Cabbage, celery, onion, peas, strawberries	
Squash	Marigolds, onion, sweetcorn	Potatoes
Strawberries	Dwarf beans, lettuce, onion	
Sweetcorn	Beans, cucumber, potatoes, pumpkin, squash	
Tomato	Asparagus, basil, cabbage, marigold, onion, parsley, sage	Fennel, potatoes
Turnip/swede	Peas	

Case Study 5.1

A COTTAGE GARDEN IN LINCOLNSHIRE

My previous cottage garden of approximately three-quarters of an acre is where I first practised companion planting. I was determined not to use any form of chemical spray in the garden as I had three young children, and instead researched the idea of companion planting as an alternative. It quickly became evident that it was practised in old cottage gardens and therefore it seemed the ideal solution for my own.

The first major decision was not to have separate areas for flowers, herbs, vegetables or fruit, but instead to mix all these elements together within the borders. I was lucky enough to inherit a large Victoria plum tree and this became the first major area where a mixture of plants that enjoyed dry shade positions were trialled to create a large shade-loving bed.

Planting herbs into borders is not unusual, with many gardeners planting rosemary, lavenders, catmints, achilleas, thymes and various other herbs in the borders or by the back door. I simply extended this idea throughout the whole garden, planting herbs as companions in all the borders. However, I was extremely lucky, as my soil was very sandy and free draining, and the garden faced south – ideal for herbs.

The one decision that initially took me out of my comfort zone was that of planting vegetables in amongst the flowers throughout the garden. Like most people, I had always had a vegetable patch separate from the main garden, but then I started experimenting with vegetables in the borders. To my astonishment it worked – there was a clear reduction in pests and diseases throughout. I used asparagus as a hedge within the garden as well as a crop, I used rhubarb as a large-leaved plant incident as well as a crop, and I often planted quick crops such as lettuce, spring onions or radish in available spaces at the front of borders. One particular year, I planted some leeks in the middle of a border. Most found their way to the kitchen, but I did allow a few to go to seed, and the resultant onion heads in the midst of other planting looked wonderful and attracted the attention of passers-by or visitors to the garden.

Having such a dry soil I extensively used many plants as ground cover companions. Underplanting taller plants, shrubs and trees helped retain moisture and assisted in general weed suppression throughout the garden. My general policy was always to tightly pack plants together in the borders, covering every available piece of ground (in the old cottage garden manner), with this knitting together of groups of plants resulting in the plants supporting one another and preserving moisture. This meant I rarely had to stake plants within the garden. I would often grow climbers through other plants, whether they were trees, shrubs or perennials. In as many cases as possible, I had a second later-flowering climber growing over the first.

This companion planting approach worked extremely well in my cottage garden, and although I did have a few pests to contend with, I don't remember having any serious disease problems on plants. In conclusion, I found this method both fascinating and effective, and would encourage every cottage gardener to think about implementing some of the ideas put forward in this chapter.

Quinces and peaches appreciate garlic being planted around their base, which is believed to help prevent 'peach leaf curl'. Nectarine and peach trees will benefit if underplanted with either asparagus, onions or strawberries.

With small gardens, space can be maximized by growing fruit trees on walls or fences. There are two methods to train trees – 'fan' and 'espalier'. Fan-trained, where the branches radiate out like a fan, is suitable for most types of fruit – apples, pears, plums, peaches and cherries. Espalier, where the branches run in horizontal tiers is a method more widely used just for apples and pears. Nowadays, you can buy trees 'ready-trained', which makes life a lot easier. To assist in pollination of the fruit and deter pests, these wall- or fence-trained trees should be companion planted. As suggested above, plant foxgloves, lavender, chives or garlic chives at the base of the tree to aid it in a natural way. You could also grow a non-vigorous clematis as a companion up through the tree to utilize the structure.

Soft fruit bushes were always a welcome addition to the old cottage gardens. Blackberries were simply collected from the wild or allowed to ramble through the cottage hedge, their prickles helping to keep animals getting into the garden. The cottage favourites were gooseberries, blackcurrants and raspberries. All soft fruit likes sun but also benefits from certain companion plants. Currant bushes love wormwood (*Artemisia absinthium*) which deters aphids and attracts beneficial insects. Tansy (*Tanacetum vulgare*), likewise, repels a host of pests but can be rather invasive. Gooseberries have a liking for tomatoes which assist in repelling pests that attack the bush.

The Maze Garden, a room of this cottage garden, illustrates the mixture of cottage flowers, herbs and vegetables grown together in one area. In the foreground at the bottom right is *Salvia officinalis* 'Berggarten', a particularly good variety of sage which is a good clumping salvia with lovely flowers that is also useful in the kitchen.

Looking back across the Maze Garden towards the gravel herb garden with the seat against the outbuildings. The rhubarb crown and asparagus hedge are evident in the garden.

The Summer Garden facing due south with various herbs distributed throughout the borders, including lavenders, artemisias and the outstanding *Salvia sclarea* var. *turkestanica*.

The Summer Garden looking towards the road, with companion herbs in the borders: *Nepeta* 'Six Hills Giant' cascading over the gravel in the foreground, *Rosmarinus* 'Benenden Blue' on the corner next to the pale-yellow flowers of *Anthemis* 'Sauce Hollandaise', and a lovely drift of terracotta and pale yellow-coloured achilleas.

Chapter 6

Green Structure

HEDGES

The cottage hedge which enclosed the garden was a stock-proof barrier that kept the precious vegetables safe from the animals grazing on the common land in the village. This surrounding boundary hedge was commonly hawthorn (quickthorn) or a mixed hedge (hawthorn, blackthorn, elder, wild rose, holly). However, the variety of available hedging material today is far greater and chosen more for decorative than protective purposes.

Hedging, either for boundaries or subdivision of the garden should be selected carefully. A well-kept hedge helps filter wind and noise, prevents plants drying out too quickly, creates a suitable background to display plants against, and – unlike a solid fence – doesn't create turbulence.

The main requirement for modern garden hedges is to create privacy, with the most important hedges being the side boundary hedges with the neighbours and the front hedge facing onto the road or pavement. Hedging creates an oasis of privacy in the back garden, and at the front deters passers-by from peeping in through the window. In consequence, the fast-growing conifer hedge is the popular choice of most gardeners wanting to effectively establish a tall barrier to give themselves privacy; however, conifer hedges are not a good choice for cottage gardens. Cottage hedges were always of a type that allowed native shade-loving plants to thrive beneath them, gave structure for climbers (honeysuckle, roses, clematis) whose roots enjoyed the shade whilst flowering along

A thatched cottage with a neatly clipped hedge and picket gate.

the top, and created a wonderful habitat for wildlife. The typically sold 'Leyland cypress' (*Cupressocyparis leylandii*), although rapidly forming an evergreen hedge, has many disadvantages that make it totally unsuitable for cottage gardens. The Leyland cypress is an exceedingly hungry tree with shallow roots that will suck up every drop of moisture from the surrounding soil, and in consequence, dry out the ground and prevent most plants from surviving anywhere near it. It is highly toxic and once neglected cannot be restored. Not only that, they just don't look right! There are far better alternatives for cottage hedges, some being traditional, and others modern equivalents.

Hebe 'Mrs Winder' near the cottage acts as a feature shrub, its dark green foliage and purple flowers contrasting well with the surrounding white flowers.

What type of hedge?

Before deciding on plants for hedging, consider what type you require. Firstly, do you want an evergreen or deciduous hedge? Evergreen hedges provide year-round privacy and a great background for planting schemes, but often require more in the way of maintenance (clipping), whereas deciduous hedges need less attention and offer better filtering of the wind throughout the year. You may also have a specific soil (heavy clay or light sand) or a certain situation (cold or exposed site) to consider. Perhaps you would enjoy a flowering hedge, maybe one more suitable for wildlife, a low-maintenance hedge that requires just one prune a year or perhaps a coloured hedge (purple/variegated) to create a contrasting background. Growth rate might be a consideration too, as might the final height you wish the hedge to achieve. Also think about whether you would rather have a formal (clipped) hedge or an informal (mixed) hedge.

Evergreen hedges

The most commonly used evergreen hedges are yew and box, which in part is due to the popularity of the gardens of Hidcote and Sissinghurst. Yew, the most architectural of all hedging, has many advantages for use as a taller hedge. Although slow to get going, yew only requires one clip per year, and its dense clipped dark foliage creates a wonderful background hedge for plants. It can be restored if left neglected, even re-growing if taken right back to its trunk. Yew can also be clipped to make a narrow hedge and therefore take up very little space, whereas many hedges all too quickly become very wide. This makes yew ideal for smaller sized cottage gardens.

Box is probably the most widely grown evergreen hedge used to give formality to gardens, whether used along paths as an edging, to subdivide the garden or vegetable patch, or to make a knot pattern. There is a vast range of *Buxus sempervirens* available apart from the usual dwarf 'Suffruticosa' form, and it is worth doing a little research before buying a quantity of hedging plants. One particularly stunning variegated form worth considering is *Buxus sempervirens* 'Elegantissima'.

Our native privet *Ligustrum vulgare* is also evergreen, or semi-evergreen in colder areas, and although some gardeners turn their noses up at it, this old cottage hedge does have its virtues. Yes, it does grow fast, and yes, it does need regular clipping; however, it looks excellent when clipped into shape and if it gets out of hand can be recovered by careful cutting back. The native variety, though, is not the usual type sold for hedging. Instead, *Ligustrum ovalifolium*, which looks much the same but doesn't have the black berries and is a slightly faster grower, is the main variety sold in nurseries and garden centres. There is also a brighter form with variegated leaves, *L. ovalifolium* 'Aureum', known as the 'golden privet'.

The evergreen bush honeysuckle *Lonicera nitida* is not as popular as it once was, but is excellent for dwarf hedging purposes. Also known as 'Wilson's honeysuckle' or 'box honeysuckle' and coming from China, it became a useful hedging material in the twentieth century, when its erect nature, glossy leaves and ease of clipping gave it widespread appeal. A fast grower that gets to 1.5m (5ft) in height, it will get floppy if allowed to get too tall. However, it has some distinct advantages – it is both drought resistant and tolerant of pollution. There is also a popular golden version – 'Baggesen's Gold' – should you wish for something a little more colourful.

Terraced cottages with clipped hedges of Portuguese laurel and box (with pyramidal ends).

Traditional privet clipped at a height to give privacy for the house and garden.

If a prickly evergreen hedge is what you require, then holly could be the answer. This traditional hedge is wider, more open and informal, but can also be purchased in a variegated form. You'll also have a ready supply of berried branches for Christmas decoration so long as you are aware that you require both male and female plants within the hedge.

Another medium-sized thorny evergreen is berberis. Ideal for smaller front gardens and subdivision of garden spaces, the very versatile *Berberis darwinii* has orange or yellow flowers which stand out well against the small dark green glossy foliage. Extremely tough and easy to clip to the required height, this plant will tolerate any soil or situation.

For dry sunny positions, you can't beat either rosemary or lavender as evergreen hedging. An upright variety of rosemary is best chosen for hedging and creates a good-looking aromatic barrier. Lavender hedges can either be tall or dwarf depending upon the variety chosen, and will come in a range of coloured flowers, leaf sizes and growth habit. Another grey-leaved evergreen hedging plant for dry positions is *Brachyglottis* 'Sunshine'. It has large silky grey/silver leaves with bright yellow flowers in summer and can be clipped loosely to a height of 1m (3ft).

A more recent and increasingly popular plant for hedging is *Photinia fraseri* 'Red Robin'. It is not a traditional cottage hedging plant but has value as an evergreen, with the new season's growth being a beautiful coppery red/orange colour. It is tough and suitable for most positions in the garden.

For drier shady positions within the garden there is no better choice than *Euonymus fortunei*. Two good varieties which are tough, easy to clip and add a touch of lightness, are *Euonymus* 'Emerald Gaiety' and *Euonymus* 'Emerald 'n' Gold'. The first has bright variegated leaves; the latter has bright gold and green variegated leaves which turn pinkish in the winter. Both are excellent not only for hedges but as ground cover. In colder areas these plants may lose some of their leaves during the winter, but bright new leaves will appear in the spring.

Other evergreens that could be worth considering include *Elaeagnus ebbingei*, a fast-growing silvery evergreen shrub; some varieties of *Escallonia*, with glossy green leaves and either pink, white or red flowers; *Osmanthus × burkwoodii*, with small leathery dark green glossy leaves and highly scented white flowers in spring; and *Viburnum tinus* 'Eve Price', a compact shrub that has tight pink buds in early spring that open into fragrant white flowers and clusters of deep blue berries in the autumn.

Deciduous hedges

The most traditional of all cottage hedges, hawthorn, falls into this category. Although deciduous, it is a good option as a hedge, being fast to grow and establish, hence the common name 'quickthorn'. It is obviously thorny, which was a requirement of a good hedge for the old cottage gardens, but perhaps not such an advantage today when collecting up the very thorny prunings off the ground. It does, however, give a well-shaped and good dense hedge if trimmed regularly, is excellent for wildlife and birds, and has those lovely white flowers in spring.

Beech (*Fagus sylvatica*) is another possible option if you require a formal hedge that has structural branches and good leaf form, or if you require a hedge for a chalky soil. Although deciduous, the beech leaves once dried turn a lovely golden-brown colour and remain on the hedge throughout the winter, thus retaining its structure and assisting in filtering the wind effectively.

For year-round colour, *Berberis thunbergia* 'Atropurpurea' is an excellent choice. A medium-sized shrub that is easy to establish and clip, it boasts red-purple foliage throughout most of the year which contrasts well with the pale-yellow flowers in spring. In the autumn, the leaves will turn an even more brilliant red before dropping.

A long cottage border backed by a hedge of *Photinia* 'Red Robin'.

A wide curving hedge of the bright evergreen *Euonymus* 'Emerald Gaiety'.

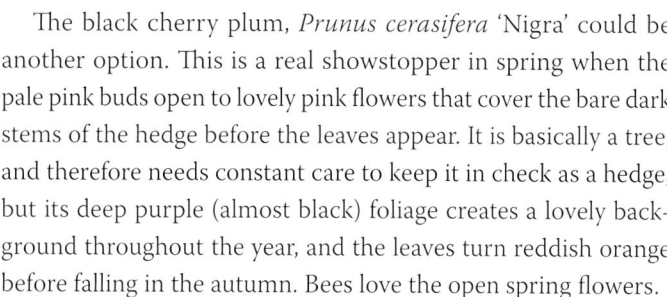

A double dwarf variegated box hedge adds structure to this cottage garden.

Dwarf evergreen hedges of *Teucrium chamaedrys* enclose old roses at Kelmarsh Hall, near Kettering.

The black cherry plum, *Prunus cerasifera* 'Nigra' could be another option. This is a real showstopper in spring when the pale pink buds open to lovely pink flowers that cover the bare dark stems of the hedge before the leaves appear. It is basically a tree, and therefore needs constant care to keep it in check as a hedge, but its deep purple (almost black) foliage creates a lovely background throughout the year, and the leaves turn reddish orange before falling in the autumn. Bees love the open spring flowers.

Dwarf hedges

Dwarf hedges can be used to create compartments within the garden, define a vista down a straight path or be a front edging along a border to aid in the holding up of floppy-headed flowers. Dwarf evergreen hedges work well in both large and small gardens giving green structure throughout the year, creating a framework and adding interest.

Box is the 'king' of dwarf hedging. Box found favour and was considered the only worthwhile dwarf hedging plant during the creation of the great formal gardens in Britain in the late sixteenth and early seventeenth centuries. It returned to favour in the Victorian period and has ever since been the go-to dwarf hedge for formality within gardens. Unfortunately, box blight has started to make people wary of using it, but in my opinion, it is still the best hedge for holding a crisply cut shape, and looks terrific in the winter with either frost or snow across the top.

A possible alternative to box is Christmas box – *Sarcococca hookeriana* var. *humilis*. This will make a dwarf hedge nearly as good as box but with darker, narrower leaves. *Sarcococca confusa* is a slightly larger variety but just as viable for hedging, and like all Christmas boxes has a wonderful sweet heady fragrance in January/February.

Euonymus fortunei varieties make great variegated dwarf hedges and do well in shady positions. There is a whole host of cultivars to choose from, all with slightly different variations on the theme of either white and green, or gold and green.

For herb gardens and dry, sunny positions within the garden you can't beat the dwarf lavender hedges. You'll require a compact variety for dwarf hedges and there is quite a variety to choose from if you go to a lavender specialist. The two most popular are 'Hidcote' and 'Munstead' but you might prefer white- or pink-flowered lavenders depending upon the colour scheme within your garden; 'Arctic Snow' or 'Nana Alba' would be suitable white-flowered varieties (height 45–50cm), and 'Little Lottie' if a delicate pink flower is required. Other dwarf blue-flowered varieties to look out for include 'Little Lady', 'Imperial Gem' and 'Beechwood Blue'.

A seldom grown evergreen dwarf hedging plant is 'wall germander' – *Teucrium chamaedrys*. Sometimes sold as *Teucrium × lucidrys*, this plant was commonly used in the Tudor period for edging knots, but seems to have fallen from grace – perhaps because the fashion in formal gardens changed to use box hedging exclusively. This is a shame, as this lovely dwarf plant makes a delightful loose dwarf flowering hedge of only 30cm (1ft) high. It has bushy aromatic mid-green foliage and erect stems carrying many dark-pink lipped flowers that attract bees. It prefers sun and a well-drained soil.

Another possibility is a dwarf barberry hedge. Either *Berberis buxifolia* 'Nana' or 'Pygmaea' will provide a good compact evergreen hedge of dark green leaves to a height of 75cm (2½ft) if required. In addition, a mass of bright yellow flowers arch along the stems in April and May. This hedging is drought tolerant, easy to grow in any situation, pest free and a great alternative to box.

TABLE 6.1: HEDGING PLANTS

Tall hedges	Description	Height
Hawthorn (*Crataegus monogyna*)	Traditional thorny deciduous hedge requiring two or more clips a year. White flowers in May/June. Good for wildlife.	2–5m (6–18ft)
Privet (*Ligustrum* species)	Traditional cottage hedge requiring at least two clips per year. White flowers in June/July.	2–5m (6–18ft)
Yew (*Taxus baccata*)	Dark evergreen foliage, excellent dense background hedging needing only one clip a year (late summer). Sun or shade.	1–3m (3–10ft)
Holly (*Ilex aquifolium*)	Thorny evergreen barrier needing two clips a year (May and September). Great for wildlife with red berries in the winter.	12m (39ft)
Beech (*Fagus sylvatica*)	Structurally formal deciduous hedge with attractive foliage that turns golden-brown. Purple beech variety needs full sun.	Height to suit garden.
Portuguese laurel (*Prunus lusitanica*)	Evergreen, drought-resistant tree that can be clipped to form a dense barrier. White flowers in early spring.	12m (40ft)
Medium hedges		
Rosemary 'Miss Jessop's Upright'	Attractive evergreen flowering hedge with culinary uses, scented foliage and blue flowers. Dry sun position required.	1m (3ft)
Old English lavender (*Lavandula angustifolia*)	Aromatic evergreen hedge with fragrant flowers. Prune after flowering. Prefers well-drained poor soil. Good for bees.	1m (3ft)
Evergreen honeysuckle (*Lonicera nitida*)	Extremely fast-growing hedge requiring many clips to maintain its shape. Copes with shade, sun and chalky soils.	1–3m (3–10ft)
Darwin's barberry (*Berberis darwinii*)	Prickly, dense evergreen shrub with dark leaves and yellow/orange flowers. Tolerant of all soils. Purple berries.	1m (3ft)
Spindle (*Euonymus fortunei*)	Bushy variegated evergreen hedging, ideal for dry shade or sun. Easy to maintain. *E*. 'Emerald Gaiety' a popular choice.	1m (3ft)
Dwarf hedges		
Box (*Buxus sempervirens*)	Box is an evergreen hedging material that is ideal for edging, subdivision of gardens and taller barriers. There are numerous varieties.	
Dwarf lavenders	There are many available varieties, with the most popular being *L*. Hidcote (purple flowered) and *L*. Munstead (mid-blue flowered).	
Wall germander (*Teucrium × lucidrys*)	Evergreen bushy perennial with delicate pink flowers. Used in Tudor knot gardens of the past, it makes attractive low hedging.	
Christmas box (*Sarcococca confusa*)	Evergreen hedging with dark glossy leaves. The small white flowers perfume the air gloriously in January and February and lift the spirits.	

Mixed hedges

For a large cottage garden, a mixed hedge is an option that deserves serious consideration. The oldest hedges in Britain are mixed native species hedges which formed boundaries but also supplied wood, berries and fruits to cottagers. As opposed to a single species hedge, a mixed hedge looks very different (informal and natural), its makeup being a combination of evergreen and deciduous shrubs, small trees and flowering climbers (roses, honeysuckle, clematis). This type of hedge has a greater width, with taller trees/shrubs erupting through at intervals along its length, with the advantage of different species within the hedge flowering at varying times and producing berries or fruits in the autumn, thus ensuring interest throughout the whole year. This type of hedge is extremely beneficial to wildlife – providing materials, food and thorny protection for nesting birds; flowers for bees, foliage for caterpillars and hiding places for hedgehogs.

You can mix and match, creating your own 'mixed hedge', and there is no reason why such plants as buddleia, *Viburnum tinus*, flowering currant or lilac couldn't be added. In fact, you don't have to plant a truly traditional native mixed hedge, you could design a 'mixed flowering hedge' or a 'mixed fragrant hedge' – the choice is entirely yours! The following trees and shrubs are worth considering:

- Blackthorn (*Prunus spinosa*) – Deciduous thorny hedge with white flowers appearing on bare branches. The large berries called 'sloes' provide food for birds and gin for humans.
- Damson (*Prunus institia*) – Small native tree, with 'Shropshire Prune Damson' being a wonderful variety. The plums form in late August and make great jams and jellies.
- Dog rose (*Rosa canina*) – A thorny native scrambler with large pink five-petalled flowers in May/June. Clusters of brilliant red hips follow in September and October.
- Elder (*Sambucus nigra*) – A small tree commonly seen in hedgerows, with distinctive flat umbels of creamy-white flowers in early summer, followed by shiny dark black berries. The flowers are used to make elderflower cordial, and the vitamin C-rich berries for wine.
- Guelder rose (*Viburnum opulus*) – A native shrub with three-lobed leaves and masses of white flowers from May to July. It provides shelter and red berries for birds.
- Hawthorn (*Crataegus monogyna*) – A thorny barrier, a home for birds and insects, and a source of food for birds. The scented white flowers (loved by bees) appear in May.
- Hazel (*Corylus avellana*) – Deciduous native tree with catkins on bare branches in spring, followed by toothed leaves. The nuts provide food for squirrels, birds and dormice.

- Holly (*Ilex aquifolium*) – An evergreen tree with prickly dark green leaves that can live up to 300 years. Deep red berries remain throughout winter, if not eaten by birds!
- Spindle tree (*Euonymus europaeus*) – Thriving on chalky soils, this tree has stunning autumn-coloured leaves and spectacular winged capsules with vivid orange seeds.

Bright red seed capsules of our native spindle tree *Euonymus europaeus*.

Flowering hedges

Rather than just a plain green boundary hedge, or a mixed hedge, another option is an attractive 'flowering hedge'. Flowering hedges tend to be more informal and open and will create a colourful divide which is quite often fragrant, and can be chosen to tie in with a particular colour scheme. Obviously, some research is always worthwhile, as this ensures the pruning or clipping is done at the correct time of year to help guarantee a good flowering display. However, as a general rule, most flowering hedges should be trimmed straight after flowering has finished. The following plants will all create good flowering hedges.

Caryopteris × clandonensis 'Heavenly Blue'
A deciduous late season (September to October) flowering hedge with particularly attractive dark blue flowers. A compact but upright shrub with lovely grey-green leaves enjoying well-drained full sun positions. Reaching 1m (3ft) in height, it is drought tolerant and good for division within the garden.

Choisya ternata
A medium-sized dense evergreen shrub that is reasonably fast growing, reaching 2m (6½ ft). Fragrant white flowers in spring and glossy foliage. *Choisya* 'Aztec Pearl' has narrower leaves.

Fuchsia magellanica

This fuchsia makes an attractive late season flowering hedge, and is semi-evergreen in mild parts. Growing to about 2m (6½ft) its pendent flowers of red and purple resemble earrings or ballerinas. It should be cut back hard yearly to ensure it doesn't get too large and maintains a good shape. The variety 'Alba' is a stunning delicate form, having single white flowers tinged with pink.

The delicate hanging flowers of *Fuchsia magellanica alba* make a lovely addition to the late summer garden.

Hebe

These evergreen shrubs are good as hedging, particularly for seaside gardens, being salt tolerant. They much prefer sunny sites and can be short-lived but give a mass of flowers yearly. Some good choices:

* *Hebe* 'Green Globe'– white flowers, 40cm (1ft) high.
* *Hebe* 'Nicola's Blush'– pale pink flowers, 60cm (2ft) high.
* *Hebe* 'Great Orme' – bright pink flowers, 150cm (5ft) high.
* *Hebe* 'Red Edge' – lilac flowers, 45cm (1–2ft) high.

Hydrangea paniculata 'Limelight'

A large striking informal hedge for late-season elegance in cool part-shade areas of the garden. Plant has a bushy upright habit, eventually achieving 2.5m (8ft). Many large dense conical flowers open in lime-green and gradually turn brilliant white.

Lavandula angustifolia

An aromatic silver-grey leaved hedge and cottage favourite with *L. × intermedia* having later flowers. This form is the hardiest in Britain and reaches 90cm (3ft), having dark blue flowers. Bees and butterflies adore lavender, which does best on well-drained sandy (even chalky) soils.

Potentilla fruticosa

Medium shrub which is particularly useful for seaside gardens and sunny positions. Useful hedging due to its long flowering period and distinctive five-petalled saucer shaped flowers. Reaching 1m (3ft) in height, the flowers can be white, pink, red, apricot, orange or pale yellow.

Ribes sanguineum

A tough, easy to grow medium upright shrub that makes a good spring flowering hedge. Preferring a sunny position, and attaining about 1.8m (6ft), it has clusters of red tubular flowers. Being deciduous, it is possibly not ideal as an external boundary hedge. Although *R.* 'Pulborough Scarlet' is common, the variety *R.* 'Tydeman's White' is available too.

Rosa rugosa

Although many shrub roses can be used for hedging, rugosas are the best possible choice. Rugosas form a dense, fast-growing barrier, are resistant to drought, disease and wind, and are salt tolerant. Only one prune a year is required, and they grow to 1.5m (5ft) with stunning red ornamental hips. The fragrant flowers are large and bowl-like, coming in colours of white, pink and red.

Weigela florida

First introduced in 1848, weigelas are showy shrubs with many forms worthy as hedging. *Weigela florida* 'Variegata' is a compact form with attractive foliage and delicate pink flowers. Ideal in all situations and reaching 2m (6½ft), bees love the tubular flowers.

Herb hedges

Herb hedges can be extremely useful in cottage gardens, softening hard path lines and providing an edible culinary resource simultaneously. As most herbs used for hedges are of Mediterranean origin, they're best planted in open sunny situations on well-drained or poor soil. Herb hedges are particularly appropriate for kitchen gardens, subdividing vegetable patches, small formal knot gardens or edging paths in gardens that generally receive full sun. Herb hedges probably provide more than any other hedge; being aromatic, beneficial for insects, culinary, informally decorative and

Dwarf *Lavandula* 'Hidcote' hedges spill informally over the path to the front door.

If hedges are trimmed at an angle, with a slightly narrower top than base, the hedge will benefit from being denser and more wind resistant. The slight slope allows for sunlight to hit every part of the hedge, top to bottom, and this in turn prevents those bare patches appearing all along the bottom of the hedge.

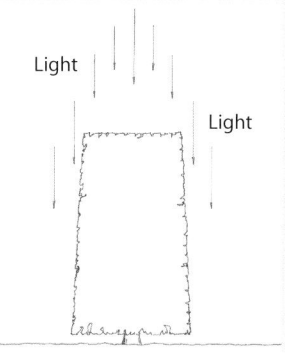

Consider the path of light when hedge trimming.

a good companion for neighbouring plants. Most herbs used for hedging are evergreen, and therefore create a permanent scented structure that also benefits the kitchen year-round.

The most obvious choice is of course, lavender. Varieties of lavenders useful for hedging have been mentioned previously, with the exception of French lavender, *Lavandula stoechas*. If you want a compact hedge with a little more pizzazz, a French lavender, with its purple bracts on top of the lovely flowers, might be worth considering. The downside with French lavenders is that they are tender and short-lived.

Rosemary makes a good medium-height aromatic evergreen hedge; choose an 'upright' rather than a prostrate variety. Rosemary has a long history of being used for hedging in England, with Elizabethans delighting in clipping it as high as they could up against the walls of palaces and manor houses. Even when considered more as a structural hedge within the garden, it can still be used throughout the year for use in the kitchen. Two excellent varieties for hedging are 'Miss Jessop's Upright' and 'Benenden Blue' (which has very large flowers).

Cotton lavender, *Santolina chamaecyparissus*, was a favourite Elizabethan herb for hedging in knot gardens, being much admired for its foliage and unusual bright yellow button flowers. Somewhat fallen from grace, it is rarely used in gardens today unless a knot garden is again required. Unfortunately, the plant has a tendency to be less compact than other herbs, is short-lived and can get unruly! However, the feathery evergreen silver foliage creates a lovely contrast with other plants, and the flowers don't necessarily have to be the vivid yellow pompoms – there are varieties with pale yellow flowers.

Hyssop, although little used, can be clipped to provide a lovely flowering hedge of approximately 60cm (2ft). Semi-evergreen, upright and compact, the tubular dark blue flowers are adored by bees. *H. officinalis roseum* is a lovely delicate, pink-flowered variety.

The low-growing shrubby thymes also make excellent dwarf herb hedges; avoid the creeping or prostrate forms. Common thyme and lemon thyme (*T. vulgaris*, *T. citriodorus*) are ideal as culinary aromatic dwarf hedging, whether for the herb garden or simply edging a path or border. A beautiful silver-leaved variety with lilac flowers in early summer is *Thymus* 'Silver Posie'.

Catmint isn't often considered as hedging, but on a poor soil in a very sunny cottage garden it's certainly worth bearing in mind. Tough, easy to grow, drought tolerant, and having masses of showy blue flower spikes on distinctive grey-green foliage, this perennial is an attractive option. Catmints have a lax habit, so your hedge will be low and bushy, and have that informal cottagey look. A good catmint for low hedging would be *Nepeta racemosa* 'Walker's Low'.

TOPIARY

Topiary, which was invented by the Romans, only became popular in Europe with the designing of vast formal gardens during the Renaissance period. It quickly lost favour in England during the English Landscape Movement but regained its position as an important element within gardens in the Victorian period, where it was considered particularly useful as green structure to tie in with the geometric displays of the 'new' bedding schemes. During this same period, the suburban Victorian garden, the Picturesque garden and the Arts and Crafts garden style, also embraced the clipped evergreen structures which topiary could provide.

Following the fashion, those cottagers who could afford the time, decided to create something similar to the manor house or vicarage garden. With no room in the precious vegetable garden, cottage garden topiary was confined either to the surrounding hedge or a shrub up against the wall of the cottage. Allowing the hedge to grow up either side of the cottage gate so that it could be clipped into a shape was common and can still be seen in villages today. Sometimes the old holly or yew trees were clipped and shaped in an abstract manner up against a cottage wall, to create interest but also to give protection against unforeseen evil. Topiary shapes differed from cottage to cottage, and from region to region, with often a simple abstract shape being sufficient; however, clipped peacocks and pheasants have always been popular.

For the modern cottage garden there are many options for topiary, with a variety of shapes available for purchase ready-clipped. Nurseries and garden centres will commonly have box balls in varying sizes on offer, either for the garden or for pots. Pyramids, cones and spirals are also available, if a little more expensive! But there is nothing stopping you making your own cottage garden more unique by simply shaping an evergreen already growing in your garden.

Hedges lend themselves to some kind of shaping. The norm is of course, straight sides and a flat top, but there are all kinds of variations which can enhance the boundary hedges. Changing the top of the hedge is fairly straightforward. The 'battlement' style has been commonplace for many years, as has the 'wavy' effect, but you could simply clip abstract mounds along the length of the hedge. Creating an imposing entrance by clipping the hedge into the form of a green arch over the front gate has been popular with cottagers for a long time and can add a touch of character to the garden. This structural entrance may well have originally been the cottager trying to emulate the entrance gates to the big house. Topiary shaped birds, of one form or another, have always been popular – although these require a little more in the way of expertise. Cake stands, simple abstract shapes and more quirky or amusing topiary can be found clipped in cottage gardens. I have seen a topiary 'train' and a topiary 'pig' recently! And, although

A topiary yew column adds height and evergreen structure near the garden gate.

The trimmed box ball in the terracotta pot acts as a feature within the cottage border.

topiary came late to the cottage garden, it is now considered a valuable addition that adds year-round structure and interest.

CLIMBERS

Traditional cottage gardens welcomed native climbers into the plot, as they took up little space but provided flower, fragrance and seasonal interest. Most commonly used were honeysuckles, native roses, ivy and 'old man's beard' (the native clematis), which resulted in cottages being called 'Ivy Cottage', 'Honeysuckle Cottage' or 'Rose Cottage'.

A greater variety and number of climbers have been introduced and become permanent features within the cottage garden since the nineteenth century. Their versatility for creating immediate height, covering walls and fences, climbing over and through a range of structures, perfuming the air and being wonderful companion plants, makes them indispensable in any cottage garden. In small gardens in particular, using climbers as a way of 'greening' the fences takes away the closed-in feel. Climbers can also be used to add instant height in borders by the use of obelisks or rustic tripods, rather than waiting for a shrub to attain the required height. As in the past, climbers are also ideal as companions for growing up through large fruit trees or over arbours. Climbers also create a softening influence around doors and windows, and this very cottagey effect helps to unify house and garden.

Your choice of climbers is dictated by a number of things: aspect, soil, region of the country, flowering season, annual or perennial climber and your personal requirements of colour, scent and flower size.

Climbers generally require support, and there are numerous ways to provide this. The obvious ones include horizontal wires on walls and fences, pergolas, arches, obelisks and trellising. Trellis is an ideal supporting structure for climbers to weave their way through and comes in various styles. Trellis can be attached to walls or used as the sides of an arbour. A more elegant form of trellis is 'treillage', which is a free-standing form of trellis for roses or other climbers, and is a great way to subdivide a garden or create a 'garden room'. Trellis panels allow a partial view through to another area of the garden but at the same time define the area they enclose, creating a wonderful structure for climbers.

Scented climbers were traditionally grown in cottage gardens, and still remain highly popular. Roses and honeysuckles continue to be the favourite climbers for scent, but jasmine and some clematis can also be considered, depending on the situation and aspect.

Clematis 'Crystal Fountain' climbs up an elegant metal arch.

A rose and clematis both climb the same structure at Wild Rose Cottage.

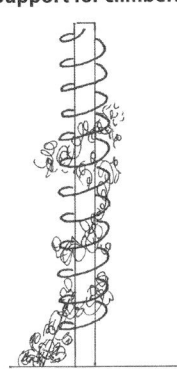

Post cemented into the ground with either a wrought iron or a thick galvanized wire spiral.

Strong metal hanging basket turned upside down and fixed to the top.

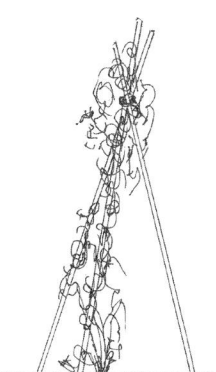

Simple rustic tripod of pokes tied together at the top.

A golden hop romps across a piece of trellis that subdivides the cottage garden.

What could be more delightful than catching an intoxicating fragrance from a climber when entering a doorway or walking under a pergola?

Climbers grown up a structure in a pot make a wonderful feature, but less vigorous climbers will need to be chosen. Perhaps a large-flowered clematis or an annual climber would be best; and it must be remembered they will require more attention than climbers in the ground, in terms of watering and feeding.

Climbing plants that come to mind immediately include roses, clematis, honeysuckle, wisteria and jasmine. However, let's not forget runner beans and hops; these were popular climbers in cottage gardens, being both useful and decorative. When the runner bean first arrived in England, it was known as the 'arber bean' and was deliberately grown over Elizabethan arbours to display its attractive flowers and give a private garden room. So why not grow these beans up over a tripod or a group of canes at the back of the border, thus creating height and flowering interest, with the addition of a good crop of beans. Perhaps grow your runner beans in a large pot as a feature.

The hop too, although not generally used for homemade beer today, makes a good, vigorous climber either as a stand-alone feature or a background plant. There is also a golden hop, if you require a change from green; the hops, of course, could be dried and used for decoration in the cottage or house, particularly if you have a few beams available. Squashes, gourds and cucumbers also lend themselves to being trained to climb up structures, and not only look effective with hanging fruits, but growing in this way protects the fruits from possibly sitting on soggy ground.

Lastly, bear in mind that climbers don't always have to climb! In the past I have deliberately planted climbers so that they trail or ramble through certain drifts of perennials. If the right combination of climber and perennial is chosen, the contrast of colours, or possibly flower colour and foliage, can be quite delightful.

Roses

Climbing and rambling roses are so much a part of the traditional cottage garden that it is impossible not to grow at least one or two. Although these roses often only flower for brief periods, the scent and appearance of the flowers make them indispensable for walls, fences, arches, porches, pergolas, outbuildings, large trees (fruit) and particularly arbours.

What is the difference between a climber and rambler? Climbing roses are generally less vigorous and will often repeat flower, or have a sprinkling of flowers on and off for a period throughout the summer. Rambling roses are far more vigorous and can easily cover large structures, having clusters of smaller flowers covering the whole plant in one magnificent flush.

Diagonal trellis panels act as a type of 'treillage' to support roses at Cressing Temple Barns.

Climbing and rambling roses require support, whether natural (tree) or artificial (pergola or wall), and will need tying in initially until they get going. Arches, obelisks and pergolas made of metal or wood can be purchased ready-made. A stretch of trellis or 'treillage' (*see* illustrations in Chapter 2) on posts makes a fabulous framework for roses. This will subdivide the garden, allow the roses to be seen at their best and leave space beneath for cottage plants.

Climbing roses themselves make a wonderful structural companion plant, creating a framework for a later flowering clematis, honeysuckle or annual climber. This makes them ideal for smaller cottage gardens where the rose comes into flower first, followed by the secondary flowering climber (clematis). Mixing roses with other climbers in this way is a wonderful use of limited space, and gives a continuity of flowering for a longer period.

Climbers and ramblers can be found for every position and aspect within the garden and Table 6.2 lists a few recommendations. However, it is advisable to visit a specialist rose nursery to find the correct rose to suit your own specific garden situation.

Beautiful double primrose yellow flowers of *Rosa* 'Banksiae lutea'.

A profusion of flowers of *Rosa* 'Rambling Rector' cascades over and along the fence.

TABLE 6.2: CLIMBING AND RAMBLING ROSES

Climbing roses	Description	Height
Rosa 'Zéphirine Drouhin'	Old Bourbon rose with continuous semi-double scented pink flowers. One of the best climbers.	3.5m (12ft)
Rosa 'Gloire de Dijon'	An old favourite with a great scent and double cream-buff flowers. Dark glossy foliage, sometimes evergreen.	5m (16½ ft)
Rosa 'Banksiae lutea'	Clusters of double primrose-yellow flowers over glossy thornless foliage in May. Requires a south-facing position.	7m (22ft)
Rosa 'Constance Spry'	Excellent climber from David Austin (1961) with double pink scented flowers. Disease resistant and long flowering.	6m (20ft)
Rosa 'Mermaid'	Lovely fragrant single primrose-yellow flowers, being up to 12cm in diameter. Dark glossy semi-evergreen thorny foliage.	8m (26ft)
Rosa 'New Dawn'	Fast-growing popular climber with glossy foliage and semi-double scented pink flowers. Happy in poor soils.	2.5m (8ft)
Rosa 'Paul's Scarlet'	Clusters of deep red semi-double flowers which hold their shape. Very few thorns and a long flowering period.	3m (10ft)
Rosa 'Mme Alfred Carrière'	Double creamy-white scented flowers with a hint of pink in the centre. Good for north-facing positions and ideal for trees.	5m (16ft)
Rosa 'Blairii Number Two'	Long flowering smaller climber with large pale pink scented flowers, being deeper pink in the centre. Excellent for arches.	4m (13ft)
Rosa 'Paul's Himalayan Musk'	Vigorous scented rose for a large garden, being ideal for a big tree or to cover a shed. Double pink flowers in midsummer.	12m (40ft)
Rosa 'Madame Grégoire Staechelin'	A vigorous climber with large semi-double pale-pink flowers, followed by good hips. An ideal choice for poor soil or shade.	5m (16ft)

Rambling roses	Description	Height
Rosa 'Albertine'	Highly scented delicate pink flowers on stems with vicious thorns. Has old world charm, but not recommended for arches.	6m (20ft)
Rosa 'Félicité Perpétue'	Vigorous rambler developed in 1827, with cream-white flowers opening from pinkish buds. Almost thornless.	6m (20ft)
Rosa 'Wedding Day'	Vigorous, fast growing rose with clusters of highly scented single white flowers. Tolerant of poor soils.	9m (30ft)
Rosa 'Sander's White'	Although bred in 1912, it is a gem for cottage gardens. Many old type white rosette flowers continue for a long period.	4m (13ft)
Rosa 'Rambling Rector'	A rampant rose for large trees and sheds which is happy in sun or shade. Semi-double white flowers last from June to September.	6m (20ft)
Rosa filipes 'Kiftsgate'	A vigorous hybrid developed at Kiftsgate Court, having fragrant single white flowers followed by decorative hips.	10.5m (34ft)
Rosa 'Lady of the Lake'	A more subdued rambler with loose clusters of semi-double pink flowers. Tolerant of shade.	4m (13ft)

A variety of our native honeysuckle *Lonicera periclymenum* 'Graham Thomas' climbs up through a tree.

Lonicera periclymenum 'Graham Thomas'
Stunning scent from July to September on large white flowers that fade to pale yellow. Vigorous deciduous honeysuckle. Height 5m (16ft).

Lonicera periclymenum 'Serotina'
Another beautifully scented honeysuckle but highly vigorous, with large white flowers with red streaks from July to October. An ideal companion for a climbing rose or to cover a pergola. Height 7m (23ft).

Lonicera × heckrottii 'Gold Flame'
A vibrant honeysuckle, the flowers having pink outer whorls and orange/yellow inner. A late summer flowerer with red berries to follow. Height 4m (13ft).

Lonicera fragrantissima (winter-flowering honeysuckle)
A smaller bushy deciduous honeysuckle that has creamy-white highly scented flowers from January to March. Good for winter borders or the wall next to a door. Height 2m (6ft).

Lonicera × purpusii 'Winter Beauty'
This smaller semi-evergreen honeysuckle is rather insignificant during the summer and is therefore best planted amongst or over a shrub, but in the winter has a lovely, sweet fragrance borne on white flowers between December and March. Height 2m (6ft).

Lonicera periclymenum 'Belgica' (Dutch honeysuckle)
This highly fragrant vigorous honeysuckle that will scent the air on warm evenings, has flowers that are yellow and raspberry red. Flowering early, it often flowers again in late summer. Height 6m (20ft).

Honeysuckle

What cottage garden, however small, could be without this highly scented climber? In fact, honeysuckles are wonderful for small gardens or garden rooms, for enclosure ensures their scent will be the stronger. Growing in sun or shade, the scent of a climbing honeysuckle is heavenly on a still summer's evening. There are numerous options for growing honeysuckles – they'll happily grow on a fence or wall, be guided up through a tree, grow over an arbour or pergola, or over an arch or a seat. Where possible, honeysuckles should be positioned in a warm spot in the garden and close to an area where the evening scent can be appreciated.

Clematis

Clematis weren't traditionally part of the cottage garden, with the exception of the rampant native 'old man's beard' (*Clematis vitalba*) which cascaded over the cottage hedge or climbed through a large fruit tree. This vigorous clematis looks stunning covered in its silky seed heads later in the year, but is certainly not suitable for today's small cottage gardens. However, there is a huge variety of clematis to choose from today, and their beauty and versatility have made them a permanent feature in every cottage garden.

For sheer flower power and diversity of shape and colour, these climbers are difficult to beat. A clematis can be found for every season of the year, which as a result means you can achieve continuous flowering on one or other structure or fence throughout the whole year. A clematis can be found for every aspect and soil situation, and they will happily ascend arches, walls and fences, trees and large shrubs, trellis and arbours, or even simply cascade over the ground amongst the flowers. There are also evergreen varieties, which will provide a year-round green structure. Their one main preference is to have 'cool' roots but with their 'heads in the sun'. Smaller flowered clematis are generally very vigorous and will soon take over, and are best used for long stretches of fence, sheds, pergolas and large trees. The large-flowered varieties are more suitable for obelisks and companion planting with roses.

Clematis are divided into three groups.

Group 1

Group 1 clematis are the early-flowering types (late winter and spring). These clematis flower on previous year's growth and don't need pruning but can be cut back (tidied up) to contain their vigour after flowering. This group includes:

- *C. alpina* – vigorous and exceedingly tough with attractive seed heads
- *C. montana* – a sun-loving rampant clematis that will cover walls, fences, large trees and structures
- *C. armandii* – an evergreen clematis with highly fragrant star-shaped white flowers in March/April
- *C. macropetala* – vigorous clematis with semi-double or double flowers (blues, pinks and whites)
- *C. cirrhosa* – an evergreen clematis that prefers a sunny position and has delicate bell-shaped flowers from December to March.

The rich-purple-flowered clematis looks perfect scrambling up through a small tree.

The early-flowering *Clematis macropetala* 'Albina Plena' looks stunning climbing through the diamond-shaped metal trellis.

Group 2

Group 2 clematis are early summer flowering (May/June) but often re-flower in August. They have large single or double flowers in different permutations of colour and design, and require just a light prune in late winter/early spring. Another pruning however, after the first flush of flowers is beneficial, as it promotes a secondary flowering period. The stems are best cut back by half to a pair of buds. This group includes those listed below, and many more large-flowering hybrids:

- *C.* 'Nelly Moser'
- *C.* 'Niobe'
- *C.* 'Miss Bateman'
- *C.* 'Multi Blue'

The large-flowered *Clematis* 'Perle d'Azur' on a trellis panel underplanted with a drift of *Knautia macedonica*.

Group 3

Group 3 clematis are the late summer flowering types which produce their flowers on the present season's growth. The stems require a simple total cut back in February or March, down to approx. 30cm (1ft) above ground level. If this isn't done, you end up with a sporadic flowering on top of a tangled mass of stems. This group includes:

- *C. viticella* – flowering from July to September in a range of colours and excellent for growing up through early flowering shrubs
- *C. texensis* – with trumpet or bell-like flowers that hang in small clusters and flower from July through to October

- *C. tangutica* – which has golden-coloured lantern-like hanging flowers from July to October, and showy, fluffy seed heads
- *C. flammula* – known as 'virgin's bower', a vigorous clematis with masses of sweetly scented small white flowers from August to October, followed by fluffy seed heads.

Dwarf clematis

Recently, breeders have started to come up with a range of dwarf clematis which are ideal for pots for small or patio gardens, and which could also be extremely valuable for smaller cottage gardens. With maximum heights at around 1.2m (4ft), these new introductions could be used in a number of ways – perhaps up rustic tripods in borders, in pots near the house or either side of a door, scrambling through small shrubs, being mid-border ground cover or even planted in large hanging baskets.

Dwarf clematis worth looking out for include *C.* 'Cezanne', *C.* 'Picardy', *C.* 'Bourbon' and the evergreen variety *C.* 'Fragrant Oberon'. Two varieties that only reach approx. 30cm (1ft) are *C.* 'Filigree' with semi-double lilac flowers, and *C.* 'Bijou' with dark blue flowers. A particularly stunning dwarf variety well worth sourcing is *Clematis* 'Little Lemons'. This is a *tangutica* hybrid that only grows to 45cm (18in) and has nodding bright yellow bells from May to September, followed by silvery seed heads.

Jasmine

Jasminum officinale, the common summer jasmine, has been grown for centuries in cottage gardens, as it bears fragrant white star-shaped flowers throughout the summer, given a warm sunny position. It was considered a good choice for the arbours of stately homes and rustic porches of cottages, and is still an excellent choice as a wall or fence climber (with some support) where the scent can be appreciated. *Jasminum nudiflorum* (winter jasmine) is really a tall shrub that requires support, although it does sort of climb! The bright yellow flowers light up those dark winter days, often from November to February.

More readily available now is the 'star jasmine', *Trachelospermum jasminoides*. This vigorous dark-leaved evergreen has heavily scented white flowers in late summer. Hardier than at first believed, it is worth considering for a fence or wall, and perhaps even a large pot. Height is 6m (20ft).

A summer jasmine climbing over the porch at Wild Rose Cottage.

A vigorous passionflower climbing through and along horizontal wire supports.

Passionflower

Looking at the amazingly complex flower of the climber *Passiflora caerulea*, it seems unlikely that it was grown in cottage gardens, but actually it has been popular in southern county cottage gardens since its introduction in *c.*1609. It does of course require a south-facing wall and protection during the winter, but once established will give flower throughout summer and into autumn. Can eventually become rather invasive if not pruned back.

Sweet pea

With their love for fragrance, cottagers grew the lovely annual sweet pea, *Lathyrus odoratus*, on rustic structures within the garden. Most of the wonderful varieties we buy today were developed in the nineteenth century and require an early start to ensure a good display and plenty of flowers for cutting.

Lathyrus latifolius, the everlasting pea, is a native of Europe and was happily tucked into and amongst other plants and simply

An evergreen sweet pea at the apex of the trellis-topped fencing.

allowed to do its own thing. It is a good companion climber for rambling up through other climbers such as roses, and will give plenty of pinkish-purple flowers throughout the summer, to a height of about 2m (6½ft). Unfortunately, this pea has no scent at all!

Annual climbers

Annual climbers often have longer flowering periods, and can be utilized to help cover the bare areas at the bottom of more permanent climbers. Although later blooming, once they start flowering in the summer they simply go on for months on end, only being stopped by the first frost. Normally giving a brilliant burst of colour, they are ideal for rustic wigwams, companion planting through shrubs, or giving temporary colour on a trellis whilst more permanent planting takes off. Needing some structural support, they also look great in containers/pots. The secret to a long, continuous flowering period for annuals is constant dead-heading to help promote further flowers.

Climbers for walls and porches

The wall of the cottage or house is a prime vertical space that has been utilized in cottage gardens for centuries. Growing a climber up the cottage wall creates a vertical garden of flowers and fragrance and a home for nesting birds. Climbers help unify cottage (or house) and garden, creating a smooth transition from one to the other.

'Black-eyed Susan' making excellent headway up and over an arbour in a cottage garden.

'Morning glory' showing off its marvellous blue flowers at the top of a diamond trellis panel attached to the cottage wall.

Name	Description	Height
Canary creeper (*Tropaeolum peregrinum*)	A fast-growing annual that likes sun, with bright yellow flowers that resemble small canary birds. Ideal for trellis.	4m (13ft)
Cup-and-saucer plant (*Cobaea scandens*)	Enjoying sunny positions, the large purple bell flowers look terrific if trained over a fence, archway or pergola.	Possible height 10m (33ft)
Morning glory (*Ipomoea tricolor*)	Another sun-lover with big blousy blue trumpet flowers that open up in the morning and then fade.	4m (13ft)
Black-eyed Susan (*Thunbergia alata*)	Extremely recognizable yellow flower with a black eye in its centre. This annual vine does well in a pot.	2.5m (8ft)
Climbing nasturtium (*Tropaeolum majus*)	The large leaves create a base for the vivid orange or yellow flowers that bees love. Good as ground cover or climber.	1.5m (5ft)
Purple bell vine (*Rhodochiton atrosanguineus*)	This annual from Mexico has long strings of purple bells that hang down from summer through to autumn. The flowers look particularly effective on arches and trellis.	3m (10ft)

Few climbers are self-clinging, exceptions to the rule being ivy and Virginia creeper. Both of these are quite rampant and need constant attention to keep them in check, but although they can disturb some mortar, in general they actually protect the wall. These apart, support for wall climbers is therefore essential, and is either wire or trellis.

It should be remembered that the base of a wall will always be extremely dry, so give climbers a good start to help them get away by adding some compost and bonemeal into the prepared hole, which should be approx. 30cm (1ft) away from the wall and the cane angled towards the wall. Water well until the climber has settled in. Planting depth should be the same as in the purchased pot, unless the climber is a clematis. Clematis need to be buried about 5cm (2in) below the soil level to help avoid 'clematis wilt'. Try not to plant vicious thorny roses against cottage walls, near doors or over the porches.

Ivy, a native woodland climber, has been used for centuries on cottage walls, and is still very useful as long as you are aware that it is rampant. The advantages of ivy are that it is self-clinging, evergreen, good for nesting birds and will happily thrive on a north-facing wall (where a variegated form looks good). Search out less vigorous and more unusual forms of ivy with interesting and attractive leaf shapes.

The Virginia creeper, *Parthenocissus quinquefolia*, which was introduced in the early seventeenth century, is a rampant self-clinger with large glossy green leaves but very inconspicuous flowers. Its main attraction is the stunning autumnal colour of leaves, which turn brilliant red/orange.

Another popular choice for cottage walls and porches is *Wisteria sinensis*. Although not traditional, this large, vigorous climber looks the part. However, you might have to be patient, as it can

This Lincolnshire cottage boasts two climbers on its walls: *Rosa banksiae lutea* on the end south-facing wall, and *Wisteria sinensis* on the longer east-facing wall.

take up to six years before it gets into its stride and starts to flower profusely. Wisteria does best on a sunny wall, and 'correct' pruning helps flowering, ensuring you don't end up with masses of foliage and the odd flower or two!

Often found growing up against the cottage wall which helps support the shrub is Japanese quince (*Chaenomeles japonica*). Although not attaining the height of other climbers, the attractive large red or pink-white flowers blossom on the bare branches in the late winter and early spring, making it a very attractive addition to the garden. Not a natural climber, it can easily be trained to a height of 90cm (3ft). Hardy, easy to prune and liking any aspect, the Japanese quince will appreciate the warmth of a wall.

Cotoneaster and *Pyracantha* (firethorn) aren't climbers as such and should probably be classed as 'wall shrubs' that require some initial support. Both will cover a wall fairly quickly and are generally grown for their highly attractive autumn berries. Cotoneasters range from ground cover varieties through to small trees, some being evergreen, and some also being ideal for hedging. The variety *Cotoneaster rhytidophyllus* is a medium-sized evergreen with attractive, long, pointed leaves on arching stems and berries that turn from orange to red; whereas the variety *Cotoneaster frigidus* 'Cornubia' is a huge shrub with dense clusters of white flowers followed by very large red berries, ultimately reaching 6m (19ft) if allowed to do so.

Pyracanthas are thorny evergreen shrubs which are usually covered in masses of white flowers in early spring, having wonderful autumn berries in colours of red, orange or yellow – which are loved by birds. Their vicious thorns don't make them easy to prune but they will happily grow on a north-facing wall up to a height of 2.5m (8ft).

The stunning feature shrub *Sambucus nigra* 'Black Lace' with delightful contrasting pink umbels.

SHRUBS FOR THE COTTAGE GARDEN

With the exception of the lilac and the rose, the popular and well-known shrubs that are found in most gardens nowadays were never part of traditional cottage gardens. Until the nineteenth and early twentieth centuries shrubs were few and far between. It was during the Victorian period that shrubs began to filter into the cottage gardens of southern counties, but even then, they were generally dismissed as a waste of valuable space unless they had exceptional qualities (scent or winter flowers) that made them an asset to the garden. The huge flood of new plants sent back by plant-hunters from all over the world (particularly China) quickly changed the makeup of the English garden, and eventually shrubs became an integral and essential structural part of all cottage gardens.

There is a massive choice of shrubs available and this often results in gardeners being tempted to buy too many when starting a new garden. Wishing to fill the bare spaces, create some structure and make a low maintenance garden, shrubs seem the obvious choice. However, virtually all shrubs become very large very quickly and soon outgrow their allotted space. They then require constant cutting back or trimming to keep them under control and in the end become 'high maintenance' plants.

For smaller cottage gardens, it is best to have no more than two or three shrubs. Ornamental trees and shrubs, although now viewed as a vital structural element within gardens, should be used carefully in cottage gardens. The cottage garden has always been a glorious mixture of flowers, climbers, trees, herbs and vegetables; and although the style has changed over the course of time, too many modern shrubs will overwhelm the 'cottagey feel' and simply create a 'shrubbery' – not a cottage garden!

Shrubs, however, do offer relatively fast height and structure within a garden and can be used as a background for other plants within a border, particularly if a coloured foliage shrub is chosen. Shrubs offer seasonal interest when nothing much else is in flower, create a natural structure for cottage climbers to scramble up through, can be used to 'green' walls and fences, can possibly be

TIP FOR CREATING SPACE UNDER SHRUBS

In relatively small cottage gardens, the valuable space under shrubs can be utilized once the plant is established (after three to four years). Simply take off some of the shrub's lower branches, which will enable you to underplant with some cottage favourites that require light shade – pulmonarias, vincas, hardy geraniums, epimediums, columbines or lily-of-the-valley.

a stand-alone specimen or feature, or create a partial screen so that the whole garden is not seen all at once.

Do some research and decide what you require in your choice of shrubs; for example, an evergreen shrub, a spring- or late-flowering shrub, a compact or large shrub, a shrub with coloured foliage or one chosen for its colourful late season berries. Consider the position within the border (back, middle or front), aspect and soil situation.

Spring-flowering shrubs

Choisya ternata (Mexican orange blossom)
This medium evergreen shrub which produces fragrant white star-like flowers in April/May has become a popular background plant in recent years. Requiring full sun and a more sheltered position, its glossy mid-green palmate leaves create a contrast for summer climbers. Height 2.5m (8ft).

Forsythia 'Spectabilis'
Possibly the best-known spring flowering shrub. This deciduous shrub became popular in the mid-nineteenth century with an introduction from China by the plant-hunter Robert Fortune. With its brilliant yellow flowers in mid-spring, the shrub is considered the 'wake-up' call after the dull winter. Cut back the shrub after flowering, otherwise it becomes an unruly plant. Height 3m (10ft).

Garrya elliptica (silk tassel bush)
A David Douglas introduction from North America in 1828, this large evergreen shrub became a garden favourite as it produces beautiful long silky tassels when little else is in flower. Particularly attractive trained up against walls, the plant can also be used as a framework for later flowering climbers. Height 4m (13ft).

Kerria japonica 'Pleniflora' (bachelor's buttons)
The bright yellow button-like flowers make a distinctive display in early spring on this tall shrub. It is generally grown up against a wall, fence or shed, due to its long arching stems that require some tying in to help support the plant. Height 2m (6–7ft).

Magnolia stellata (star magnolia)
A slow-growing, medium-sized shrub which has become more popular recently and is ideally suited to the cottage garden. The shrub is covered in large, white, slightly scented 'star-like' flowers in spring, making it an attractive plant for the border or a large pot. Happy in sun or part-shade, it prefers a neutral to acid soil. Height 2–2.4m (6½–8ft).

Prunus incisa 'Kojo No Mai'
This deciduous dwarf cherry is a shrub that has it all! The stems have an unusual zigzag structure and are covered with masses of pink-tinged white flowers in spring before the leaves form. The plant is useful as a specimen in a spring border or even placed in a pot on the patio, and often has a good autumn colour to the leaves. Height 2.5m (8ft).

Ribes sanguineum (flowering currant)
Like the forsythia, this easy-to-establish shrub has been a popular introduction into gardens, arriving from North America in 1826. The hardy deciduous shrub has currant-like leaves and grows in any soil but prefers sun. The variety 'Pulborough Scarlet' has deep red flowers. Height 1.8m (6ft).

Skimmia japonica
A smaller evergreen shrub for light shade positions having leathery foliage and a range of coloured flowered forms (white, red, cream, green). Good for year-round interest, skimmias are just as happy in pots as the ground, and their fragrant flowers are followed by an impressive display of either red or white berries. The variety 'Kew Green' is a particularly attractive variety. Height 0.9–2m (3–6ft).

The useful slow-growing evergreen shrub *Skimmia* 'Kew Green' in a cottage border.

Spiraea 'Arguta' (bridal wreath)

This hardy and easy-to-grow deciduous shrub is an absolute picture in May when the arching stems are literally covered in white flowers. Needing a sunny position, this fast-growing shrub can be hard pruned, which makes it ideal for smaller gardens, as it can be kept in check. Height 2.5m (8ft).

Arching stems of the brilliant white flowers of 'bridal wreath' (*Spiraea* 'Arguta') light up this dark cottage garden corner.

Syringa vulgaris cultivars (lilac)

The lilac has been grown in cottage gardens for centuries and can be classed as a large shrub or small tree. It became immensely popular with cottagers due to the delightful scent on the mauve-purple cone-shaped flowers from late spring to early summer. Height up to 3m (10ft).

Traditional and commonly grown lilac in a cottage garden.

Summer-flowering shrubs

Buddleia davidii (butterfly bush)

Although not introduced until 1890, this butterfly-attracting shrub has become popular in all gardens extremely quickly. Easy to grow, with large conical flower heads in colours ranging from white and pink to purple and deep purple (*B.* 'Black Night'), it is a popular choice for dry sun positions in cottage gardens. The previous year's growth requires cutting back in early spring. Height 2.4m (8ft).

Cistus × purpureus (purple rock rose)

These small evergreen shrubs prefer a full sun position and poor soil. The attractive five-petalled flowers are large and have distinctive dark blotches at the centre. Other forms are available, with white or pink flowers. Height 1m (3ft).

Deutzia species

These deciduous early summer-flowering shrubs don't get the attention they deserve. There is a good range of species and varieties, most having elegant arching stems which are covered with an abundance of fragrant flowers (single and double) ranging from white to dark pink. With no pest or disease problems, and preferring a sunny position, this medium-sized shrub is worth considering for the border – the compact form *Deutzia* 'Strawberry Fields' being an excellent choice. Height 1.2–1.8m (4–6ft).

The compact *Deutzia* 'Lavender Time' which only gets to 1m (3ft) in height, is ideal for small cottage gardens.

Exochorda × macrantha 'The Bride'

This wonderful medium-sized shrub is also known as the 'pearl bush'. It has masses of gorgeous clear white flowers in May/June that light up any garden. Preferring a sunny, well-drained site, it is an ideal shrub for the cottage garden, having an open structure ideal for a late-flowering clematis to climb through. Height 2m (6ft).

Exochorda 'The Bride' in full flower in the front of a Lincolnshire cottage garden.

Hebe species

Like deutzias, the very underrated hebes are not grown enough. There is a vast range of possibilities with these evergreen shrubs, from compact dome-forming varieties through to tall mid-border types. The larger varieties in particular fit in beautifully with cottage gardens, often producing their long brush-like flowers from late summer through to early winter. Attractive to bees and butterflies, their structure is an open invitation for a non-vigorous companion climber to ramble through. Some varieties also have attractive purple or variegated foliage. Height 0.3–2m (1–6ft).

Leycesteria formosa (Himalayan honeysuckle or pheasant berry)

This extremely vigorous deciduous shrub is a good addition to the back of the border for late summer/early autumn colour. It produces very long erect stems which bear hanging racemes of white flowers with red bracts, followed by clusters of purple berries. Height 2.5m (8ft).

Philadelphus (mock orange)

An old favourite, these medium-sized deciduous shrubs are good for the back of the border in sunny positions in retentive soil. Flowering in early summer, their large cupped white flowers are beautifully scented. 'Belle Etoile' is a good variety to source, being more compact than most – height 1.5m (5ft).

Physocarpus (ninebark)

These shrubs are grown, not for the flowers (although they are attractive), but for the beautiful coloured foliage. The red- and purple-leaf varieties are particularly striking and create wonderful foils in borders for surrounding perennials. The leaves themselves are interestingly toothed and if red in colour turn a lovely amber-orange when the sun shines through them. Clusters of white flowers appear in summer, often followed by red berries. Two varieties to look out for are 'Lady in Red' and 'Diabolo'. Height 2.5m (8ft).

Weigela florida

Another Robert Fortune introduction, in 1844, these easy-to-grow and accommodating shrubs give plenty of summer joy, having large funnel-shaped flowers covering the bush in a range of colours depending upon the variety. Doing well in sun or part-shade, they are good bee plants. *Weigela florida* 'Variegata' is a lovely bright foliage form with delicate, large pink flowers that adds light in part-shade positions. Height 1–2m (3–6ft).

The unusual *Weigela florida versicolor* with large pink and white flowers on the one shrub.

Late summer and autumn-flowering shrubs

Caryopteris × *clandonensis* 'Heavenly Blue' (blue spiraea)
This highly attractive dwarf shrub is ideal for the front of borders. It has narrow grey-green aromatic leaves with beautiful mid-blue flowers which bloom continuously from summer into late autumn. This well-known variety was discovered in a garden in Clandon, Surrey. Height 60cm (2ft).

Ceratostigma willmottianum
Another dwarf shrub with stunning blue flowers throughout the autumn. Preferring a sunny position, the green leaves will also turn a rich autumn red before they fall. The first seed was sent to Ellen Willmott from China in 1908, and from this all of today's plants have been raised. Height 60cm (2ft).

The large mophead hydrangea has a range of flower colours, from pink through to blue, due to the rust flaking down off the shed behind (which alters the pH of the soil).

The distinctive and beautiful flowers of a lace-cap hydrangea.

Fuchsia (lady's eardrops)
Hardy fuchsias are informal late-season shrubs that are ideal for mid-border cottage plantings, and although getting fairly tall, can be pruned back hard in the winter/early spring. Given a position in the sun on well-drained soil, fuchsias produce masses of elegant ballerina-looking pendant flowers of two colours (normally pink and purple). The two good varieties are *F*. 'Ricartoonii' and *F*. 'Hawkshead', the former having brilliant red and purple flowers, and the latter white flowers – both having long flowering periods from late summer through to the autumn. Height 1.2–1.5m (4–5ft).

Hydrangea macrophylla
Many cottage gardens had a mophead hydrangea, and they are still highly popular shrubs for borders or pots. There are many new recent introductions of the big round-headed types which generally come in the colour range of pinks, darker pinks and white. The blue-coloured hydrangeas will only remain blue on acid soils, unless of course you take things into your own hands and add a 'bluing' solution to the soil. Also gaining in popularity are the 'lace caps' (with a ring of large petals surrounding a central area of tiny flowers) and 'paniculata' types (having stunning conical heads). Hydrangeas are very thirsty plants, so any planted in pots will need plenty of water regularly. Height 1–2.5m (3–8ft).

Winter-flowering shrubs

Daphne mezereum
This small deciduous shrub, first introduced *c*.1560, has been grown in cottage gardens for centuries due to the wonderfully perfumed flowers that lift the spirits in the month of February. The tubular pink-purple flowers cluster up along the bare stems and are followed by bright red berries nestled in amongst the

Two *Hydrangea* 'Annabelle' have been placed in the cottage border to tie it together.

leaves. *Daphne odora* is more widely grown today, and – like all daphnes – tends to go barer nearer the base of the shrub, with the foliage and flowers seeming to form a top-heavy structure. Underplanting the shrub helps alleviate this bare bottom structural problem. The plant looks good in a spring border or planted in an attractive pot placed near the door, with 'Marginata' being an attractive variegated alternative. Height 1m (3ft).

Jasminum nudiflorum (winter jasmine)

Often flowering from November through to February (when little else is in flower), this medium shrub was quickly accepted into cottage gardens after its introduction in 1844. It has gained a reputation as a wall shrub as it requires some initial support, but once tied in soon takes off and produces bright green stems covered in star-like yellow flowers which can be cut as decoration for the house. Happy in any soil, the shrub will require a good pruning after flowering to promote new long flowering stems for the end of the year. Height 1.5–2.5m (5–8ft).

A winter jasmine in mid-December, adding much needed colour in the garden.

Mahonia aquifolium (Oregon grape)

A go-anywhere, exceedingly tough evergreen shrub that will even tolerate dry deep shade. It has distinctive, large, spiky, glossy foliage that turns an attractive red colour on poor soils, and yellow flowers that cluster above the leaves from late winter through to early spring, brightening up the dull winter days. *Mahonia japonica* from the Far East is a little more refined and prefers a part-shade situation to prosper. Both these mahonias have a somewhat architectural look and are best planted at the back of the border. A particularly good hybrid is *Mahonia* 'Charity' which has more erect, quite outstanding yellow flowers. Height 2.1m (7ft).

Viburnum tinus

This large evergreen shrub needs space, as it grows at a very fast rate, but does provide a solid dark green background at the back of the border, which will give good contrast for summer-flowering plants. The clusters of white flowers (breaking from pink buds) stand out beautifully against the dark glossy foliage and flower from late autumn to early spring. The variety 'Eve Price' is a slightly more compact form, and 'Gwenllian' has smaller, more ovate leaves. These shrubs are worth considering for evergreen hedging or a free-standing shrub having a summer-flowering clematis growing up through it. Height 3m (10ft).

The long, distinctive, yellow flowers of mahonia brighten up the garden on dull winter days.

Viburnum × bodnantense 'Dawn'

This large winter-flowering shrub is a cross that originated in Bodnant Garden, North Wales, in the 1930s. Extremely useful in the cottage garden, the upright structure of bare branches produces highly fragrant clusters of pinkish-white flowers from November through to January. Place the shrub near a path, entrance or arch to make the most of the perfume throughout the winter period, and perhaps grow an annual climber over the plant in the summer. Height 2.5–3m (8–10ft).

Shrubs for autumn and winter foliage colour

Acers (Japanese maples)

The trend towards using these plants in gardens has recently accelerated and is due to their elegant shape, lovely leaf forms, but more than anything else, stunning autumn foliage colours. However, let's be clear, these plants were never grown in cottage gardens and their presence in any garden is distinctively oriental. But if you wish for brilliant autumn colour in a large cottage-style border you could incorporate an acer at the back if you wish. A word of caution though: acers are trees or large shrubs, and although slow growing will eventually take up a great deal of space. To keep the acer a reasonable size you could plant it in a large container as a feature shrub. *Acer palmatum* 'Little Princess' is a lovely small variety which only grows to about 1.5m (5ft) and has leaves that in autumn change to a beautiful yellow inner surrounded by a vivid orange outer margin.

Berberis thunbergii 'Atropurpurea Nana'

This wonderfully compact purple barberry only reaches 60cm (2ft) and is an ideal small shrub for either the cottage border or as a dwarf hedge. It has lovely pale-yellow flowers and red berries; however, the autumnal change to its leaves is nothing short of show stopping!

Cotinus coggygria (smoke bush)

Smoke bushes are either green- or purple-leaved deciduous shrubs with smoky plumes of pinkish flowers in summer. As autumn arrives the leaves change to beautiful vivid colours of reds or oranges before finally dropping. An outstanding variety is *Cotinus* 'Grace'.

The *Acer palmatum* 'Garnet' creates a fabulous contrast within the cottage border and, growing only to approx. 1m (3ft), is ideal for small gardens.

The purple smoke bush makes an eye-catching statement in this cottage garden.

The two rowan trees standing either side of this Scottish cottage gate make a wonderful entrance and also protect the cottage and croft from witches.

TREES FOR THE COTTAGE GARDEN

In the past, cottage gardens didn't have ornamental trees. Fruit and other 'useful' native trees were the only ones deliberately planted in the cottage garden with the exception of the lilac, which was planted near the cottage for its delightful scent. Fruit trees were mainly apples and pears, and only grown in the garden if it was large enough to accommodate them. In Lincolnshire, the back gardens were very long and roughly subdivided into three sections: closest to the cottage was the vegetable patch, followed by a small orchard and then a bean field.

Useful trees also found their way into the cottage garden, or to be more precise, more often in the mixed hedge that enclosed the garden. These highly useful trees might well have been holly, rowan, hazel, spindle, damson or elder. Rowan and holly were grown because they were believed to be 'protective' trees – keeping evil and local witches away! Both trees have vivid red berries, and the colour red was considered a protection. Scottish cottages often had two rowan trees standing sentinel (one either side of the gate) to protect the croft from witches. In England, the holly tree gave the same protection and also provided winter decoration.

In the nineteenth century, ornamental trees started to be planted in middle-class gardens as specimen trees in lawns, with the need to have the newest ornamental tree fuelled by the continual discoveries of plant-hunters. Eventually, as the cottage garden changed from its productive garden to its contemporary cottage style, ornamental trees have become an essential element within the garden.

For today's small cottage garden, large ornamental trees are out of the question, however, there are plenty of suitable small trees now available. Only 'one or two' small trees should be considered for gardens of limited space. Care needs to be taken when choosing a tree for a small garden as it should be required to provide more than just spring blossom. If you have room for just 'one' tree, try to choose one that either has flowers followed by berries, or flowers and a good autumnal colour, or flowers and an interesting bark. Take time and find the right tree for your garden – consider the situation, soil, height and requirements you particularly want (scent, flower, autumn colour).

Table 6.4 lists a number of small trees that are worth considering for small cottage gardens. If you are lucky enough to have a larger garden, you could think about two or three of the suggested trees.

TABLE 6.4: TREES FOR THE COTTAGE GARDEN

Name	Description	Height
Acer griseum	This slow-growing deciduous tree, known as the 'paperbark maple', is generally grown for its hugely attractive peeling papery chestnut-coloured bark, which after peeling back reveals the smooth shiny new red bark beneath. If planted in full sun, the leaves will turn a brilliant red colour in the autumn.	10m (33ft)
Amelanchier lamarckii	This tree would be an excellent choice for any garden, having white blossom in the spring that looks stunning against the young bronze foliage. Deep red berries appear in June, and in the autumn the leaves turn an orange colour. If you require a smaller variety, then either *A.* 'R.J. Hilton' which reaches 4m (13ft) or *A.* × *grandiflora* 'Ballerina' reaches 5m (16ft), could be an option.	10m (33ft)
Arbutus unedo	Known as the 'strawberry tree', this is a slow-growing evergreen with an interesting reddish bark. It bears clusters of white flowers in the autumn, followed by wonderful red fruits. Best on acid soils.	9m (30ft)
Betula utilis var. *jacquemontii*	Renowned for its exceptionally white bark and pyramidal shape, this tree is hugely popular. The ordinary birches are too big for a small garden, but this medium-sized tree is worth thinking about and can be used as a focal point in the garden. *B.* var. *jacquemontii* 'Moonbeam' reaches only approx. 6m (20ft).	15m (49ft)
Corylus avellana	The native hazel has always been a valued cottage tree for its wood and edible nuts, and looks attractive in the early spring with its hanging male catkins. The purple-leaved variety, *C. maxima* 'Purpurea' is particularly striking, and the corkscrew hazel, *C. avellana* 'Contorta' is an eye-catching addition to any garden, and the twisted stems useful for winter decoration.	8m (26ft)
Euonymus europaeus	The 'spindle tree' is another native, and was valued for its hard wood which was used for the shafts of spindles. The insignificant white flowers are followed by stunning pink seed capsules in the autumn, which open to reveal bright orange seeds. The leaves turn a lovely red/orange colour in the autumn.	6m (20ft)
Laburnum anagyroides	The 'golden rain tree' was an early entrant into English gardens (1560) but not commonly grown in cottage gardens. The attractive hanging chains of bright yellow flowers brighten up gardens in the spring, but every part of this tree is poisonous. The best variety is *L. watereri* 'Vossii'.	7m (23ft)
Liquidambar styraciflua	The 'sweet gums' are renowned for their maple-like leaves having a remarkably long period of autumnal colour, usually of oranges and deep reds. Often too large for small gardens, there are one or two medium-sized varieties – *L.* 'Corky' and *L.* 'Stared' being approx. 8m (26ft) after 10 years. However, the compact sweet gum *Liquidambar* 'Gum Ball' only reaches 3m (10ft).	12m (39ft)
Malus sylvestris	The native crab apple is a small deciduous tree that has white flowers followed by distinctive yellow fruits. All crab apples have lovely spring blossom and a great autumn colour to the leaves, making them a terrific year-round tree. *Malus* 'John Downie' and *Malus* × *robusta* 'Red Sentinel' are both heavy fruiting varieties that are ideal for making crab apple jelly.	7m (23ft)
Prunus species	The 'flowering cherries' are a large family of trees that are known for their wonderful spring blossom. Luckily, there are some varieties of flowering cherry that are suitable for small gardens, these being: *Prunus incisa* 'The Bride' *Prunus* 'Accolade' *Prunus* 'Pink Perfection' *Prunus incisa* 'Oshidori'	 4–8m (13–26ft) 4–8m (13–26ft) 3–4.5m (10–15ft) 4m (13ft)
Sorbus aucuparia	The rowan (mountain ash) with its vivid red berries is a traditional cottage tree, that often has remarkable autumn colours. Smaller popular choices are *Sorbus* 'Joseph Rock' which is an upright, yellow-berried variety with clusters of white flowers in the spring, and stunning coloured orange/red leaves in the autumn; and *Sorbus* 'Eastern Promise' which has unusual pink berries in the autumn followed by leaves that turn a stunning red-purple colour. Both attain a height of 4–8m (13–26ft).	8–15m (26–33ft)

The purple hazel makes a lovely individual feature and contrasts well with the *Iris sibirica*.

The small spindle tree *Euonymus alatus* 'Compactus' (burning bush) has the most amazing autumn colour.

The beautiful delicate pink flowers of *Prunus incisa* 'Oshidori'.

The fascinating corkscrew hazel *Corylus avellana* 'Contorta' with lovely male catkins in February.

Prunus incisa 'Oshidori', a stunning early double-flowered form which only reaches approx. 4m (13ft).

Chapter 7

Traditional Features

PATHS

Paths are an essential element within the cottage garden allowing easy movement from one area to another. Paths are there to help keep your feet dry, to avoid treading on the soil and to facilitate the movement of wheelbarrows, mowers and other such equipment. However, for the keen cottage gardener, paths can also take you on a journey around a garden in order to appreciate the flowers in the borders throughout the seasons.

Primary paths should be laid down where you 'need' to go – the garage, shed, washing line or vegetable patch. Practicality of primary paths is most important. These main routes should be wide enough (1m/3ft) to accommodate equipment but also to allow for the cottage plants to spill over the edges in random profusion. All major paths should be constructed of hard landscaping materials (slabs, bricks, concrete) to ensure safe and dry access to all vital areas of the garden throughout the year.

Secondary paths (often non-functional) have a different role to play, perhaps twisting and turning around different parts of the garden, criss-crossing a large island border, taking routes around the back of the vegetable patch, leading into a small orchard, taking you through a specifically created area burgeoning with flowers that can then be admired more closely or leading down to a seat or summerhouse. These paths, with less traffic, can be softer – perhaps grass, gravel or woodchip, or possibly slabs laid in the grass.

The back path of a Lincolnshire cottage garden with the clipped box cone in a pot acting as a vista-closer.

Paths are either straight or curved. In the past, all cottage garden paths tended to be straight, but in today's cottage garden curved paths that disappear behind a large shrub or under an arch add an air of mystery and help enhance the planting schemes. Straight paths should always lead somewhere – down the garden to the shed, the vegetable patch or a summerhouse. They create a strong visual line that leads the eye and the feet. In old cottage gardens, the back-garden path either ran close to the hedge on one side of the garden, or ran straight down the middle of the garden. Straight paths can be enhanced with pergolas, arches, dwarf hedges, repeated pots and vista-closers.

Gardens with central paths can be quartered, as was normal in medieval monastic layouts. The cross paths then create the opportunity for a central feature, whilst the surrounding square paths allow easy access to the whole garden. Quarters can then be subdivided if needed.

Curved paths can be the main path snaking down the garden, but are often better as secondary paths, where they can be deliberately narrower, slowing down movement and allowing the chance to take in the surrounding flower schemes.

Path materials

Cottage garden paths were originally just beaten earth with ashes spread on top, but were gradually improved upon during the nineteenth century when local stone or bricks were used for the main path from the gate to the front door. During the Arts and Crafts garden movement it was stressed that materials used in gardens needed to be local, so that both cottage and garden were

A straight path running down to the back door, wide enough for exuberant cottage plants.

Traditional path running from the cottage in the village of Edensor near Chatsworth House.

Circular stepping stones set into the grass in Rosie Wilson's cottage garden in Cambridge.

Bricks laid in a basketweave pattern between box hedging at Hill Close Gardens, Warwick.

Gently winding grass path in Marian's cottage garden in Colsterworth, Lincolnshire.

in harmony with the surroundings and locality. This is something that might well be considered today.

Any materials discovered in sheds and out-buildings or half-hidden amongst weeds can be used in combination to create a cottagey path. However, whatever materials you decide to use, try not to go for anything too fancy or modern. Old bricks, stone slabs, cobbles, tiles or a mixture of these materials, create a more authentic cottage-garden feel. Good places to search for such materials are reclamation yards or antique shops that deal with old garden materials.

Slabs

Slabs can either be expensive 'proper' stone slabs or cheap alternatives from the local garden centre. Both have pros and cons. Proper stone slabs are exceedingly heavy and thick and once down are not

likely to ever be moved again! Ordinary concrete slabs from DIY or garden centres are easier to lay and come in a range of colours, designs and sizes (square or rectangular) but will require a firm base to sit on to prevent rocking, tilting or any future movement.

Concrete slabs can also be used as stepping-stones through grass areas, adding an informal yet solid route to other parts of the garden; circular slabs work particularly well here.

Bricks

Bricks are a great material for cottage paths with the option of being laid in different interesting patterns (soldier, herringbone, basketweave) and being a lovely warm red colour. They are useful for both primary and secondary paths, and are in general a fairly cheap material.

Cottage plants gloriously spilling over the edge of a wide gravel path.

A path linking two areas in this Lincolnshire cottage garden constructed entirely of materials discovered in the garden (old bricks, cobbles, tiles).

The herringbone patterned path leads into another garden room at The Bridges Garden, Woolpit.

The brick-edged cobbled path ties in beautifully with the cottage style, creating a weed-free route.

Gravel

Gravel is certainly the cheapest material available and provides a loose bright path that feels cottagey. It looks good with an edging, and if used for a major path will require a hardcore base beneath to give a solid path to walk on that doesn't move around under your feet. There is nothing worse than trying to walk through a deep gravel area where the gravel has simply been poured over a matting – it's like trying to walk in treacle! Any gravel should only be 2–3cm (1in) deep but laid over a good firm limestone sub-base of 10–15cm (4–6in) and thumped down with a vibrator plate. This ensures a solid path that will be generally weed free and can easily be raked to maintain its looks.

Gravel has the advantage of coming in a vast range of sizes, shapes and colours. Pea gravel is commonly used but often encourages weed seedlings, and this in turn means time spent hand weeding or the use of chemical sprays (which is not an approach I would endorse). The 'up-side' is that this gravel also gains many plant seedlings that can be potted up to give extra plants to use or give away. Larger gravels (20mm) have fewer weed problems and look extremely attractive, although they are normally more expensive.

Cobbles

A cobbled path is very effective, particularly when wet, as the different coloured cobbles create a fascinating routeway. It is best if the cobbles are cemented in, giving a more solid, weed-free path to walk on. This can be achieved by firstly cementing in some form of edging, then pouring in cement between the two sides, and finally, carefully pushing in the cobbles, which should have only a small area of 'each cobble' showing above the surface of the cement.

Wood chippings

Paths made of wood chippings are ideal for secondary paths in wooded areas of the garden. Use edging to prevent the loss of too much material under the shrubs, and it will require topping up regularly unless the path itself has a fabric matting underneath the chippings. Chippings come in a variety of sizes and colours which can be chosen according to your own garden situation.

Grass

Grass paths are in my opinion one of best solutions for secondary paths. There is nothing better than seeing a neatly mown grass path snaking off around a border or under an arch. Mowing grass paths in large cottage gardens is best achieved with either a petrol or battery mower, as the length of extension cables required for long paths running off into the garden makes electric mowers unsuitable.

Path edgings

Edgings along paths aren't always necessary but often improve the look of a path. Edgings assist in retaining loose path materials such as gravel and wood chippings, reducing the need for continual topping up of materials (which can become costly).

Brick and tile edging

Bricks are a traditional choice, and were often seen 'sunk at an angle' running up either side of the cottage path leading to the front door. However, bricks can also be used lengthways and in an upright manner for edging, being ideal for both straight and curved paths.

Victorian edging tiles (scalloped or scrolled) can still be found if you wish for a little nostalgia, or – if these are too expensive – the modern equivalents of these edgings. These types of tile can simply be dug into the soil alongside a path, and are ideal for straight or curved paths, being excellent for retaining gravel areas and holding soil back. Terracotta floor tiles can also be used as path edgings.

Wooden boards/edging

Long wooden boards are fairly inexpensive and easy to place, but have the major disadvantages of limited life span and being useful only for straight paths. The length of board life can be extended by either painting or preserving before they are positioned. They are really suitable for paths around the vegetable patch or for edging wood chipping paths through shrubby areas. Garden centres now sell wooden edging in rolls which might be worth consideration; these do actually go round bends!

Tiles with their corners pushed into the soil create an unusual yet attractive edging.

Brick edging retaining the gravel in the path with self-set *Verbena bonariensis*.

Concrete edging

Many different designs of concrete edging are available, being both affordable and long lasting. They come in a range of colours and designs, and can either be placed into the soil directly, or, for more permanence, be cemented into place.

Other alternatives

There are other edging materials that could be used – Elizabethans often used shells or stones to edge their 'privy' gardens. Metal edgings are a possibility but are expensive. The green plastic corrugated edging that comes in a roll (often used for lawns) is not suitable, and quickly becomes brittle and breaks apart. In an age when we are now trying to reduce this type of plastic, steer clear of it!

GARDEN STRUCTURES

Simple, rustic structures have always had a place in cottage gardens, possibly being just a plank seat set under a wooden arch to create a resting place near the vegetable patch. Shade has always been valued in the garden, and a shaded (and often scented) retreat or flowery shaded walk has been a vital element since medieval times, when these structures were called arbours, bowers and shaded alleys.

The Elizabethans also considered bowers and shaded walks essential structures, but added ornaments such as sundials, water features and statuary to their gardens. Eventually, the Arts and Crafts garden movement of the late nineteenth century gathered together and used these earlier features as formal structural elements within the design, which were then informalized by the cottage-style planting schemes. A typical Arts and Crafts garden would probably include a pergola, sundial, various pots and urns, arches, seats and a summerhouse. The purpose of these architectural elements was to link the house and garden, add height,

Concrete rope-top edging used to separate the cottage borders from the gravel path.

climbing structures for plants, create a year-round framework to the garden, give rests and retreats within the garden and perhaps even an interesting surprise (a beautifully planted pot just around the corner).

Nowadays, these structures and features have become an integral part of the cottage garden, and although the emphasis is still very much on flowers, with outdoor spaces being considered more for entertainment and enjoyment, garden furniture and features have become ever more important within gardens.

Pergolas

A pergola might sound as though it should be in a stately home rather than a cottage garden, but in fact, doesn't need to be anything like the vast structures that Edwin Lutyens provided for Gertrude Jekyll's climbers. A pergola is simply an open framework structure over which plants can climb and create a shaded walk for hot summer days – what could be more appropriate for those cottage climbers if you have the space?

A simple but strong pergola in a cottage garden is a structure with many possibilities, and once covered with scented roses, honeysuckles or clematis will give the garden quite a different feel. A pergola immediately gives year-round structural height and creates a feature that can change as the seasons pass. Shadows forming on the ground as the sun moves round are in themselves of interest, but it is the climbers that provide the main source of enjoyment, and choosing a varied selection is very satisfying.

As a structural feature, a pergola can be attached to the house to lead you out into the garden and simultaneously create a shaded outdoor entertaining area for meals or drinks on warm summer evenings. Alternatively, the pergola could be used as a flowery shaded tunnel leading around a particular part of the garden, or be constructed up against a wall to create a frame for climbing plants and a shaded seating area. Another possibility would be to use a pergola to help subdivide the garden instead of using hedging or trellis.

Materials for pergolas can vary. If you wish to be cottagey, a rustic pergola formed of wooden poles would be ideal. But even if you buy an 'off-the-shelf' wooden pergola, once the plants scramble over it, it'll look as almost as good. Metal pergolas create a more elegant look, whereas wooden ones seem more homely and honest in a cottage garden, but the choice is entirely yours.

When planting up pergolas, climbing and rambling roses, honeysuckles and clematis spring to mind and are best suited to the cottage style. However, there are other options, such as wisteria or annual climbers. For a pergola dividing the garden from the vegetable patch, you might also consider growing runner beans or squashes.

Arches

Traditionally, arches were constructed over the gate of the cottage garden that opened onto the path leading to the front door. They took up no space within the garden, yet created a flowery approach and allowed the cottager to grow scented climbers. The same applies today, this feature taking up little or no space in a small garden but creating height and structural support that offers the opportunity for climbers. An arch also acts like a picture frame, enabling you to engineer a view to be seen to its best advantage, whether that be into the garden itself, or from one area of the garden into another. An arch is a welcoming green door that is inviting you to go through to see what delights lie beyond; it provides a link between two different areas and acts as a focal point.

For arches, it's best to source non-vigorous climbers that will give a good display of flowers and scent without pulling the structure down or making it impossible to walk through. A smaller climbing rose or a later flowering clematis are ideal choices for an arch.

A rustic pergola linking two areas within a cottage garden and providing a frame for climbers.

Pergola with a vigorous rambling rose cascading over the structure.

A traditional rose arch positioned over the cottage garden gate.

This rustic arch with the lovely climbing rose looks perfect in Wild Rose Cottage, Lode.

This intricate black metal arch is beautifully informalized by the perennial pea and the clematis.

An arch with trellis sides linking two garden rooms and making a good framework for climbers.

Wooden arches tie in wonderfully with cottage gardens, but metal alternatives can look more elegant, being lighter in structure and coming in a greater range of designs. The arch doesn't need to be an 'arch' design as such, either; alternative available designs include arches that have straight wooden poles across the top (squaring them off) and others that form a triangle at the top. All types will look just as good when the climbers get going and cover the structure. The style is a purely aesthetic thing!

Arches can be stand-alone structures at the start of a path, or as a feature half-way down a path; or they can form an entrance in a stretch of hedge or trellising that creates a subdivision within the garden. To emphasize an arch as an entrance, two pots can be placed on either side.

Arbours

An arbour is an open trellised structure, with neither the sides nor roof being solid, but instead, designed for climbers to clothe it totally, so as to create a hidden seated retreat for shelter and shade. An arbour in a cottage garden can be positioned away from the house either at the end or in the middle of the garden. It creates a shaded retreat where you can take a break from the weeding, reflect on the day's work or allow visitors to rest awhile and admire your garden.

An arbour fills two criteria – being both a useful seating space and a feature within the garden. It could be quite a simple structure, perhaps just a wooden seat with trellised sides and wooden poles across the top, or possibly something more elaborate (perhaps in metal).

Shakespeare points out that in his time all arbours were covered with scented climbers, and this is still the best and most obvious choice for cottage gardens. Traditionally roses and honeysuckles were used; however, clematis is another excellent climber for arbours, particularly if the right variety is chosen that has both scent and a long flowering period.

GARDEN ORNAMENTS

Garden ornaments are an 'added touch' that bring some individualism to the cottage garden and, if placed correctly, help visitors to focus in on a particular planting scheme or part of the garden. Garden ornaments include statues, sundials, bird baths, urns, butler's sinks, chimney pots and even dolly tubs. The secret is

A hop-covered arbour is tucked away at the bottom of this narrow Cambridge cottage garden.

The urn on a plinth surrounded by alliums acts as an eye-catcher in the gravel garden.

The urn at the end of variegated clipped box hedges acts as wonderful vista-closer.

The decorative urn acts as a focal point and draws attention to the cottagey planting of ferns, epimediums, columbines and dicentra.

to choose ornaments that tie in and don't look out of place with the cottage garden style. Many ornaments can either be used as a stand-alone feature or be planted up with complementary foliage or flowers to create an eye-catcher within the garden.

Sundials were a vital feature in the gardens of Tudor and Elizabethan manor houses and often formed the central feature at the cross-point of the quartered garden, back then being not only a decorative feature but a tool to tell the time. Towards the end of the nineteenth century, the Arts and Crafts garden movement re-introduced the sundial as a prominent feature within the garden, as it tied in with the style they were aiming to create. I doubt sundials were ever part of the traditional cottage garden, as they were an expensive showcase piece for those with money.

More at home in the cottage garden is the bird bath, which is particularly useful as a centrepiece in small front gardens of cottages. An important aspect of all cottage gardens is to encourage wildlife, and a bird bath will of course encourage birds into the garden. Simple designs in stone (or concrete) work best.

Statues can be a bit tricky! There is now a vast array of statuary on offer at garden centres and nurseries, but choose carefully: a Greek goddess with her arms lopped off doesn't sit right in a cottage garden; neither do concrete unicorns, lions, Chinese warriors and other such-like churned out pieces. If you must have a statue, then choose an appropriate metal or stone statue that can be partially tucked away in amongst the foliage.

My own favourite ornament is the classic beehive. Half-hidden amongst plants, a beehive makes a lovely focal point, and being painted white can be used to advantage as a contrast for darker flowers. It also makes an ideal focal point within vegetable and herb gardens.

There are many other objects which could be considered for ornamentation, including old urns, galvanized wash tubs, old wheelbarrows, metal watering cans and old animal troughs. Even an old tin bath can be converted into a feature, perhaps turning it on end and placing a plank inside to create an unusual feature seat within the garden. Ornaments are extremely useful as incidental elements of surprise within a cottage garden, and if small enough can be moved around so as to create different scenes in the garden as the season changes.

Eye-catchers and vista-closers

Certain ornaments make excellent eye-catchers or vista-closers. An 'eye-catcher' is an object placed in the garden as a focal point to gain attention and draw the eye, but also forming a decorative feature. Urns, sundials, beehives, or even a modern piece of art, can be used in this respect. Depending on the situation and requirement, an eye-catcher can be placed in the border, on a gravel area, at cross-paths or in front of a wall.

In a garden, a 'vista-closer' is an object that ends a long straight view down a path. By placing an ornament or feature at the end of a path, you are effectively drawing the eye (and the feet) down the path. Placing an arch or a pergola over the path running down to the vista-closer creates an even better picture, as these structures form a frame that defines the view. Alternatively, the vista can be enhanced by a continuous formal hedge on either side (possibly box or yew) or perhaps a series of repeated box balls. Tall urns are probably the most effective vista-closers, although ornaments are not the only objects that can work. A seat, an arbour, a piece of topiary or even an attractive summerhouse, can all be used to create a vista-closer.

In cottage gardens, make sure vista-closers are in keeping with the feel of the garden. A Greek temple, Greek statue or stone dragon will not look right. Something simple that won't detract but actually complements the cottage planting is what is required.

A wooden bench in a cottage garden with the background provided by a thalictrum, an obelisk with clematis and a dark-leaved physocarpus.

The simple wooden seat underneath this homemade structure creates a lovely shady retreat.

This metal and wooden slatted seat fits in well with the cottage-style planting surrounding it.

SEATS

A seat or a simple wooden bench was often part of the traditional cottage garden. Generally placed by a door, they were left out all year as a permanent place to sit and rest awhile between gardening work, or for the older members of the cottager's family to watch village life pass by.

A seat is vital in a cottage garden. It's a place to take a break from the weeding, appreciate your own garden and give somewhere for family and friends to sit when they visit.

Seats create focal points or features within the cottage garden in addition to being a piece of furniture to sit and have a cup of tea on. With this in mind, their position needs to be thought about carefully. Do you wish for a shady retreat, a sunny spot, a seat to take in a particular view of the garden, a seat to look outwards beyond the garden to a fine view, a seat for a morning cuppa or a seat placed to catch the last rays of the evening sun? If you are lucky enough to have a large cottage garden, you'll be able to have more than one seat.

Seats in a cottage garden should be permanent features, as opposed to a table and chairs set for outside dining which will need to be stored over winter in a shed or garage. A permanent seat will be a vital contribution to the aesthetics of the cottage garden, and therefore the design is important. In terms of material, wood is probably most suitable, being the common material used in the old cottage gardens. Then comes the question – to paint or not to paint? Both plain wood and painted seats look attractive, so this will be entirely your decision. If you have other features such as a gate and wooden planter that need painting, then paint the seat, gate and planter the same colour, as this will help unify the garden. Of course, there is nothing to say a 'metal and wooden slatted seat' isn't just as good as a wooden one; it is the placing of the seat, and in particular, the planting around the seat, that actually creates the cottagey feel.

When siting your seat, place it on a paved or gravel area to help with its permanence. Seats on lawns require continual moving around to enable the lawn to be mowed and could sink into the lawn during wet periods of weather, so it's generally best to avoid this positioning. Seats placed against a south-facing wall are ideal for late evening relaxation, as the wall soaks up the warmth of the sun during the day and then releases the heat in the evening. Many gardeners like to have a seat in the shade to sit on during the hottest part of the day in summer, in which case an enclosed seat or arbour is the answer.

Seats designed around (under) large fruit trees work exceptionally well and have a charm that lures visitors to them. You could either design and build your own wooden one or buy a circular metal one (which normally comes in two halves). If your tree is on the edge of the garden, your seat needn't totally encircle it, but could instead be semi-circular in design.

POTS AND CONTAINERS

Many old cottage gardens had a few terracotta pots, particularly for the deep cottage windowsills, where a selection of their favourite scented plants or florist flowers were frequently grown. Pots and containers used in today's cottage garden serve many purposes – some simply for ornamental use to create a focal point in the garden, some for herbs by the back kitchen door, some for plants that require specialist soil conditions (acid lovers), some for seasonal displays, some for tender plants that require protection over winter and some for vivid displays of annuals by the front door or on the patio.

Pots and containers, whether planted up or left empty, are in reality another form of garden ornament. They should be carefully positioned to create a focal point within the garden or on the patio or terrace. In some cases, the decorative pot itself is the focus; but in other cases, the focus will be the vibrant planting arrangement. A single pot or container might well constitute the required feature but at other times an attractively grouped collection of pots can create the desired effect.

In general, pots are used to contain either a specimen plant or varied display, however, an empty ornamental pot or urn does have a role to play within the garden as a focal point or feature. Often more decoratively designed pots are used as eye-catchers to bring a particular area within a border into sharp focus or emphasize a delightful grouping of flowers.

In traditional cottage gardens the only pots used were terracotta as stone urns used on big estates were far too expensive for cottagers. Terracotta remained the popular choice up until the 1950s and therefore seems the most appropriate type to be used for modern cottage gardens. There are, however, other options. Wooden planters are fairly cheap to buy (sometimes flat-packed), they last a reasonable amount of time and can be painted to tie in with the garden design. An advantage of large wooden planters is that they are lighter than stone or terracotta. During the great European fashion for orangeries, the white painted wooden planter was considered the best way to grow and display the clipped orange trees, and gave rise to the wonderful Versailles tub. Even lighter than wood, is of course, plastic. Plastic pots are used universally for 'point of sale' plants, but larger more decorative plastic pots are also available for planting up. From a distance these can fool you

An effectively planted pot of a dark-leaved heuchera and *Allium cristophii*.

into believing they are real terracotta pots and have the advantage of being exceedingly light and therefore very much easier to move around. Albeit easier to handle, they are plastic, and with plastic pollution very much on everyone's mind, it is surely better to stick to terracotta pots and add 'pot wheels' to aid movement.

When it comes to pots, size matters! Larger pots are a far better option than small ones as they require less watering and keep the roots healthier. With a large pot there is a greater volume of compost but less surface area to dry out, whereas in small pots, the volume of compost is smaller but the surface area greater. The result is that smaller pots dry out extremely quickly during hot spells and require watering continually (sometimes two or three times a day).

Any plants in pots will require the right compost and regular feeding to keep them healthy and promote flowering. Feeding is something many people forget. They wrongly assume that once the plant is placed in the pot it will look after itself. The compost will of course have some food incorporated into it, but once this has been taken up, the plant will start to suffer. There are very few plants that will thrive on neglect in pots; most require some attention. Using the right compost is vital.

Frost can be problem. It is always worth checking the terracotta pots you purchase are frost proof, otherwise you could be making an expensive mistake. Ones produced in Britain are far better and usually guaranteed frost-proof. During a harsh winter the sides of the pots will get exceedingly cold and affect the roots up against the inside of the pot, causing damage to the plant. Insulating the pot before putting the compost in and planting up is a good idea, particularly in really cold areas of the country. I use bubble plastic (from parcels) which I then wrap around the inside of the pot which provides insulation.

Designing with pots

Pots are hugely versatile and give the cottage gardener many options. They are not purely for show-casing annuals throughout the summer/autumn months. If you have a chalky soil, a pot will enable you to grow plants that prefer an acid soil; and if you have a heavy clay soil it will give you the option of growing herbs and plants that enjoy a light, well-drained soil. You could possibly grow tender or more exotic plants in pots that need to be taken in and protected over the winter. If, like many people, you have a small cottage garden but wish to grow a specimen shrub, planting it in a pot helps to keep it smaller. Of course, you can move a pot around the garden and create a different sort of effect with varying planting schemes.

Grouping pots together makes a very effective feature within the garden, especially if displayed upon a paved or gravelled area. A group of pots by the front or back door works well and creates an attractive entrance feature. Pots grouped close to a door could simply be a mixture of lovely seasonal annuals and bulbs, or alternatively, a group of herbs in pots useful for the kitchen. When grouping pots together always try to have an odd number of pots as it seems to give a better effect. A group of three is highly effective but you can have far more! Make sure the pots are all different shapes, sizes and heights when grouping, as it

A group of pots in the corner of a small garden being used for acid-loving shrubs, perennials and herbs.

gives a better display, and try to mix some plain pots with some decorative pots.

If you're using a tall urn (or a chimney pot) whether singly or as part of a group, try to use plants that cascade down over the side. Never use tall perennials in a very tall urn as they look absurd. Tall perennials are better suited to large, wide pots.

A good-sized feature pot can be planted in a variety of ways. It could have a specimen shrub or small tree to provide spring flowers and autumn colour, a 'wow' summer display of annuals, a large textured-leaf perennial or an obelisk planted with a climber. A single display pot is highly useful as a vista-closer or a feature pot within a border.

Pots need not only be used as single features; the same design of pot can be repeated within a garden to either create movement

Two pots with clipped box balls create a formal statement at the end of the path.

A tall urn used as a focal point for linking brick circles in The Bridges Garden, Woolpit, Suffolk.

Two old chimney pots act as an entrance and help to distinguish between two garden rooms.

or help define an area or room. If you have a squared area and place four identical pots, one at each corner of the square, the effect of the pots will be to tie this area together and define the space. It makes the area (garden room) whole and lifts it out of the ordinary. If you wish to create the effect of movement down a straight path, which will assist in drawing the eye down to the end, you could place pairs of identical pots down along both sides (with or without planting). It is a tried-and-tested method that works particularly well under pergolas. To emphasize the movement of the pots even more, you might like to plant clipped box balls or spirals within the pots, as this will ensure evergreen structure throughout the year.

'Hot pots' are pots planted up with vivid flowers in colours of yellow, orange and red. These 'hot' colours stand out, create impact and draw attention to themselves. Place 'hot pots' in specific spots in the garden where they look their best but don't disrupt the flow of borders. They look stunning placed either side of front doors, drawing the eye to the entrance; or used to create warmth and light if placed in a shady corner or dull spot within the garden.

The right plants for pots

Some plants are better suited to pots than others. Herbs are a good example, as in general, they can be planted in pots and pretty much be left to their own devices, requiring very little in the way of watering. Herbs love free-draining soil, so ensure the pot has drainage holes, and put plenty of broken crocks in the bottom before planting. Herbs also require sun, so place the pots in a full sun position if possible. A group of pots with different culinary herbs for the kitchen is highly useful and extremely pleasing. You could have some permanent pots of lavender, thyme, origanum, sage and rosemary; and then smaller pots of annuals, such as basil, parsley and coriander. Mint can also be grown in a pot, in fact, it's probably better planted in a pot to prevent it from taking over the whole garden; however, it prefers a slightly shady position rather than full sun and needs to be kept moist.

If you're not blessed with an acid soil, but desperately wish for a rhododendron or blueberry bush, then you'll have no other choice but to use pots. Any acid lovers can be contained using an ericaceous compost, but be aware you may need to re-pot a large shrub four or five years later and in the meantime feed regularly. The advantage of planting acid lovers in pots is that the pot can be placed in the position within the garden that best benefits the plant; for instance, the correct aspect and right amount of sun or shade – as most ericaceous plants dislike direct sunlight. As well as rhododendrons and azaleas being ideal for pots, other acid lovers that make good pot plants include camellias, *Pieris*

This fern stands out brilliantly against its black pot and does well in the cool, shady corner.

japonica, Japanese maples, magnolias, *Calluna vulgaris* (heather) and *Kalmia latifolia*.

One plant that seems ready-made for pots is the hosta. Grown for their exceedingly attractive foliage, the big ribbed or variegated heart-shaped leaves contrast well with large red terracotta pots. A group of hostas in pots can look terrific in semi-shade positions or placed down the dingy side passage of the house. Easy to grow, they are generally low maintenance and have good flowering stems in spring. Their only problem is slug damage, but a good amount of sharp gravel around the top of the pot after planting helps. And if this doesn't solve the problem, then try beer traps (real ale is best) or repeated sprays of garlic water.

Ferns also look the part in pots, with their wonderful feathery leaves arching over the sides, and will be an excellent choice for a really shady corner in the garden or behind the house, as they require very little light to survive. You could simply have one large spectacular fern in a pot, or alternatively, place a fern in combination with other shade-loving plants, such as epimediums, brunneras, tiarellas, hostas or *Alchemilla mollis*. Another possibility is to have three different types of fern together in one pot.

Clipped evergreens in pots will give you year-round structure. Box balls are extremely popular and relatively cheap nowadays, and will make a definitive formal statement if used in pots either side of a doorway or archway, or at the four corners of a flower bed or garden area. A formal box ball in a pot can be juxtaposed with loose cottage planting up against and around the base of the pot. Other clipped topiary shapes such as spirals, pyramids, pillars, and even cubes, also look great in pots.

Alpines are specialist plants that can be best displayed in large, shallow pots either on a paved or gravel area. Troughs and shallow pots of alpines look best grouped together informally, and being difficult to admire down near the ground will benefit from being placed on a stand so as to allow the plants to be seen easily and aid any work that is required.

One particular alpine that became a favourite florist flower of cottagers in the north of Britain is the auricula. These specialist alpines require a lot of attention and an extremely careful watering regime which was the primary reason these beautiful show plants were grown in terracotta pots. The traditional pots were all of a uniform design and size for show purposes and often displayed in lines on wooden shelving or in an 'auricula theatre'.

There are two plants that were traditionally grown in pots from the medieval period onwards: the lily and the carnation. Care and attention would have been lavished on these beautiful and very expensive show plants, with the lily being considered the only equal to the rose. Placing these plants in pots meant they could be admired at all times and be a focal point within the garden. Often, either carpenter's work or hazel sticks were pushed elegantly around the plants to hold up their long stems and graceful flowers. Although these two flowers seem to have fallen out of favour somewhat, they still look their absolute best in pots rather than jostling with other flowers in the borders.

If you wish for low-maintenance pots, then you need to choose plants that actually thrive on neglect and require very little in the way of watering. Certain plants pretty much look after themselves. These include most Mediterranean plants, and particularly those with silver leaves, which is a result of the tiny hairs on the leaves which reflect the sun's rays and help slow evaporation. The best low-maintenance pots for hot, sunny positions will therefore include lavenders, santolinas, sages and lamb's ears (*Stachys byzantina*).

Further plants needing very little attention and watering include: cistus, rosemary, agapanthus, sedum, Russian sage (*Perovskia atriplicifolia*), the Mexican daisy (*Erigeron karvinskianus*) and the perennial wallflower (*Erysimum*). The perennial wallflowers aren't really perennial, they are short lived, but for sheer flower power are worth putting in pots – *Erysimum* 'Bowles's Mauve' being a good choice. Scented pelargoniums which are already widely grown in pots throughout the summer are also extremely drought tolerant, and will happily continue to give pleasure for a very long period with very little attention.

Seasonal pots

Seasonal pots are probably the most frequently planted style of pot used for gardens, patios, terraces and front doors. In spring, bulbs are usually the preferred choice for pots, with tulips being the fashionable bulb of choice. Tulips have long been admired and grown in pots, and what could be better than to have pots of tulips either side of the front door, or a group of different sized pots of tulips on the back terrace or patio. Although tulips are possibly the most fashionable bulb, there are others worth considering for

pots, including daffodils, hyacinths, dwarf iris, crocus and muscari (grape hyacinth).

Once spring bulbs are finished the pot will look tatty and will require replanting with summer bedding or annuals. A good method for making sure you don't compromise the look of a decorative pot, is to use interchangeable plastic pots that can be easily lifted in and out of the main terracotta display pot. This enables you to simply take out the plastic inner pot of spring bulbs when they are finished, and swap it for another planted pot of the summer bedding. This will maintain the focal point without the distress of having to look at a pot of unsightly foliage! Once the summer bedding pot is coming to an end, this can then be swapped again with another prepared pot of winter pansies or a decorative selection of winter foliage plants.

Other containers

There are many different types of container that can be planted up apart from usual terracotta pots. In the past cottagers would use any available container once its original purpose was no longer possible. Metal buckets and wash tubs after being thrown out were ideal candidates for re-purposing as containers for plants. Used wooden barrels could be cut in half and become plant holders for herbs or plants that were rather more invasive.

Objects that once had a use in the old cottages or gardens add an air of authenticity. Old stone troughs, galvanized buckets, circular pig feeding troughs, butler's sinks and other containers (previously mentioned) can all be planted up and add a kind of cottage quirkiness. Be innovative, and make use of old objects to create interesting focal points within the garden.

Window boxes are immensely popular nowadays, particularly in towns and cities where space is limited. It is doubtful that window boxes were used in old cottage gardens, as terracotta pots were normally placed on the wide sills. However, they are ideally suited to the deep outer sills of cottages and houses and can create that wonderfully exuberant cottage-style feeling. For gardens with little space, they are a must, creating extra planting space and ensuring a long flowering display that frames the window. There are all kinds of options for window boxes: a spring flowering display with bulbs, a box full of herbs for culinary use, a seasonal summer display with annuals or a more permanent low-maintenance display (common houseleeks could be an option). Even a vegetable/salad type window box with frilly lettuces at the front can look attractive, and additionally, provide produce for the kitchen. The most common window boxes are those full of bright summer bedding and annuals (pelargoniums and the like) which should always include some cascading plants such as lobelias or petunias.

A balanced group of seasonally filled spring pots (tulips, daffodils, hyacinths, muscari and dark blue violas) outside the entrance to the walled garden at Kelmarsh Hall, Northamptonshire.

A group of hanging baskets delightfully placed in an old apple tree.

Cottage gardens don't generally have hanging baskets, as their intrusive gaudy colours scream for attention and detract from the overall picture of the garden. But perhaps there is a place, if carefully selected, where these suspended containers can be used to great effect. In small cottage gardens where space is at a premium they could be suspended from a pergola or an arch.

Neither are hanging baskets required to be a composition of brightly-coloured bedding! Perhaps something more subdued, like a basket of ferns or a simple basket of the lovely *Erigeron karvinskianus*. And perhaps for the winter, a delightful hanging basket of a particular viola.

Many years ago, I came across a group of baskets hung in an old apple tree half-way down a cottage garden. These baskets filled that gap between the ground and the canopy of the tree and made it look as though the tree itself was dripping with hanging fuchsias – wonderful!

An interesting group of rescued galvanized containers, all planted with herbs.

Appendix I:
Gardens to Visit

Historical gardens

Weald & Downland Living Museum

Town Lane, Singleton, Chichester, West Sussex PO18 0EU

An open-air museum showcasing cottages and houses and their gardens from the south-east region of the country, from medieval through to the nineteenth century.

Cressing Temple Barns

Witham Road, Cressing, Braintree, Essex CM77 8PD

Grade I listed Barley and Wheat Barns with a recent recreated Tudor walled garden with period features, flowers and herbs.

Hill Close Gardens

Bread and Meat Close, Warwick CV34 6HF

Grade II listed restored Victorian gardens which provided both produce and pleasure for the shopkeepers in the town who didn't have gardens attached to their premises.

Hill Top (National Trust)

Near Sawrey, Hawkshead, Ambleside, Cumbria LA22 0LF

Small farmhouse cottage garden that belonged to Beatrix Potter, full of old cottage flowers, herbs and vegetables.

Thomas Hardy's Cottage and Garden (National Trust)

Higher Bockhampton, near Dorchester, Dorset DT2 8QJ

A thatched cottage enclosed in woodland with a recreated romantic cottage garden packed with roses and traditional cottage flowers.

Anne Hathaway's Cottage

22 Cottage Lane, Shottery, Stratford-upon-Avon, Warwickshire CV37 9HH

Large cottage garden attached to the Tudor farmhouse, which has been recreated in a romantic cottage style.

Dove Cottage

Town End, Grasmere, Cumbria LA22 9SH

Home of William and Dorothy Wordsworth, the cottage-style garden has been restored as a semi-wild garden.

Alfriston Clergy House (National Trust)

The Tye, Alfriston, Polegate, East Sussex BN26 5TL

Grade II fifteenth-century thatched cottage, with front cottage garden crammed with traditional flowers, small orchard at the side and lawned terraced garden at the rear.

Large gardens in the cottage style

Sissinghurst Castle Garden (National Trust)

Biddenden Road, Cranbrook, Kent TN17 2AB

The famous garden of Harold Nicholson and Vita Sackville-West has a formal layout subdivided into rooms, each being treated differently. Vita created sumptuous cottage-style plantings with old-fashioned roses and traditional cottage perennials. The White Garden is particularly stunning.

Coton Manor Garden & Plant Nursery

Coton, near Guilsborough, Northamptonshire NN6 8RQ

Designed in the 1920s, these stunning gardens have a series of rooms and water features, with lovely cottage-style herbaceous borders, some of which are colour-schemed. It has charm in abundance and a wonderful nursery full of unusual plants.

Elton Hall and Gardens

Elton Hall, near Peterborough, Cambridgeshire PE8 6SH

The gardens date back to the 1670s and have been developed at different periods. The result is a formal Arts and Crafts style garden with various rooms each carefully designed with exceptional planting schemes.

Kelmarsh Hall and Gardens

Main Road, Kelmarsh, near Kettering, Northamptonshire NN6 9LY

The gardens are designed around the unusual triangular walled kitchen garden. Norah Lindsay, the great colourist, was called in to add loose cottage-style borders, a rose garden and a long herbaceous border. Incredible spring displays make this garden a must-see early in the year.

Helmingham Hall Gardens

Helmingham Park, near Stowmarket, Suffolk IP14 6EF

The early sixteenth-century moated hall is surrounded by glorious gardens which have recently been redesigned, and include an old walled kitchen garden with vegetables, herbs and flowers, and a central double herbaceous border. Unusual and wonderful plant combinations shine throughout the garden.

Parcevall Hall Gardens

Skyreholme, near Appletreewick, North Yorkshire BD23 6DE

A wonderful example of an Arts and Crafts garden in a spectacular setting. The terraced rooms and 'red borders' are particularly well designed, with a good use of green structure and harmonious colour schemes.

Stillingfleet Lodge Gardens and Plant Nursery

Stewart Lane, Stillingfleet, near York YO19 6HP

A garden of different rooms, but very much a cottage garden with the emphasis on traditional cottage plants and wildlife. Wonderful borders with much to admire and plenty of planting ideas to take away.

East Lambrook Manor Gardens and Plant Nursery

East Lambrook, South Petherton, Somerset TA13 5HH

The beautiful cottage garden of Margery Fish, which is packed with stunning plant combinations and treasures. The very epitome of a cottage garden, full of traditional cottage plants spilling over paths in effortless profusion.

Barnsdale Gardens and Plant Nursery

Barnsdale Avenue, Exton, Oakham, Rutland LE15 8AH

Barnsdale has a series of designed gardens dotted across an 8-acre site. Many of these gardens were created by Geoff Hamilton for the BBC *Gardeners' World* programmes, two of which were specifically designed as cottage gardens – 'The Artisan's Cottage Garden' and 'The Gentleman's Cottage Garden'.

Beth Chatto's Plants & Gardens

Elmstead Market, Clacton Road, Elmstead, Colchester, Essex CO7 7DB

Fabulous gardens designed by the renowned plantswoman Beth Chatto. The gardens include different areas and the plants most suited to these particular areas – the Dry Garden, the Damp Garden, the Woodland Garden, the Reservoir Garden, Long Shade Walk and the Gravel Garden. Excellent nursery.

Bluebell Cottage Gardens and Nursery

Lodge Lane, Warrington, Cheshire WA4 4HP

The gardens surround the cottage and have been designed as a series of rooms in the cottage garden style, providing year-round interest, and focusing on plant associations and wildlife.

Small cottage gardens

The Cottage Garden in Birmingham Botanic Gardens

Westbourne Road, Edgbaston, Birmingham B15 3TR

Behind the children's playground is the most magical cottage garden, which is wrapped around an old lodge built in 1847. The garden delightfully overflows with seasonal traditional cottage flowers.

The Mill Garden

55 Mill Street, Warwick CV34 4HB

Lying alongside the banks of the River Avon and just a stone's throw from Warwick Castle, the small cottage garden is full of surprises and stunning plant combinations. Combine your visit with Hill Close Gardens, Warwick.

Appendix II:
List of Plants for Dry Sun

Acanthus – *longifolius* and *spinosa* (both small varieties)
Achillea – 'Forncett Fletton' and *sibirica* 'Love Parade'
Agapanthus
Allium* – *senescens*, *cristophii*, 'Purple Sensation', *schoenoprasum* (giant chives)
Anthemis – 'E.C. Buxton' and 'Sauce Hollandaise'

Artemisia* – *vallesiaca*, *vulgaris* 'Cragg Barber Eye', *douglasiana* 'Valerie Finnis', 'Powis Castle', 'Filigree Queen', 'Oriental Limelight'
Calamintha* – *nepetoides* 'Blue Cloud'
Centaurea* – *nigra* subsp. *rivularis*, *cheiranthifolia*, *nervosa uniflora*, *dealbata* 'Steenbergii', *hypoleuca* 'John Coutts', *bella* (ground cover)
Centranthus – valerian

Cephalaria – giant scabious
Convolvulus – *tenuissimus* (creeping, silver leaves, pink flowers) and *cneorum*
Diascia – *rigescens* and 'Lilac Belle'
Dierama – *igneum* (smaller form, delicate pink flowers)
Echinops – *ritro*
Erigeron* – *karvinskianus* (long flowering period) and 'Schneewittchen'

*Eryngium** – *variifolium, bourgatii, tripartitum*

*Euphorbia** – *myrsinites, polychroma* – NOT for use in gardens with children

Geranium – *renardii* varieties

Helianthemum – rock roses

Iris (bearded) – love to have their rhizomes baked

Knautia macedonica – very dark scabious-like flower with very long flowering period

Lavandula – 'Hidcote', 'Munstead Dwarf', 'Old English' and many more

Lupinus versicolor – low, spreading lupin with silvery foliage

Lychnis coronaria – Oculata Group

*Nepeta** – *nervosa*, 'Dawn to Dusk', 'Six Hills Giant', 'Souvenir d'André Chaudron'

*Origanum** – 'Rosenkuppel', *laevigatum*, 'Dingle Fairy'

*Osteospermum** – hardy ones!

Penstemon – 'Pink Endurance', 'MacPenny's Pink', 'Claire de Moore'

Perovskia – 'Blue Spires' is the best variety

Rosmarinus

*Salvia** – *sylvestris* 'Superba', *sylvestris* 'Rose Queen', *nemorosa* 'Ostfriesland', *nemorosa* 'Plumosa', 'May Night', *sclarea* var. *turkestanica*, 'Berggarten', *verticillata* 'Purple Rain', *uliginosa* (late-flowering), *guaraniitica* 'Blue Enigma'

Santolina – *chamaecyparissus* and *virens*

*Saponaria** – *officinalis* 'Flore Pleno'

Scabiosa – 'Bressingham White', 'Pink Mist', 'Butterfly Blue'

Sedum

Senecio – *compactus*

Stachys – *lanata* (lamb's ears), *officinalis* 'Rosea' and *macrantha*

*Thymus**

Verbascum – *chaixii* 'Album', *phoeniceum* 'Album', 'Southern Charm'

Verbena – *hastata, bonariensis* and *rigida*

* Indicates plants that the author feels will be drought-resistant in full sun.

Appendix III:
List of Plants for Dry Shade

PERENNIALS

Ajuga reptans 'Burgundy Glow' or 'Catlin's Giant'

Alchemilla conjuncta – native small version with silver to the back of leaves, quite lovely

Alchemilla erythropoda (small, neat variety)

Alchemilla mollis or *vulgaris*

Aquilegia vulgaris – use white/cream-flowered varieties to light up area

Brunnera 'Jack Frost' – lovely variegated foliage with forget-me-not blue flowers in spring

Convallaria 'Hardwick Hall' – a leaf with a gold edge and has largest flowers of any lily of the valley

Dicentra eximia

Dicentra 'Stuart Boothman'

Digitalis alba

Digitalis grandiflora – a primrose-yellow foxglove that is a perennial variety

Disporum longistylum – interesting Chinese perennial, tall arching stems with hanging bells

*Epimedium sulphureum × versicolor** – good yellow flowers in late February

*Epimedium × rubrum** – stunning red and white flowers

*Epimedium × warleyense** – slightly taller than two above with orange/yellow flowers

Erythronium 'Pagoda' – a fantastic spring bulb which has the greatest numbers of nodding yellow flowers in early spring

Erythronium 'White Beauty' – a superior variety of the above with pure white flowers over wonderful spotted leaves; very much slower growing than 'Pagoda'

Galium odoratum – sweet woodruff; lovely spring ground cover, excellent for shade but can take over

Geranium nodosum – will tolerate dense, dry shade and has glossy mid-green leaves with blue flowers

Geranium macrorrhizum – strong smell to leaves which turn red/orange in autumn; pink/white flowered forms

Geranium 'Sherwood' – taller geranium with starry pink flowers that float at 1m (3ft) high

Geranium versicolor – good clumps of foliage with cathedral-window-lined flowers

Lathyrus vernus – the ground cover/clump-forming perennial pea; ideal front of border or part-shade in pink/blue/white forms

Leucojum vernum – 'snowflake', tall perennial with snowdrop-type flowers in late spring

Liriope muscari – grass-like perennial with rocket-like dark blue berries in late part of year

Lunaria variegata – variegated leaves with white flowers

Pachysandra – evergreen ground cover; variegated version is good but very slow to expand

Peucedanum 'Daphnis' – a beautiful large-leaved variegated perennial with stunning creamy cow-parsley like flowers in the spring; non-invasive (although it looks like larger variegated ground elder)

Paeonia 'Rubra plena' – does really well in part-shade situations

Polemonium carneum 'Lambrook Mauve'

Tellima grandiflora – simply one of the best perennials for dry shade with beautiful nodding heads of cream flowers in the spring

Teucrium scorodonia 'Crispum' – small green flowers over lovely foliage

Tiarella cordifolia – the foam flower; requires just a little moist soil but will settle in dry positions

Tradescantia virginicum – 'spiderwort'; easy perennial that bulks up easily in dry part-shade

Tricyrtis formosa – the ordinary toad lily; good for late colour in part-shade

Veronica gentianoides – excellent evergreen ground cover for right at the front, forming an evergreen mat of foliage with beautiful tallish – 15cm (6in) – pale blue spires of flowers

Vinca – 'periwinkle'; good for shade but can become invasive – choose wisely, as there are some good large-flowered varieties

Viola labradorica – purple leaved violet

*Note: the epimediums make excellent ground cover at about 30cm (1ft) height. They flower in late February/early March followed by the new heart-shaped leaves, which give lovely ground cover (for bulbs to erupt through) which then turn to beautiful autumn colours in November. After the autumn the leaves dry, leaving a lovely ground cover of bronze-like appearance. I then cut down the leaves to the ground in the first week of February ready for the flowers to emerge just a little later.

FERNS FOR DRY SHADE

Asplenium scolopendrium
Blechnum penna-marina
Cystopteris falcatum
Dryopteris filix-mas
Polystichum setiferum 'Pulcherrimum Bevis'
Matteuccia struthiopteris

SHRUBS

Berberis 'Apricot Queen'
Daphne pontica

Elaeagnus × ebbingei 'Limelight' – lights up well and evergreen, but large

Euonymus fortunei – evergreen variegated

Fatsia japonica – good large-leaved shrub with good white flowers

Fuchsia magellanica alba – late-flowering hardy fuchsia that does well in part-shade, 1.5m (5ft) high

Hydrangea quercifolia (oak-leaved hydrangea) – white flowers with great autumn leaf colour

Itea virginica – evergreen with late white spires of flowers, 1.2m (4ft) height and spread

Lonicera nitida 'Baggesen's Gold'

Mahonia 'Charity' or 'Apollo'

Sarcococca hookeriana var. *humilis* (Christmas box) – highly scented white spring flowers

Skimmia japonica – prefers part-shade but likes a little acid in soil

Weigela florida variegata – variegated with pink flowers in spring to light up under part-shade

Viburnum davidii

Viburnum × hillieri 'Winton' – bushy evergreen, 2.5m (8ft) height and spread

Appendix IV:
The Cottage Garden Society

Founded in 1982 when cottage garden style of gardening was considered unfashionable, it brought together like-minded gardeners who loved to grow traditional cottage flowers, herbs and vegetables in an attractive yet haphazard manner of dense plantings.

The National Society benefited from the support of BBC *Gardeners' World* presenter Geoff Hamilton, who was the society's first president (his son Nick having taken over the mantle). The society has a presence at most of the country's garden shows, often with a display garden created by one of the regional groups.

The regional groups are at the heart of the society, with members meeting up for talks, seed and plant exchanges, and garden visits. The groups vary in size, but all bring together gardeners who wish to exchange ideas and discuss the ongoing development of this style of gardening.

A quarterly magazine, full of interesting and informative articles, deals with everything from favourite cottage flowers and how to deal with certain pests, to seasonal cottage recipes and keeping chickens.

I would strongly urge anyone interested in cottage gardens to join the society. For further information go to the website (www.thecottagegardensociety.org.uk) or write to: The Cottage Garden Society, 'Brandon', Ravenshall, Betley, Cheshire CW3 9BH.

Bibliography

Baker, Margaret, *The Folklore of Plants* (Shire Publications, 1999)

Bayard, Tania, *Sweet Herbs and Sundry Flowers* (Metropolitan Museum of Art, 1985)

Bird, Richard, *Companion Planting* (Greenwich Editions, 1996)

Bisgrove, Richard, *The Gardens of Gertrude Jekyll* (Frances Lincoln, 1992)

Blackburne-Maze, Peter, *The Apple Book* (Collingridge Books, 1986)

Chivers, Susan, and Woloszynska, Suzanne, *The Cottage Garden: Margery Fish at East Lambrook Manor* (John Murray, 1990)

Clark, Timothy, *Margery Fish: Country Gardening* (Garden Art Press, 2001)

De Bray, Lys, *Elizabethan Garlands* (Brockhampton Press Ltd, 1997)

Fish, Margery, *We Made a Garden* (The Garden Book Club, 1956)

Flowerdew, Bob, *Companion Planting* (Kyle Cathie Ltd, 2010)

Genders, Roy, *The Cottage Garden and the Old-Fashioned Flowers* (Pelham Books, 1970)

Gerard, John, *Gerard's Herball* (Minerva, 1974)

Gordon, Lesley, *Poorman's Nosegay: Flowers from a Cottage Garden* (Collins & Havill, 1973)

Grey-Wilson, Christopher, *Clematis: The Genus* (Batsford Ltd, 2000)

Hamilton, Geoff, *Cottage Gardens* (BBC Books, 1995)

Harvey, John, *Medieval Gardens* (Batsford Ltd, 1981)

Hill, Thomas, *The Gardener's Labyrinth* (Oxford University Press, 1987 reprint)

Houston, Fiona J., *The Garden Cottage Diaries* (Saraband, 2009)

Hughes, Sophie, *Carnations and Pinks* (Crowood Press, 1991)

Hyams, Edward, *English Cottage Gardens* (Whittet Books, 1970)

Innes, Miranda, and Perry, Clay, *Medieval Flowers* (Kyle Cathie Ltd, 2002)

Jekyll, Gertrude, *Colour Schemes for the Flower Garden* (Penguin Books, 1983)

Landsberg, Sylvia, *The Medieval Garden* (British Museum Press, 2003)

Lane, Clive, *The Cottage Gardener's Companion* (David & Charles, 1993)

Lane, Clive, *Cottage Garden Annuals* (David & Charles, 1997)

Lloyd, Christopher, *The Cottage Garden* (Dorling Kindersley, 1990)

Lord, Tony, *Planting Schemes from Sissinghurst* (Frances Lincoln, 2003)

Martin, Tovah, *A Heritage of Flowers* (Gaia Books Ltd, 1999)

McLean, Teresa, *Medieval English Gardens* (Viking Press, 1981)

Moody, Mary, *Roses* (Murdoch Books, 2006)

Nicolson, Philippa, *V. Sackville-West's Garden Book* (Michael Joseph Ltd, 1968)

O'Rush, Claire, *The Enchanted Garden* (Greenwich Editions, 1996)

Philbrick, Helen, and Gregg, Richard, *Companion Plants* (Robinson & Watkins, 1977)

Phillips, Sue, *The Cottage Garden* (Conran Octopus Ltd, 1994)

Riotte, Louise, *Roses Love Garlic* (Storey Books, 1998)

Robinson, William, *The Wild Garden* (Century Publishing, 1983)

Scott-James, Anne, *The Cottage Garden* (Penguin Books, 1981)

Scott-James, Anne, *Sissinghurst: The Making of a Garden* (Michael Joseph Ltd., 1975)

Tusser, Thomas, *Five Hundred Pointes of Good Husbandrie* (Forgotten Books, 2015 reproduction)

Verey, Rosemary, *The Scented Garden* (Michael Joseph Ltd, 1981)

Ward, Bobby J., *A Contemplation Upon Flowers* (Timber Press, 2005)

Way, Twigs, *Carnation* (Reaktion Books, 2016)

Whitaker, Jane, *Gardens for Gloriana* (Bloomsbury, 2019)

Willes, Margaret, *Pick of the Bunch* (Bodleian Library, 2016)

Index